RAILS™ ANTIPATTERNS

D0573215

Addison-Wesley
Professional Ruby Series

Obie Fernandez, Series Editor

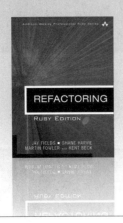

REFACTORING
RUBY EDITION

JAY FIELDS ■ SHANE HARVIE
MARTIN FOWLER with KENT BECK

**RAILS
ANTIPATTERNS**

BEST PRACTICE RUBY ON
RAILS REFACTORING

CHAD PYTEL ● TAMMER SALEH

**DISTRIBUTED
PROGRAMMING
WITH RUBY**

MARK BATES

THE RAILS 3 WAY

Foreword by David H. Hansson

OBIE FERNANDEZ

✦Addison-Wesley

Visit **informit.com/ruby** for a complete list of available products.

The **Addison-Wesley Professional Ruby Series** provides readers
with practical, people-oriented, and in-depth information about
applying the Ruby platform to create dynamic technology solutions.
The series is based on the premise that the need for expert reference
books, written by experienced practitioners, will never be satisfied solely
by blogs and the Internet.

✦Addison-Wesley **Cisco Press** EXAM/**CRAM** **IBM** Press. **que·** ‖ PRENTICE HALL **SAMS** | Safari·› Books Online

RAILS™ ANTIPATTERNS
Best Practice Ruby on Rails™ Refactoring

Chad Pytel

Tammer Saleh

✦ Addison-Wesley

Upper Saddle River, NJ • Boston • Indianapolis • San Francisco
New York • Toronto • Montreal • London • Munich • Paris • Madrid
Capetown • Sydney • Tokyo • Singapore • Mexico City

Many of the designations used by manufacturers and sellers to distinguish their products are claimed as trademarks. Where those designations appear in this book, and the publisher was aware of a trademark claim, the designations have been printed with initial capital letters or in all capitals.

The authors and publisher have taken care in the preparation of this book, but make no expressed or implied warranty of any kind and assume no responsibility for errors or omissions. No liability is assumed for incidental or consequential damages in connection with or arising out of the use of the information or programs contained herein.

The publisher offers excellent discounts on this book when ordered in quantity for bulk purchases or special sales, which may include electronic versions and/or custom covers and content particular to your business, training goals, marketing focus, and branding interests. For more information, please contact:

U.S. Corporate and Government Sales
(800) 382-3419
corpsales@pearsontechgroup.com

For sales outside the United States please contact:

International Sales
international@pearson.com

Visit us on the Web: informit.com/aw

Library of Congress cataloging-in-publication data is on file with the Library of Congress

Copyright © 2011 Pearson Education, Inc.

All rights reserved. Printed in the United States of America. This publication is protected by copyright, and permission must be obtained from the publisher prior to any prohibited reproduction, storage in a retrieval system, or transmission in any form or by any means, electronic, mechanical, photocopying, recording, or likewise. For information regarding permissions, write to:

Pearson Education, Inc.
Rights and Contracts Department
501 Boylston Street, Suite 900
Boston, MA 02116
Fax: (617) 671-3447

ISBN-13: 978-0-321-60481-1
ISBN-10: 0-321-60481-4
Text printed in the United States on recycled paper at RR Donnelley in Crawfordsville, Indiana.
First printing, November 2010

Editor-in-Chief
Mark Taub

Acquisitions Editor
Debra Williams Cauley

Development Editor
Michael Thurston

Managing Editor
John Fuller

Project Editor
Elizabeth Ryan

Copy Editor
Kitty Wilson

Indexer
The CIP Group

Proofreader
Linda Begley

Technical Reviewers
Jennifer Lindner
Pat Allen
Joe Ferris
Stephen Caudill
Tim Pope
Robert Pitts
Jim "Big Tiger" Remsik
Lar Van Der Jagt

Publishing Coordinator
Kim Boedigheimer

Cover Designer
Chuti Prasertsith

Compositor
The CIP Group

To my wife, Rachel, and son, Noah.
Thanks for letting me steal away to get this book finished.
—Chad

To Heather, Ralph and Rochelle, James,
and my mother, Judith.
—Tammer

Contents

Foreword

It's hard to believe that it will soon be three years since Zed Shaw published his infamous (and now retracted) rant "Rails Is a Ghetto." Even though Zed's over-the-top depiction of certain well-known people was wicked and pure social satire, the expression he coined has stuck like the proverbial thorn among certain higher echelons of the community. It's an especially piquant expression to use when we're called on to fix atrocious Rails projects. Occasionally, we'll even use the phrase with regard to our own messes. But most commonly, this expression is applied to code written by the *unwashed masses*. The rapid ascension of Rails as a mainstream technology has attracted droves of eager programmers from both outside and inside the wide sphere of web development. Unfortunately, Rails doesn't discriminate among newcomers. It offers deep pitfalls for bearded wise men of the object-oriented world and PHP script kiddies alike.

Frankly, I would have written this book myself eventually, because there's such a need for it in the marketplace. At Hashrocket, we do a lot of project rescue work. Oh, the agony! We've seen every AntiPattern detailed in this book rear its ugly face in real-life projects. Sometimes we see almost every AntiPattern in this book in a *single* project! My good friends and consultants extraordinaire Chad and Tammer have seen the same horrors. Only fellow consultants like these two could write this book properly because of the wide variety of coding challenges we face regularly. The solutions in this book cover a wide range of sticky situations that we know any professional Ruby developer will run into on a regular basis.

If you're new to Rails (and, based on the demographics, you probably are), then you're now holding one of the most valuable resources possible for getting past the chasm that separates an ordinary Rails developer from greatness. Congratulations and good luck making the leap.

—Obie Fernandez
   Author of *The Rails 3 Way*
   Series editor of the Addison-Wesley Professional Ruby Series
   CEO and founder of Hashrocket

Introduction

As Rails consultants, we've seen a lot of Rails applications. The majority of the AntiPatterns described in this book are directly extracted from real-world applications. We hope that by formalizing their descriptions here, we can present you with the tools you'll need to identify these AntiPatterns in your own code, understand their causes, and be able to refactor yourself out of the broken patterns.

What Are AntiPatterns?

AntiPatterns are common approaches to recurring problems that ultimately prove to be ineffective.

The term *AntiPatterns* was coined in 1995 by Andrew Koenig, inspired by Gang of Four's book *Design Patterns*, which developed the concept of design patterns in the software field. The term was widely popularized three years later by the book *AntiPatterns: Refactoring Software, Architectures, and Projects in Crisis* (William Brown, Raphael Malveau, Skip McCormick, and Tom Mowbray). According to the authors of *AntiPatterns*, there must be at least two key elements present to formally distinguish an actual AntiPattern from a simple bad habit, bad practice, or bad idea:

- A repeated pattern of action, process, or structure that initially appears to be beneficial but ultimately produces more bad consequences than beneficial results

- A refactored solution that is clearly documented, proven in actual practice, and repeatable

What Is Refactoring?

Refactoring is the act of modifying an application's code not to change its functional behavior but instead to improve the quality of the application itself. These improvements are intended to improve readability, reduce complexity, increase maintainability, and improve the extensibility (that is, possibility for future growth) of the system.

This book makes extensive reference to the process of refactoring in order to fix code that is exhibiting an AntiPattern. In an attempt to increase readability and understandability of the AntiPatterns and solutions in this book, we've left out the automated test suite that should accompany the code. We want to draw extra attention to the fact that your code should be well tested. When you have tests in place, some of the solutions we've presented will be much easier to implement with confidence. Without tests, some of the solutions might not even be possible. Unfortunately, many of the applications you encounter that exhibit these AntiPatterns will also be untested.

How to Read This Book

Each AntiPattern in this book outlines the mistakes we see in the wild and the negative effects they have on developer velocity, code clarity, maintenance, and other aspects of a successful Rails project. We follow each AntiPattern with one or more solutions that we have used in practice and that have been proven as proper fixes for the AntiPattern.

While you can read this book straight through from front to back, we've taken great pains to make each solution stand on its own. Therefore, this book is both a strong technical publication as well as a quick source of reference for Rails developers looking to hone their techniques in the trenches.

The following is a brief outline of what's covered in each chapter:

- **Chapter 1, "Models"**: Because Rails encourages code to be pushed down the Model-View-Controller (MVC) stack to the Model layer, it's fitting that a chapter on models is the largest chapter in the book. Here, we focus on a variety of AntiPatterns that occur in Model layer code, from general object-oriented programming violations to complex SQL and excessive code duplication.

- **Chapter 2, "Domain Modeling"**: Going beyond the nitty-gritty code at the Model layer in a Rails project, this chapter focuses on overall schema and database issues. This chapter covers issues such as normalization and serialization.

- **Chapter 3, "Views"**: The Rails framework gives developers a large number of tools and conventions that make code in the Model and Controller layers consistent and maintainable. Unfortunately, the required flexibility in the View layer prevents this sort of consistency. This chapter shows how to make use of the View layer tools Rails provides.

- **Chapter 4, "Controllers":** Since the integration of a RESTful paradigm in the Rails framework, the Controller layer has seen some significant improvements. This chapter goes through the AntiPatterns we've seen in Controller-layer-related Rails code.

- **Chapter 5, "Services":** Dealing with and exposing APIs requires tenacity. This chapter walks through all the common pitfalls we've seen, including timeouts, exceptions, backgrounding, response codes, and more.

- **Chapter 6, "Using Third-Party Code":** This short chapter reviews some of the AntiPatterns that can come from incorporating community plugins and gems into your applications.

- **Chapter 7, "Testing":** One of the strengths of Rails is the strong push toward test-driven development. Unfortunately, we've seen as many AntiPatterns inside test suites as in production code. This chapter outlines these AntiPatterns and how to address them.

- **Chapter 8, "Scaling and Deploying":** Developing a Rails application locally is a great experience, but there are many factors to consider once it's time to release an application to the world. This chapter will help you ensure that your applications are ready for prime time.

- **Chapter 9, "Databases":** This chapter outlines the common issues we've seen with migrations and validations.

- **Chapter 10, "Building for Failure":** Finally, the last chapter in the book gives guidance on general best practices for ensuring that an application degrades gracefully once it encounters the real world.

Acknowledgments

As any published author will tell you, writing a book is a difficult task. It's also one that cannot be done in isolation. Two people deserve the majority of our gratitude. Obie Fernandez was with us when the idea for this book formed, and he believed in us enough to help us get it published. After that, it was up to Debra Williams Cauley, an incredible editor, and now an incredible friend, to whip us into shape whenever progress slowed. This book never would have been published without their help.

There were many other people who also had a hand in getting this book to our readers. Both Pat Allan and Joe Ferris worked hard to contribute solutions involving Thinking Sphinx and unit-testing techniques, respectively. Michael Thurston and Jennifer Lindner worked hand-in-hand with us to make sure what we delivered to you is as high caliber as possible. Special thanks also to Stephen Caudill for rounding up the "volunteers" from Hashrocket and coordinating the review push.

Thanks also go to the entire crew at thoughtbot, who provided inspiration and feedback throughout the writing of this book. Your passion for excellence and quality in everything you do was the initial light shined upon many of these AntiPatterns.

Finally, we'd like to thank all the readers who gave us such incredibly useful feedback during the Safari beta program, as well as all the hardworking people at Addison-Wesley who have made this book a reality.

About the Authors

Chad Pytel is the founder and CEO of thoughtbot, a software development firm specializing in Ruby on Rails, and creators of Paperclip, Shoulda, FactoryGirl, and Hoptoad, among other projects. thoughtbot embraces both agile development methodologies and a "getting real" project philosophy. Chad coauthored *Pro Active Record: Databases with Ruby and Rails* (Apress, 2007) and has presented at various conferences around the world. Chad lives with his wife and son in Boston. When not managing projects and writing code, Chad enjoys spending time with his family. To follow along with Chad and the rest of the thoughtbot team's ideas on development, design, technology, and business, visit their blog at http://robots.thoughtbot.com.

Tammer Saleh is the director of engineering at Engine Yard. He wrote the Shoulda testing framework, was the primary developer and project manager for thoughtbot's fantastic Hoptoad service, and is an experienced Ruby on Rails trainer and speaker. In previous lives, he's done AI development for the NCSA and the University of Illinois, as well as systems administration for both Citysearch.com and Caltech's Earthquake Detection Network. You can find him online at http://tammersaleh.com.

CHAPTER 1
Models

The Model layer of your Rails application often provides the core structure of your application. Especially if you're following a RESTful application design pattern, the structure that is initially laid out in your models will carry through to your controllers and views.

The Model layer should also contain the business logic of your application. Therefore, the models of your application will often receive the majority of developer attention throughout a project's lifecycle.

Because so much attention is paid to the models, and because so much responsibility is contained within them, it's relatively easy for things to get out of hand in the models as an application grows and evolves. Also, because of the powerful nature of the Model layer of Rails, and specifically the Active Record ORM, it's fairly easy for things to get out of hand.

Fortunately, Rails provides the structure and tools necessary to stop this slow (or quick!) downward spiral, and it's often just a matter of effectively using them in order to keep the peace. In addition, it's important to always keep your guard up. In particular, it's incredibly important to have good unit test coverage of your models (and coverage of your entire application) to not only ensure that they function properly but to provide a test harness that will assist in maintenance, refactoring, and modification down the road.

In this chapter, we will cover many of the common pitfalls that can occur in the Model layer of the application, and we present proven techniques for recovering from these issues—and avoiding them in the first place.

AntiPattern: Voyeuristic Models

If you're reading this book, you're probably familiar with what object-oriented programming is and its basic tenets—such as encapsulation, modularity, polymorphism, and inheritance—as well as some of its other core concepts, such as use of classes and methods.

Both Ruby and the Ruby on Rails framework use these object-oriented programming tenets and concepts. Let's quickly review some of these concepts that you'll use as you build applications using the Ruby language and the Ruby on Rails framework:

- **Class:** A class defines the characteristics of an object, including the details of what it is (its attributes) and what it can do (its methods).

- **Method:** A method exists on a class and defines what the class can do. For example, a `Post` class can be published, and the method that is called to cause the class to publish itself may be the `publish()` method.

- **Encapsulation:** A class provides the modularity and structure of an object-oriented computer program, and often a class will be recognizable to a non-programmer familiar with the computer program's problem domain. For example, a banker would be familiar with most of the characteristics of a Bank class in a banking computer program. Ideally, the code for a class should be relatively self-contained through *encapsulation*, which is the concealment of functional details of a class from the other objects that call its methods. This is typically done by limiting the methods other objects are allowed to call and exposing a public interface through which an object is exposed to the world. In Ruby, this is done with the `public`, `protected`, and `private` keywords.

- **Model:** In the Ruby on Rails Active Record ORM library and the Model-View-Controller (MVC) architecture to which Ruby on Rails subscribes, models are the classes that make up a program and the classes that will be persisted to the program's database layer. We'll continue to use the term *model* nearly interchangeably with the word *class* throughout this book. It's important to remember that a model is merely a class and that it should also follow the core principles of object-oriented programming.

The lifecycle functionality that Active Record provides with its callbacks and validations and the structure and organization in the View and Controller layers of the Ruby on Rails framework provide an incredibly powerful set of tools with which to build web applications. However, these powerful tools can be used to break down the principles of object-oriented programming and to create code that is strongly coupled, not encapsulated, and poorly organized. So remember that with great power comes great responsibility.

A well-intentioned programmer may create an application that breaks the fundamental tenets of object-oriented programming for a variety of reasons. For example, if the programmer is coming from a less structured web development framework (or unframework) such as Perl or PHP, she may simply not be aware of the structure that Ruby on Rails, MVC, and object-oriented programming provide. She may apply what she knows about her current environment to a program she's building using Ruby on Rails. Alternatively, a programmer very experienced with object-oriented programming and MVC may first approach the Rails framework and be distracted by the dynamic nature of the Ruby language and unfamiliar with what he might consider to be unique aspects of the Ruby language, such as modules. Distracted by these things, he might proceed to build a system without first considering the overall architecture and principles with which he is familiar because he perceives Ruby on Rails to be different. Or perhaps a programmer is just overwhelmed by what the Ruby on Rails framework provides—such as generators, lifecycle methods, and the Active Record ORM—that she may get distracted by the immense capability and build a system too quickly, too messily, and without foresight or engineering discipline.

Regardless of the reason a programmer might create an application that breaks the fundamental tenets of object-oriented programming, without a doubt, it can happen. Both experienced and inexperienced programmers alike may have this problem when they come to this new framework for the first time.

The following sections present several scenarios that violate the core tenets of MVC and object-oriented programming, and they present alternative implementations and procedures for fixing these violations to help produce more readable and maintainable code.

Solution: Follow the Law of Demeter

An incredibly powerful feature of Ruby on Rails is Active Record associations, which are incredibly easy to set up, configure, and use. This ease of use allows you to dive deep down and across associations, particularly in views. However, while this functionality is powerful, it can make refactoring tedious and error prone.

Say that you've properly encapsulated your application's functionality inside different models, and you've been effectively breaking up functionality into small methods on the models. Now you have some models, and you have view code that looks like the following:

```
class Address < ActiveRecord::Base
  belongs_to :customer
end

class Customer < ActiveRecord::Base
  has_one :address
  has_many :invoices
end

class Invoice < ActiveRecord::Base
  belongs_to :customer
end
```

This code shows a simple invoice structure, with a customer who has a single address. The view code to display the address lines for the invoice would be as follows:

```
<%= @invoice.customer.name %>
<%= @invoice.customer.address.street %>
<%= @invoice.customer.address.city %>,
<%= @invoice.customer.address.state %>
<%= @invoice.customer.address.zip_code %>
```

Ruby on Rails allows you to easily navigate between the relationships of objects and therefore makes it easy to dive deep within and across related objects. While this is really powerful, there are a few reasons it's not ideal. For proper encapsulation, the invoice should not reach across the customer object to the street attribute of the address object. Because if, for example, in the future your application were to change so that a customer has both a billing address and a shipping address, every place in your code that reached across these objects to retrieve the street would break and would need to change.

To avoid the problem just described, it's important to follow the Law of Demeter, also known as the Principle of Least Knowledge. This law, invented at Northeastern University in 1987, lays out the concept that an object can call methods on a related object but that it should not reach through that object to call a method on a third related object. In Rails, this could be summed up as "use only one dot." For example, `@invoice.customer.name` breaks the Law of Demeter, but `@invoice.customer_name` does not. Of course, this is an over simplification of the principle, but it can be used as a guideline.

To follow the Law of Demeter, you could rewrite the code above as follows:

```
class Address < ActiveRecord::Base
  belongs_to :customer
end

class Customer < ActiveRecord::Base
  has_one :address
  has_many :invoices

  def street
    address.street
  end

  def city
    address.city
  end

  def state
    address.state
  end

  def zip_code
    address.zip_code
  end
end

class Invoice < ActiveRecord::Base
  belongs_to :customer

  def customer_name
    customer.name
  end

  def customer_street
    customer.street
  end
```

```
    def customer_city
      customer.city
    end

    def customer_state
      customer.state
    end

    def customer_zip_code
      customer.zip_code
    end
  end
```

And you could change the view code to the following:

```
<%= @invoice.customer_name %>
<%= @invoice.customer_street %>
<%= @invoice.customer_city %>,
<%= @invoice.customer_state %>
<%= @invoice.customer_zip_code %>
```

In this new code, you have abstracted out the individual methods that were originally being reached by crossing two objects into individual wrapper methods on each of the models.

The downside to this approach is that the classes have been littered with many small wrapper methods. If things were to change, now all of these wrapper methods would need to be maintained. And while this will likely be considerably less work than changing hundreds of references to `invoice.customer.address.street` throughout your code, it's still an annoyance that would be nice to avoid.

In addition, your public interface on `Invoice` has been polluted by methods that arguably have nothing to do with the rest of your interface for invoices. This is a general disadvantage of Law of Demeter, and it is not particularly specific to Ruby on Rails.

Fortunately, Ruby on Rails includes a function that addresses the first concern. This method is the class-level `delegate` method. This method provides a shortcut for indicating that one or more methods that will be created on your object are actually provided by a related object. Using this `delegate` method, you can rewrite your example like this:

```
class Address < ActiveRecord::Base
  belongs_to :customer
end

class Customer < ActiveRecord::Base
  has_one :address
  has_many :invoices

  delegate :street, :city, :state, :zip_code, :to => :address
end

class Invoice < ActiveRecord::Base
  belongs_to :customer

  delegate :name,
           :street,
           :city,
           :state,
           :zip_code,
           :to     => :customer,
           :prefix => true
end
```

In this situation, you don't have to change your view code; the methods are exposed just as they were before:

```
<%= @invoice.customer_name %>
<%= @invoice.customer_street %>
<%= @invoice.customer_city %>,
<%= @invoice.customer_state %>
<%= @invoice.customer_zip_code %>
```

Thanks to this helper provided by Rails, you have the benefit of following the Law of Demeter without so much extra clutter in your models.

Solution: Push All `find()` Calls into Finders on the Model

Programmers who are not familiar with the MVC design pattern to which Rails adheres, as well as those who are just unfamiliar with the general structures provided by Ruby on Rails may find themselves with code living where it simply doesn't belong.

This section shows several examples and illustrates proper technique for getting knowledge of your domain model out of your views and controllers.

The code problem discussed in this section can present itself in all three layers of the MVC design pattern, but it is most prevalent in its most blatant form in the view or the controller. Any place where you directly call finders on a model, other than inside the model itself, is a place that decreases readability and maintainability.

For example, if you wanted to create a web page that displays all the users in your web application, ordered by last name, you might be tempted to put this call to `find` directly in the view code, as follows:

```
<html>
  <body>
    <ul>
      <% User.find(:order => "last_name").each do |user| -%>
        <li><%= user.last_name %> <%= user.first_name %></li>
      <% end %>
    </ul>
  </body>
</html>
```

While this may seem like a straightforward way to create the web page, you've put calls directly in the view; this style may seem familiar to developers coming from PHP. In PHP, it would not be uncommon to actually have SQL directly in the HTML page as well, like this:

```
<html>
  <body>
<?php
  $result = mysql_query('SELECT last_name, first_name FROM users
ORDER BY last_name') or die('Query failed: ' . mysql_error());

  echo "<ul>\n";
  while ($line = mysql_fetch_array($result, MYSQL_ASSOC)) {
    echo "\t<li>$line[0] $line[1]</li>\n";
  }
  echo "</ul>\n";
?>
  </body>
</html>
```

Based on the PHP, the concise `find` method provided by Rails certainly is a step up! However, both examples leave something to be desired.

At the very least, including the actual logic for what users will be displayed on this page is a violation of MVC. At worst, this logic can be duplicated many times throughout the application, causing very real maintainability issues. For example, it will be problematic if you want the users in your application to be ordered by last name whenever they appear in a list.

In order to get rid of the MVC violation, you need to move the logic for which users are displayed on the page into the `Users` controller. When you do this, you end up with something like the following:

```
class UsersController < ApplicationController
  def index
    @users = User.order("last_name")
  end
end
```

The following is the corresponding index view:

```
<html>
  <body>
    <ul>
      <% @users.each do |user| -%>
        <li><%= user.last_name %> <%= user.first_name %></li>
      <% end %>
    </ul>
  </body>
</html>
```

Now you don't have any logic in the presentation layer about the collection of users you're displaying; now it's just sitting in the controller.

At one time, when Rails was young and wild, many programmers would stop here, content to remove the MVC violation. However, times have changed, and most developers now realize the benefits of going one step further and moving the direct `find` call down into the model itself. With this change, the view doesn't change at all. However, you end up with a controller that calls a new `ordered` method on the `User` model:

```
class UsersController < ApplicationController
  def index
```

```
      @users = User.ordered
    end
  end
```

And the `User` model contains the call to `find`:

```
class User < ActiveRecord::Base
  def self.ordered
    order("last_name")
  end
end
```

Having the definition of what it means to retrieve an ordered list of users in a central location is beneficial. The Ruby on Rails community has embraced this concept so strongly that it has been baked into the framework itself, with `scope`. We'll go into the use of scopes later, but for now suffice to say that they are shortcuts for defining methods on a model. For example, the named scope for the `ordered` method would be written as follows:

```
class User < ActiveRecord::Base
  scope :ordered, order("last_name")
end
```

Solution: Keep Finders on Their Own Model

Moving the `find` calls out of the Controller layer in your Rails application and into custom finders on the model is a strong step in the right direction of producing maintainable software. A common mistake, however, is to move those `find` calls into the closest model at hand, ignoring proper delegation of responsibilities.

Say that while working on the next great social networking application, you find a complex `find` call in a controller:

```
class UsersController < ApplicationController
  def index
    @user = User.find(params[:id])
    @memberships =
      @user.memberships.where(:active => true).
                        limit(5).
                        order("last_active_on DESC")
  end
end
```

Based on what you've learned from the last two solutions, you diligently move that scope chain into a method on the `User` model. You think this seems like the best place for it, since you're dealing with the `UsersController`:

```
class UsersController < ApplicationController
  def index
    @user = User.find(params[:id])
    @recent_active_memberships = @user.find_recent_active_memberships
  end
end

class User < ActiveRecord::Base
  has_many :memberships

  def find_recent_active_memberships
    memberships.where(:active => true).
                limit(5).
                order("last_active_on DESC")
  end
end
```

This is definitely an improvement. `UsersController` is now much thinner, and the method name reveals intent nicely. But you can do more. In the first example, the `UsersController` knew far too much about the underlying implementation of the `Membership` model. It was digging into the database columns, accessing the `active` and `last_active_on` columns, and it was doing some other very SQL-like things. You've improved the situation a bit, but as far as delegation of responsibilities goes, you've simply moved the problem into the `User` model. The `User` model now knows far too much about the `Membership` model's implementation, which is a clue that you still haven't pushed the methods far enough.

AssociationProxy Magic

You'll learn more about association flexibility in a later AntiPattern, but knowing a bit about how Active Record associations work is important for this example.

When you access an Active Record association, what you get isn't an array but a proxy class of type `ActiveRecord::Associations::AssociationProxy` that walks and talks like an array. This is a pretty nifty object, as it lets you access all the class methods on the target class, but it limits them to the subset defined by the association.

What that means is if you have a `Membership.active` method that returns all active memberships, you can use that method through your associations. `user.memberships.active` will then return all active memberships *for that user.* This is pretty neat—and definitely useful.

By making use of the power of Active Record associations, you can trim up this example even further. You can define a finder on `Membership`, and you can then access that finder through the `User#memberships` association, as follows:

```
class User < ActiveRecord::Base
  has_many :memberships

  def find_recent_active_memberships
    memberships.find_recently_active
  end
end

class Membership < ActiveRecord::Base
  belongs_to :user

  def self.find_recently_active
    where(:active => true).limit(5).order("last_active_on DESC")
  end
end
```

This is much better. The application now honors the MVC boundaries and delegates domain model responsibilities cleanly. This is a fine place to stop your refactoring, but you can also make use of Rails 3 scopes.

A Quick Rundown on Scopes

You'll learn more about Active Record scopes later in this chapter, in the section "AntiPattern: Spaghetti SQL," but knowing a bit about how they work is important for this example.

A *scope* is a close cousin to `AssociationProxy`, but instead of referencing a separate model, a scope allows you to define a subset of the current model.

You can define a scope in your Active Record model by using the `scope` class method:

```
class Car < ActiveRecord::Base
  scope :red, where(:color => 'red')

end
```

You can now ask for all red cars by calling `Car.red`. Like the `AssociationProxy` class, the scope that's returned from `Car.red` allows you to "chain on" other class methods or other named scopes. For example, calling `Car.red.where(:doors => 2)` will return the scope for all red two-door cars.

You can make use of scopes here to produce a variety of finders on `Membership` that you can then chain together to get the results you're looking for:

```
class User < ActiveRecord::Base
  has_many :memberships

  def find_recent_active_memberships
    memberships.only_active.order_by_activity.limit(5)
  end
end

class Membership < ActiveRecord::Base
  belongs_to :user

  scope :only_active,       where(:active => true)
  scope :order_by_activity, order('last_active_on DESC')
end
```

By making the refactoring in this last step, you've generalized a lot of the code. Instead of only having a `Member#find_recently_active` method, you now have three class methods that you can mix and match to your heart's desire.

There are downsides to this approach, including problems with readability and simplicity, as well as abuse of the Law of Demeter. Whether you use this approach is a judgment call on your part. Will you use the added flexibility? Is it better than defining a handful of separate finders? Like many advanced refactorings, this one has no easy answer and depends greatly on your tastes.

AntiPattern: Fat Models

One of the key themes of this book, and something we believe in firmly, is the importance of simplicity in application development. Complexity is the number-one killer of projects today, and it comes into an application in many ways, including through excitement over new features, overly clever developers, and unfamiliarity with the Ruby on Rails framework.

This chapter deals with simplicity from a unique angle: simplifying the internals of a model by moving that complexity to new units in the application—modules and classes.

To illustrate a model that's grown beyond its means, let's examine a sample `Order` model in an online store application. The `Order` model has class methods for finding orders based on state or by using advanced and simple search interfaces. It also has methods for exporting an order as XML, JSON, and PDF (and we're sure more will creep in as the application moves along). Here is the `Order` model for this online store application:

```
# app/models/order.rb
class Order < ActiveRecord::Base
  def self.find_purchased
    # ...
  end

  def self.find_waiting_for_review
    # ...
  end

  def self.find_waiting_for_sign_off
    # ...
  end

  def self.find_waiting_for_sign_off
    # ...
  end

  def self.advanced_search(fields, options = {})
    # ...
  end
```

```
    def self.simple_search(terms)
      # ...
    end

    def to_xml
      # ...
    end

    def to_json
      # ...
    end

    def to_csv
      # ...
    end

    def to_pdf
      # ...
    end
  end
```

We've left the implementation of the various methods to your imagination because this chapter isn't concerned with them. (You might be able to refactor the methods and reduce the number of methods by using one of the other techniques we discuss in this book.) What we're concerned with here is the location of these methods.

When considering that this is just a small sample of the Order class's code, it's easy to see that models like this can quickly get out of hand. We wish we could say that it's been uncommon for us to see models like this surpassing 1,000 lines of code in a single file. But model obesity tends to creep up on new Ruby on Rails developers. The maintenance and readability issues created by these obese classes quickly become apparent.

In the next solution, you'll see how easy Ruby on Rails makes it for you to group related methods into modules. After that, you'll learn about the underlying domain issues behind overweight classes and see why some methods should be moved into another class of their own.

Solution: Delegate Responsibility to New Classes

In the last solution, we discussed the use of Ruby modules for separating out related functionality. This is a useful technique for segregating code purely for reasons of readability. It's also a technique that new Ruby on Rails developers often overuse. Let's take another look at the `Order` class, this time focusing on the conversion methods:

```ruby
# app/models/order.rb
class Order < ActiveRecord::Base
  def to_xml
    # ...
  end

  def to_json
    # ...
  end

  def to_csv
    # ...
  end

  def to_pdf
    # ...
  end
end
```

Often, the code you're about to move into a module doesn't fit in the original class in the first place. The conversion methods above aren't really part of an `Order` object mandate. An `Order` object should be responsible for order-like processes: calculating price, managing line items, and so on.

Keepin' It Classy

When code doesn't belong in the class that contains it, you should refactor the code into a class of its own. This is an application of the Single Responsibility Principle. While the spirit of this principle has always existed as part of object-oriented design, the term was first coined by Robert Cecil Martin, in his paper "SRP: The Single Responsibility Principle."[1] Martin summarized this rule as follows: "There should never be more than one reason for a class to change."

Having classes take on more than a single axis of responsibility leads to code that is brittle in the face of changing requirements. Over time, the responsibilities of a class

---

1. You can find this paper, and many other great resources, at www.objectmentor.com.

begin to intermingle, and changing the conversion behavior in `to_xml` leads to changes in the rest of the class as well.

You can apply SRP to the `Order` model by splitting those conversion methods into an `OrderConverter` class:

```ruby
# app/models/order.rb
class Order < ActiveRecord::Base
  def converter
    OrderConverter.new(self)
  end
end


# app/models/order_converter.rb
class OrderConverter
  attr_reader :order
  def initialize(order)
    @order = order
  end

  def to_xml
    # ...
  end

  def to_json
    # ...
  end

  def to_csv
    # ...
  end

  def to_pdf
    # ...
  end
end
```

In this way, you give the conversion methods their own home, inside a separate and easily testable class. Exporting the PDF version of an order is now just a matter of calling the following:

```ruby
@order.converter.to_pdf
```

In object-oriented circles, this is known as *composition*. The Order object is composed of an OrderConverter object and any other objects it needs. The Rails association methods (for example, has_one, has_many, belongs_to) all create this sort of composition automatically for database-backed models.

Breaking the Law of Demeter

Although the chaining introduced in the preceding section upholds the Single Responsibility Principle, it violates the Law of Demeter. You can fix this by making use of Ruby on Rails delegation support:

```
# app/models/order.rb
class Order < ActiveRecord::Base
  delegate :to_xml, :to_json, :to_csv, :to_pdf, :to => :converter
  def converter
    OrderConverter.new(self)
  end
end
```

Now you can retain your @order.to_pdf calls, which are simply forwarded on to the OrderConverter class. We discuss both the Law of Demeter and Rails delegation earlier in this chapter, in the section "Solution: Follow the Law of Demeter."

Crying All the Way to the Bank

The technique just described—of delegating functionality to a separate class that's included in the first class via composition—is fundamental enough to warrant a second example. This time, we'll borrow a bit from the Rails documentation, with some modifications for clarity.

The following class represents a bank account:

```
# app/models/bank_account.rb
class BankAccount < ActiveRecord::Base
  validates :balance_in_cents, :presence => true
  validates :currency,         :presence => true

  def balance_in_other_currency(currency)
    # currency exchange logic...
  end
```

```ruby
  def balance
    balance_in_cents / 100
  end

  def balance_equal?(other_bank_account)
    balance_in_cents ==
      other_bank_account.balance_in_other_currency(currency)
  end
end
```

In addition to the normal bank account actions, such as transfer, deposit, withdraw, open, and close, this class has methods for returning the balance in dollars, comparing the balances (<=>), and converting the balance to another currency. Clearly, this class is doing too much. It's taking on the behavior of bank accounts and of money in general. To follow Martin's reasoning, we would need to modify this class if there were a change to how much would be charged for a transfer—or every time a currency rate changed.

To improve the BankAccount class, you could move the balance logic into a composed object that represents money. Using composition in this way is so common that Rails provides the composed_of method as a shortcut.

composed_of takes three main options: the name of the method that will reference the new object, the name of the object's class (:class_name), and the mapping of database columns to attributes on the object (:mapping). When a model record is loaded, Active Record creates a new composed object for you, using the database columns in the constructor, and creates an accessor by which you can use it.

You can refactor the BankAccount class as follows to make use of the composed_of method:

```ruby
# app/models/bank_account.rb
class BankAccount < ActiveRecord::Base
  validates :balance_in_cents, :presence => true
  validates :currency,         :presence => true

  composed_of :balance,
              :class_name => "Money",
              :mapping => [%w(balance_in_cents amount_in_cents),
                           %w(currency currency)]
end
```

```ruby
# app/models/money.rb
class Money
  include Comparable
  attr_accessor :amount_in_cents, :currency

  def initialize(amount_in_cents, currency)
    self.amount_in_cents = amount_in_cents
    self.currency        = currency
  end

  def in_currency(other_currency)
    # currency exchange logic...
  end

  def amount
    amount_in_cents / 100
  end

  def <=>(other_money)
    amount_in_cents <=>
      other_money.in_currency(currency).amount_in_cents
  end
end
```

Now you can convert the balance of a bank account to another currency by using `@bank_account.balance.in_currency(:usd)`. Likewise, you can compare the balances by using `@bank_account.balance > @other_bank_account.balance`, regardless of which currencies the bank accounts are using.

> **Warning**
>
> There is one issue to be aware of when using `composed_of`: You cannot modify a composed object in place. If you do so, depending on the version of Rails you're using, either your change will not persist when you save the parent record or you'll receive a frozen object exception.

Wrapping Up

In summary, it's often not enough to reduce a model's complexity by simply moving methods into modules. If a class is taking on more than one responsibility, or if there is more than one reason for the class to be modified, then it likely needs to be broken up into composed classes. Each of these classes would then have its own distinct responsibilities, which decreases coupling and increases maintainability.

Solution: Make Use of Modules

Let's take another look at the Order object model, this time using Ruby modules to slim it down:

```ruby
# app/models/order.rb
class Order < ActiveRecord::Base
  def self.find_purchased
    # ...
  end

  def self.find_waiting_for_review
    # ...
  end

  def self.find_waiting_for_sign_off
    # ...
  end

  def self.find_waiting_for_sign_off
    # ...
  end

  def self.advanced_search(fields, options = {})
    # ...
  end

  def self.simple_search(terms)
    # ...
  end

  def to_xml
    # ...
  end

  def to_json
    # ...
  end
```

```
   def to_csv
     # ...
   end

   def to_pdf
     # ...
   end
end
```

Modules allow you to extract behavior into separate files. This improves readability by leaving the Order model file with just the most important Order-related code. Modules also serve to group related information into labeled namespaces.

Divide and Conquer

If you examine the Order model in the preceding section, you can see three easy groupings for the methods it contains: methods for finding all orders of a certain type, methods for searching against all orders, and methods for exporting orders. You can make those groups more obvious by moving those methods into modules, as in the following example:

```
# app/models/order.rb
class Order < ActiveRecord::Base
  extend OrderStateFinders
  extend OrderSearchers
  include OrderExporters
end

# lib/order_state_finders.rb
module OrderStateFinders
  def find_purchased
    # ...
  end

  def find_waiting_for_review
    # ...
  end

  def find_waiting_for_sign_off
    # ...
  end
```

```
    def find_waiting_for_sign_off
      # ...
    end
end


# lib/order_searchers.rb
module OrderSearchers
  def advanced_search(fields, options = {})
    # ...
  end

  def simple_search(terms)
    # ...
  end
end


# lib/order_exporters.rb
module OrderExporters
  def to_xml
    # ...
  end

  def to_json
    # ...
  end

  def to_csv
    # ...
  end

  def to_pdf
    # ...
  end
end
```

There is a difference between `include` and `extend` in this `Order` object model: `include` puts the module's methods on the calling class as instance methods, and `extend` makes them into class methods.

Move and Shake

By moving related functionality into modules, you've reduced the Order model to three lines. Of course, this "reduction" is not truly a reduction; you've simply moved the code from one place to another. Nonetheless, moving this code reduces the apparent complexity of the Order model and allows you to organize those methods into convenient groups.

As of version 2.2.2, Rails () does not automatically require the modules under lib. However, an initializer in the suspenders project template (see http://github.com/thoughtbot/suspenders) takes care of this for you:

```
# config/initializers/requires.rb
Dir[File.join(Rails.root, 'lib', '*.rb')].each do |f|
  require f
end
```

> **Note**
> Using modules in this way only touches on their potential. We'll discuss modules in greater depth in the section "AntiPattern: Duplicate Code Duplication," later in this chapter.

Solution: Reduce the Size of Large Transaction Blocks

Large transaction blocks are often unnecessary, whether they are in the controller or the model, because Active Record supplies built-in transactions as part of the saving process. These built-in transactions automatically wrap the entire save process, including all callbacks and validations. By utilizing these built-in transactions, you can significantly reduce code complexity.

The following is a significant transaction that takes place inside a custom method on an Account model, setting several values, and creating several associated models the first time an account is created.

```
class Account < ActiveRecord::Base
  def create_account!(account_params, user_params)
    transaction do
      account = Account.create!(account_params)
      first_user = User.new(user_params)
      first_user.admin = true
```

```
        first_user.save!
        self.users << first_user
        account.save!
        Mailer.deliver_confirmation(first_user)
        return account
      end
    end
end
```

This code bundles all the functionality for creating an account in a method called `create_account!` on the `Account` model. This method will be used only for creating accounts, and it contains the following functionality:

- Creates the first user for an account
- Makes the user an administrator
- Adds the user to the account
- Saves the account
- Sends a confirmation email to the user

All this functionality is wrapped inside a transaction so that if anything fails, the subsequent actions are not performed, and the proceeding database changes are reverted.

Often, developers make special create or save methods to hold custom functionality when they are new to Rails and do not have a strong understanding of the validation and callback functionality Active Record provides. By utilizing the built-in functionality, however, you can remove the custom `create_account!` method, the explicit transaction block, and the explicit call to `save!`.

Order Up

The callbacks and validations build into Active Record have a set order of operation. If any callback or validation along the way is not successful, the model's save process will be halted, and the transaction will be rolled back.

> **Note**
>
> Prior to Rails 2.2, the transaction was rolled back *only* for calls to save! and save, and the resulting callbacks that failed would not be saved, but they did not trigger a database rollback.

The following is the order of the callbacks for a call to save (and save!) on a record that has never been saved before:

```
before_validation
before_validation :on => :create
after_validation
after_validation :on => :create
before_save
before_create
after_create
after_save
```

This callback sequence provides enormous flexibility throughout the Active Record lifecycle. In addition, because this sequence of events occurs within a transaction, it often enables you to avoid manually starting and programming your own transactions. With knowledge of the callback lifecycle in hand, you can now refactor your manual transaction to fit nicely within the callbacks provided by Active Record.

Check the Controller

Although you'll be primarily making changes to the model here, it's beneficial to look at the controller that calls the create_account! method so that you can understand how this code is used:

```
class AccountsController < ApplicationController
  def create
    @account = Account.create_account!(params[:account],
                                       params[:user])
    redirect_to @account,
                :notice => "Your account was successfully created."
  rescue
    render :action => :new
  end
```

There are several ways you could improve this create action on its own, as discussed in Chapter 4. However, as a result of the model changes you are going to be making, the create action in this controller is going to be changed and improved. In the preceding controller code, the create_account! method is called, and if it fails due to a raised exception, the user will be shown the account creation form again. If it succeeds, the user will be redirected to the show page for the newly created account.

Now that you have an understanding of how the `create_account!` method is used and how it will affect the code, you can begin refactoring. You can start by moving all the functionality into callbacks and setters that occur before (and after, in the case of email sending) the creation of a new account.

Nested Attributes

The `create_account!` method takes parameters for an account, and it takes parameters for the first user for an account. However, the built-in `save` and `create` methods allow for only a single hash of attributes and values to be passed in. You need to actually create a setter on the `Account` model for setting the attributes of what you can consider the administrative user. You can do so by using the Rails method `accepts_nested_attributes_for`, as shown here:

```
accepts_nested_attributes_for :users
```

With this in place, you can modify the form in the view or other application code that builds the attributes for the `Account` object. You want this object to include a subhash of the attributes for the admin user, nested under the attributes for `Account`, with the key `users_attributes`. Then, any of the methods for creating or updating an `Account` object (`Account#new`, `Account#create`, `Account#update_attributes`) can then call the setter with a hash.

The following is the view code for this example:

```
<%= form_for(@account) do |form| -%>
  <%= form.label :name, 'Account name' %>
  <%= form.text_field :name %>
  <% fields_for :user, User.new do |user_form| -%>
    <%= user_form.label :name, 'User name' %>
    <%= user_form.text_field :name %>
    <%= user_form.label :email %>
    <%= user_form.text_field :email %>
    <%= user_form.label :password %>
    <%= user_form.password_field :password %>
  <% end %>
  <%= form.submit 'Create', :disable_with => 'Please wait...' %>
<% end %>
```

In this code, the fields for a user are nested within the fields for the account. When this form is submitted to the server, the hash for the User fields will be within the hash of fields for an account with the key users_attributes.

Again, in order for the users_attributes method to be called with the attributes for a user, you need no further code. When the hash for Account is passed to Account#new, the users_attributes method will be called.

You still need to set the admin flag on the admin user to true. You can accomplish this with a before_create callback on Account that sets this flag on all users before they are created:

```
class Account < ActiveRecord::Base
  before_create :make_admin_user

  private

  def make_admin_user
    self.users.first.admin = true
  end
```

There is no need to explicitly save the user or account within the users_attributes method. Any newly created users that are added to the account's users collection with this method will be automatically saved when the account is saved.

Confirm That Email

In the create_account! method in the preceding section, a confirmation email is sent to the created user after a successful call to save!. This can be accomplished by moving the call to the mailer into an after_create callback. If the requirements of the application specified that each user created should receive a confirmation email, then this should actually be an after_create callback on the User model itself. For our purposes, let's assume that only the admin user, who is created along with the account, receives a confirmation email, and therefore the callback should be in the Account model. This callback will be a method named send_confirmation_email, as shown here:

```
class Account < ActiveRecord::Base
  after_create :send_confirmation_email
```

```
  private

  def send_confirmation_email
    Mailer.confirmation(users.first).deliver
  end
```

This causes the confirmation email to be sent to the first user on the account (the only user at the point the account is created).

Back to Standard

With the changes you've already made to the Account model, you've actually duplicated all the functionality that was originally contained in the create_account! method. Let's take a step back and look at how things are organized now:

```
class Account < ActiveRecord::Base
  accepts_nested_attributes_for :users

  before_create :make_admin_user
  after_create :send_confirmation_email

  private

  def make_admin_user
    self.users.first.admin = true
  end

  def send_confirmation_email
    Mailer.confirmation(users.first).deliver
  end
```

You now no longer have the create_account! method. The functionality is instead encompassed by a normal call to Account#create (or Account#new, followed by a call to save). Also notice that you no longer have to explicitly create a transaction, as all of the actions taking place now occur within the transaction provided by account creation. Let's take a look at the controller code for creating an account:

```
class AccountsController < ApplicationController
  def create
    @account = Account.new params[:account]
```

```
    if @account.save
      flash[:notice] = "Your account was successfully created."
      redirect_to account_url(@account)
    else
      render :action => :new
    end
  end
```

This controller has very little custom functionality occurring; it is essentially the default scaffolding controller (with additional code actually removed from the default scaffold). The majority of deliberate improvements here were made at the model level. The changes to the controller and the view were made to facilitate the changes to the model. However, the changes made to the controller are a side benefit, as the controller is improved from its original version.

There will inevitably be times when you feel that the actions you need to perform do not fit within the built-in process of creating or saving an object. In these circumstances, it's likely that the domain model you are working with may be incorrectly structured. In such cases, you should evaluate the different entities you are working with and keep the Active Record lifecycle in mind. You may be able to reorganize your models such that your seemingly custom transaction fits nicely within the lifecycle provided by Active Record.

AntiPattern: Spaghetti SQL

Active Record is an incredibly powerful framework, and many new Rails developers fail to use it to their advantage. Not taking advantage of the incredible utility of Active Record associations is a perfect example.

Many times we've come across code like the following:

```
class PetsController < ApplicationController
  def show
    @pet = Pet.find(params[:id])
    @toys = Toy.where(:pet_id => @pet.id, :cute => true)
  end
end
```

One of the issues with this action is that it's doing a custom find call that rightfully belongs on the Toy model. You should fix this quickly so we can dig into the real underlying issue:

```
class PetsController < ApplicationController
  def show
    @pet = Pet.find(params[:id])
    @toys = Toy.find_cute_for_pet(@pet)
  end
end

class Toy < ActiveRecord::Base
  def self.find_cute_for_pet(pet)
    where(:pet_id => pet.id, :cute => true)
  end
end
```

You now have a well-named and intention-revealing method on Toy, and the controller is no longer digging into the model's implementation. But, if it wasn't already, the fundamental problem with this code should now be apparent: The person who wrote this code wasn't aware of or was uncomfortable with the full range of options that Active Record associations provide.

Solution: Use Your Active Record Associations and Finders Effectively

A common mistake we see in programmers working with all languages and frameworks is that they fail to fully learn and make use of the libraries and tools they have at their disposal. Ruby on Rails is an incredibly powerful framework that lets you build applications at a phenomenal pace. But in order to reap the benefits, you must take the time to master the framework and learn about all the time- and work-saving shortcuts it offers.

Let's take a look at some code for finding pet toys, using Active Record associations:

```ruby
class PetsController < ApplicationController
  def show
    @pet = Pet.find(params[:id])
    @toys = @pet.find_cute_toys
  end
end

class Pet < ActiveRecord::Base
  has_many :toys

  def find_cute_toys
    self.toys.where(:cute => true)
  end
end
```

While Active Record associations give you accessors on your model that look and act like instances or arrays of instances of the target model (for example, `toy.pet`, `pet.toys`), in truth what they give you is a proxy class that has a good deal of extra behavior on it. This allows you to call finder methods on the association array.

This code makes use of the tools that Rails gives you for free. The `has_many` line gives you not only the `Pet#toys` proxy array but also all the power and functionality that comes with it—more than we can outline here. See http://api.rubyonrails.org for more information.

One issue with the code that still remains is that the `Pet` model now knows the implementation details of the `Toy` model (specifically, the fact that `Toy` has a Boolean "cute" column). Let's look at a few ways we can clean it up by making good use of the `toys` association.

The first way to clean up the preceding code is a relatively little-known trick that involves placing methods on an association. If you give any association declaration a block, it will extend the association with the contents of that block. In other words, methods defined inside that block will become methods on the association. The following is an example of this:

```
class PetsController < ApplicationController
  def show
    @pet = Pet.find(params[:id])
    @toys = @pet.toys.cute
  end
end

class Pet < ActiveRecord::Base
  has_many :toys do
    def cute
      where(:cute => true)
    end
  end
end
```

The toys association now has a method on it named cute. If you call pet.toys.cute, Rails will combine the conditions into one, returning those toys that have both the pet_id and cute fields set correctly. This happens in a single SQL call and is implemented using an internal Active Record tool called scope.

While this is an interesting trick, it's of dubious utility. For one thing, this doesn't actually solve the issue outlined above; the Pet model still knows of the internals of the Toy model. Another issue is that this trick can lead to repetitive code. Say that the concept of a Toy owner is introduced:

```
class Owner < ActiveRecord::Base
  has_many :toys do
    def cute
      where(:cute => true)
    end
  end
end
```

The definition of the cute method is now repeated in both the Pet and Owner models. The second method for adding behavior to the Active Record associations works around both of these issues. All the association declarations allow you to specify a module via the `:extend` option, which will be mixed into the association. Any methods on that module will then become methods on the association, much as with the block format. You add `:extend` to the association definition, as shown in the following module and class definitions:

```ruby
module ToyAssocationMethods
  def cute
    where(:cute => true)
  end
end

class Pet < ActiveRecord::Base
  has_many :toys, :extend => ToyAssocationMethods
end

class Owner < ActiveRecord::Base
  has_many :toys, :extend => ToyAssocationMethods
end
```

This encapsulates the behavior of the Toy model in a single location, and it arguably keeps the Toy implementation at least close to the Toy model (if you consider the module to be an extension of that model).

    While this technique is useful in some very specific circumstances (which we will explain shortly), it is usually much more complex than necessary. As mentioned earlier, the toys array is really an association proxy that allows you to call `all` and `find` on it as if it were the Toy class. In fact, that proxy allows you to call any class method on Toy and scopes it properly to the subset of toys that belong to that pet.[2]

    With all this in mind, you can refactor the code once again:

```ruby
class PetsController < ApplicationController
  def show
    @pet = Pet.find(params[:id])
    @toys = @pet.toys.cute
  end
end
```

---

2. This is actually true only as long as you don't use `find_by_sql` in your finder methods. The mechanism by which the SQL statements are combined (`scope`) breaks down when a full raw SQL statement is used.

```
class Toy < ActiveRecord::Base
  def self.cute
    where(:cute => true)
  end
end

class Pet < ActiveRecord::Base
  has_many :toys
end
```

After you define `Toy#cute`, you can also make use of it through your association methods. This keeps the implementation details directly on the `Toy` model, where they belong, and makes them available to any model that is associated with it. In fact, because all methods are proxied along with the `Toy` model, you can make use of scopes as well:

```
class PetsController < ApplicationController
  def show
    @pet = Pet.find(params[:id])
    @toys = @pet.toys.cute.paginate(params[:page])
  end
end

class Toy < ActiveRecord::Base
  scope :cute, where(:cute => true)
end

class Pet < ActiveRecord::Base
  has_many :toys
end
```

Here you have the `@pet.toys.cute.paginate(params[:page])` line as a single SQL call.

As mentioned earlier, there are certain times when you actually want to use one of the first two ways of extending association behavior. Both the block and the `:extend` forms allow you to access the details of the underlying proxy object directly from within your finder methods. Specifically, you have access to `proxy_owner`, which points back to the owner of the association. While this is rarely needed, it can be a life-saver in some circumstances, such as the following:

```
class Toy < ActiveRecord::Base
  # has column :minimum_age
end

class Pet < ActiveRecord::Base
  # has column :age

  has_many :toys do
    def appropriate
      where(["minimum_age < ?", proxy_owner.age])
    end
  end
end
```

The `pet.toys.appropriate` method now returns a different set of toys, based on the state of the pet (specifically, all the toys whose minimum age is less than the pet's age). Again, this is not commonly needed functionality, but it can really come in handy in some cases.

Like any other craftsman with his or her tools, a programmer who doesn't take the time to learn all the powers of libraries is neglectful in his or her trade.

Solution: Learn and Love the `Scope` Method

One of the greatest headaches of Rails application development involves writing complex finder methods—usually to back an advanced search interface. One way you can minimize the complexity of these methods while increasing the opportunity for code reuse is by leveraging the Active Record scoping methods.

Before we dive into more complex examples, let's take on a smaller refactoring to get acquainted with the Active Record scope helpers. Say that while working on a user interface for managing the processes running on your servers, you come across the following finder method:

```
class RemoteProcess < ActiveRecord::Base
  def self.find_top_running_processes(limit = 5)
    find(:all,
         :conditions => "state = 'Running'",
         :order => "percent_cpu desc",
         :limit => limit)
  end
```

```
    def self.find_top_running_system_processes(limit = 5)
      find(:all,
           :conditions => "state = 'Running' and
                           (owner in ('root', 'mysql')",
           :order => "percent_cpu desc",
           :limit => limit)
    end
end
```

Finders like this are incredibly common. If a model has one or two of them, you may be inclined to avoid refactoring them. But finders like this reproduce like rabbits. By the end of the application lifetime, you'll likely see one finder for every combination of RemoteProcess state, owner, order, and so on.

We can clean up this method and make the components reusable by employing named scopes. The scope method defines class methods on your model that can be chained together and combined into one SQL query. A scope can be defined by a hash of options that should be merged into the find call or by a lambda that can take arguments and return such a hash.

When you call a scope, you get back an ActiveRecord::Relation object, which walks and talks just like the array you would have gotten back from find. The crucial difference is that the database lookup is lazy-evaluated—that is, it's not triggered until you actually try to access the records in the array. In the meantime, you can chain on more scope calls to further refine your eventual result set.

Scopes are an implementation of the *Virtual Proxy* design pattern, which means they act as a proxy for the result set returned from find. However, they do not initialize that result set until an actual record is accessed.

You could use scopes as follows to rewrite the preceding finder:

```
class RemoteProcess < ActiveRecord::Base
  scope :running, where(:state => 'Running')
  scope :system,  where(:owner => ['root', 'mysql'])
  scope :sorted,  order("percent_cpu desc")
  scope :top,     lambda {|l| limit(l) }
end

RemoteProcess.running.sorted.top(10)
RemoteProcess.running.system.sorted.top(5)
```

Not only does this reduce the code size, which is a good goal in itself, but it also allows you to produce a much wider variety of finders by chaining named scope calls. Each of these last two lines is executed using a *single SQL query*, and this is just as efficient as using a normal finder call.

While using the `scope` method as shown above is popular with Rails 3 applications, the readability benefit is negligible compared to using simple class methods. Therefore, we recommend using the following less subtle and more traditional version:

```ruby
class RemoteProcess < ActiveRecord::Base
  def self.running
    where(:state => 'Running')
  end

  def self.system
    where(:owner => ['root', 'mysql'])
  end

  def self.sorted
    order("percent_cpu desc")
  end

  def self.top(l)
    limit(l)
  end
end
```

These class methods act identically to the methods generated by the scope calls in the first example, but they are much easier for a general Ruby developer to understand. They also allow normal parameter passing, without the need for lambdas. That being said, as the `scope` calls are more idiomatic, we continue to use them in some of the simpler code examples throughout the book.

The sprinkling of periods in the last two lines may trigger a code smell involving a Law of Demeter violation. This isn't actually the case: All the methods being called here are on the `RemoteProcess` model, so we aren't digging into the implementation of associated classes. Nonetheless, that call chain can get pretty unwieldy and is still a source of code duplication, if it's called often. You can shore this up nicely by wrapping the chain in a descriptive class method:

```
class RemoteProcess < ActiveRecord::Base
  scope :running, where(:state => 'Running')
  scope :system,  where(:owner => ['root', 'mysql'])
  scope :sorted,  order("percent_cpu desc")
  scope :top,     lambda {|l| limit(l) }

  def self.find_top_running_processes(limit = 5)
    running.sorted.top(limit)
  end

  def self.find_top_running_system_processes(limit = 5)
    running.system.sorted.top(limit)
  end
end
```

This version gives you the best of both worlds. You can now construct arbitrary finders by using the scopes you've defined, and you have consistent and well-named methods for the most common scope chains.

This technique is also useful in testing scope calls while using mocking in your tests. Mocking out a chain of method calls like this is difficult with almost every existing Ruby mocking framework. Consolidating these chains in a method on the model allows you to mock out just that method.

Now that we've taken a quick look at basic scope usage, let's return to the original problem of writing advanced search methods. In this case, you need to create an advanced search implementation for an online music database. This is a typical example of the hoops you have to jump through to make advanced searches work correctly. The complexity and size of the following method makes it a definite maintenance problem, and you've been tasked with finding a way of cleaning it up:

```
class Song < ActiveRecord::Base
  def self.search(title, artist, genre,
                  published, order, limit, page)
    condition_values = { :title  => "%#{title}%",
                         :artist => "%#{artist}%",
                         :genre  => "%#{genre}%"}

    case order
    when "name":   order_clause = "name DESC"
    when "length": order_clause = "duration ASC"
```

```
    when "genre":  order_clause = "genre DESC"
    else
      order_clause = "album DESC"
    end

    joins      = []
    conditions = []
    conditions << "(title  LIKE ':title')"  unless title.blank?
    conditions << "(artist LIKE ':artist')" unless artist.blank?
    conditions << "(genre  LIKE ':genre')"  unless genre.blank?

    unless published.blank?
      conditions << "(published_on == :true OR
                      published_on IS NOT NULL)"
    end

    find_opts = { :conditions => [conditions.join(" AND "),
                                  condition_values],
               :joins      => joins.join(' '),
               :limit      => limit,
               :order      => order_clause }

    page = 1 if page.blank?
    paginate(:all, find_opts.merge(:page => page,
                                   :per_page => 25))
  end
end
```

This technique of building up the conditions, joins, and other find options inside a series of conditionals was considered a fine way of implementing methods before scopes came into play.[3]

You can clean up the preceding method by employing scopes as follows:

```
class Song < ActiveRecord::Base
  def self.top(number)
    limit(number)
  end
```

---

3. …or before has_finder and named_scope, the predecessors to scope.

```
  def self.matching(column, value)
    where(["#{column} like ?", "%#{value}%"])
  end

  def self.published
    where("published_on is not null")
  end

  def self.order(col)
    sql = case col
            when "name":   "name desc"
            when "length": "duration asc"
            when "genre":  "genre desc"
            else "album desc"
          end
    order(sql)
  end

  def self.search(title, artist, genre, published)
    finder = matching(:title, title)
    finder = finder.matching(:artist, artist)
    finder = finder.matching(:genre, genre)
    finder = finder.published unless published.blank?
    return finder
  end
end

Song.search("fool", "billy", "rock", true).
     order("length").
     top(10).
     paginate(:page => 1)
```

While this re-implementation using scopes reduces the code size somewhat, the real benefits are elsewhere.

The new implementation separates the tasks of searching for songs from those of ordering, limiting, and paginating the results. These tasks are different from one another and were originally implemented in a single method only because of the limitations of ActiveRecord::Base#find. Now that those methods have been refactored out of the find method, they can be reused throughout the application.

Furthermore, we might argue that implementing pagination inside the model is a violation of the Model-View-Controller (MVC) pattern. The controller should be responsible for determining when pagination is appropriate (that is, when rendering the index page) and when it isn't (for example, when sending the results via XML, JSON, and so on).

You may be squeamish about creating named scope class methods if they would be used only as part of a single finder method on the model. For example, let's assume that the `published` and `matching` class methods would never be used outside the search method. You can still implement the search method cleanly, using the `where` method. In the following example, `where` acts just like `find(:all)` but returns a `Scope` object instead of a results array:

```ruby
class Song < ActiveRecord::Base
  has_many :uploads
  has_many :users, :through => :uploads

  # top and order are implemented the same as before,
  # using named_scope...

  def self.search(title, artist, genre, published)
    finder =        where(["title  like ?", "%#{title}%"])
    finder = finder.where(["artist like ?", "%#{artist}%"])
    finder = finder.where(["genre  like ?", "%#{genre}%"])
    unless published.blank?
      finder = finder.where("published_on is not null")
    end
    return finder
  end
end
```

This implementation cleanly hides the logic of finding matching and published songs inside the search method, but it still returns a `Scope` object. It is just as "chainable" as the scope version, and it involves much less code than the original method.

Scopes show what can be done with some ingenuity combined with the flexibility of a language like Ruby. They provide a means of expressing complicated SQL queries in a clean and beautiful manner, allowing you to write readable and maintainable code.

Solution: Use a Full-Text Search Engine

An effective search feature is critical to most modern web applications. Adding the ability to search for phrases in a single column isn't difficult, either. It's when things get a bit more complex that the headaches begin.

To smooth things out again, it's often worth adding a full-text search engine to your toolkit. The Rails world certainly doesn't lack options in that arena; some possibilities are Ferret (http://ferret.davebalmain.com), Sphinx (http://sphinxsearch.com), Solr (http://lucene.apache.org/solr), and Xapian (http://xapian.org). For the purpose of this chapter, though, we'll be focusing on Sphinx and the Active Record plugin Thinking Sphinx (http://ts.freelancing-gods.com).

This leads to the caveat that the solution is valid only if you're using MySQL or PostgreSQL. While Microsoft SQL Server and SQLite 3 aren't options yet, support for them is on the horizon.

Simplify Search

The following is an example of a common search approach that involves searching for results that match any of the words provided in any of the specified columns:

```ruby
# app/models/user.rb
class User < ActiveRecord::Base
  def self.search(terms, page)
    columns = %w( name login location country )
    tokens  = terms.split(/\s+/)

    if tokens.empty?
      conditions = nil
    else
      conditions = tokens.collect do |token|
        columns.collect do |column|
          "#{column} LIKE '%#{connection.quote(token)}%'"
        end
      end
      conditions = conditions.flatten.join(" OR ")
    end

    paginate :conditions => conditions, :page => page
  end
end


# app/controllers/users_controller.rb
class UsersController < ApplicationController
  def index
    @users = User.search(params[:search], params[:page])
  end
end
```

Active Record doesn't lend itself to this type of search particularly well, given that implicit conditions are joined by AND logic, and the comparisons are exact. The example therefore has untidy looping around each word token and column possibility to ensure that the tokens are escaped (something Active Record normally takes care of for us) and pattern-matched (using MySQL's syntax). After all this, you could paginate the search results by using the `will_paginate` (http://wiki.github.com/mislav/will_paginate) library.

You can slim down this example considerably. First, you need to install Sphinx. If you're using Windows, you need an installer (available for download at http://sphinxsearch.com/downloads.html), and it should be a piece of cake. If you're using package systems such as `apt`, `port`, and `yum`, you may have options available as well.

If you need (or prefer) to compile by source, though, you need to pay attention to the following pretty standard steps:

```
./configure
make
sudo make install
```

> **Note**
> The default `configure` setup excludes PostgreSQL support. To enable it, you need to use the following flag instead:
>
> ```
> ./configure --with-pgsql=`pg_config
> --pkgincludedir`
> ```

Next, you need to install the Thinking Sphinx gem:

```
gem install thinking-sphinx
```

> **Note**
> Before you get caught up with the specifics of the sample application, you need to understand the basic process for using Sphinx. It runs as a daemon that is controlled by the `thinking_sphinx:start` and `thinking_sphinx:stop` rake tasks. You need to index your data regularly (via a cron job or similar method), and the task for this is `thinking_sphinx:index` (or `ts:in`, to save some typing).

> In most cases, you do not need to stop Sphinx while the indexing occurs. The only exception to this rule is when you've changed your Sphinx setup by adding, editing, or removing indexes within models.

You need to tell Sphinx what data you want indexed—in this case, the columns you were searching against in your controller:

```
class User < ActiveRecord::Base
  define_index do
    indexes name, login, location, country
  end
end
```

Essentially, all you're doing is requesting that text columns be indexed as fields for your searches. Don't forget to index your data and then get that daemon running:

```
rake ts:in
rake ts:start
```

Now you can clean up your controller:

```
class UsersController < ApplicationController
  def index
    User.search(params[:search],
      :page       => params[:page],
      :match_mode => :any
    )
  end
end
```

This is it, really. There's no need to change the view, as Thinking Sphinx works nicely with will_paginate collections.

The one difference between the custom-defined search method and the new one provided by Thinking Sphinx is that the new code will match any full words provided in the search query against any full words in the indexed data. If you want pattern matching, then that requires a little bit of tweaking. First, you need to ask Sphinx to index infixes and allow for star syntax. You do this by editing the config/sphinx.yml file:

```
development:
  enable_star: true
  min_infix_len: 1

test:
  enable_star: true
  min_infix_len: 1

production:
  enable_star: true
  min_infix_len: 1
```

Next, because you've changed your Sphinx setup, you need to stop the daemon, re-index, and then restart:

```
rake ts:stop
rake ts:in
rake ts:start
```

Finally, you need to change the search query to auto-star each word in the search query (for example, changing "rail job" to "*rail* *job*"):

```
def index
  @users = User.search(params[:search],
                       :page       => params[:page],
                       :match_mode => :any,
                       :star       => true)
end
```

Advanced Functionality

With Thinking Sphinx, a lot of Sphinx's advanced features are kept off to the side; they're still there and usable, but only when you want them. The following sections describe a few options you might want to keep in mind.

Match Modes, Conditions, and Filters

Sometimes you'll want to limit a search to a particular field. For this, imitating Active Record's find method works fine:

```
User.search :conditions => {:location => "Melbourne"}
```

Don't expect Thinking Sphinx to handle anything beyond strings within the conditions hash, though, because Sphinx itself understands only text.

Note that the match mode is changed from the default, ALL, to EXTENDED to allow for single field matching. Earlier examples show the use of ANY to match any single word; another common mode is PHRASE. It might be worth visiting the Sphinx documentation site (http://sphinxsearch.com/docs/current.html#matching-modes) to get a solid understanding of how these different match modes work.

If you want to limit searches by integers, dates, Booleans, or floats, then what you're after is an attribute—which in Sphinx is a separate concept than text fields. Attributes are useful for filtering, sorting, and grouping, and you can set them up in your models as follows:

```
class User < ActiveRecord::Base
  define_index do
    # field definitions
    has deleted, created_at
  end
end
```

Obviously, you wouldn't want deleted users appearing in most search results, so you need to filter them out:

```
User.search params[:search], :with => {:deleted => false}
```

Filters are a bit more flexible than normal text conditions. You can use ranges and arrays as well as single values:

```
User.search(params[:search],
  :with => {:created_at => 1.week.ago..Time.now}
)
```

Sorting

As mentioned earlier, attributes are the key to sorting. For example, sorting by when users were created is pretty simple:

```
User.search params[:search], :order => :created_at
```

Or you could reverse things:

```
User.search params[:search], :order => "created_at DESC"
```

What if you wanted to sort by name, though? That's a field, not an attribute. Luckily, Sphinx can create attributes for strings, by translating them to ordinal integers. This simply means that you can sort but not filter. Thinking Sphinx abstracts this for you to keep things even simpler: You just mark a field as sortable:

```
class User < ActiveRecord::Base
  define_index do
    indexes name, :sortable => true
    indexes login, location, country

    has deleted, created_at
  end
end
```

And searching becomes a simple task again:

```
User.search params[:search], :order => :name
# or maybe something like:
User.search params[:search], :order => "name ASC, created_at DESC"
```

Searching Across All Models

In a site-wide search, you might want to have a mixture of model instances returned—users, articles, links, and so on. As long as they've all being indexed for Sphinx, you can grab them all in a single call:

```
ThinkingSphinx::Search.search params[:search],
                        :page => params[:page]
```

The same arguments on a model level apply here as well. However, if you're filtering or sorting, you need to make sure all the indexes have attributes with the same names.

Delta Indexes

One final trick to keep up your sleeve is tied to a limitation of Sphinx: Sphinx doesn't automatically update your indexed data when you create or edit your model instances.

This means your search results ignore anything that's changed since you last ran the index rake task.

Understandably, this isn't ideal. The easiest way around it is to track those changes in a delta index, which—due to its tiny size—can be re-indexed as every change is made. To get this running, you want to first flag the relevant models to use the delta approach:

```
class User < ActiveRecord::Base
  define_index do
    # fields and attributes

    set_property :delta => true
  end
end
```

Don't forget to do the stop-index-start shuffle:

```
rake ts:stop
rake ts:in
rake ts:start
```

Now your changes will be promptly reflected in your search results.

You still need to run the normal index task regularly, though. Otherwise, the delta index itself will become large and slow to index, which in turn slows down your application. The extra overhead here can be inappropriate for some high-traffic sites, so it may be worth investigating deltas via the delayed job plugin (http://freelancing-gods.com/posts/thinking_sphinx_delta_changes).

AntiPattern: Duplicate Code Duplication

Andy Hunt and Dave Thomas originally coined the term DRY (Don't Repeat Yourself) Principle in *The Pragmatic Programmer*. The DRY Principle, which is consistently misunderstood, is fundamentally *not* about reducing lines of code. The basis of the DRY Principle, say Hunt and Thomas, is that "every piece of knowledge must have a single, unambiguous, authoritative representation within a system." Therefore, the DRY Principle is about reducing both the opportunity for developer error and the effort required to make business logic changes in the application.

The DRY Principle is something that we've all understood fundamentally as being a quality of "good code." Likely half of the history of computer engineering has gone into supporting this principle, but it still takes practice and know-how to use it effectively.

For example, a very poorly written sales application may calculate the shipping in the HTML confirmation screen, in the receipt email, and in the credit card transaction module. It's clear that this calculation, which is both complex and likely to change, should be performed in a single place. The key question that we will be examining in the next three solutions is what is the simplest, most readable, and most generally effective way of applying the DRY Principle to your code. How you do this is highly dependent on the problem at hand.

The following sections cover three of the most powerful DRY Principle techniques available to a Ruby on Rails developer, in order of simplicity and locality. The first solution explains how to extract code into modules for use across multiple classes. The second solution takes you through the development of a Ruby on Rails plugin, allowing you to keep behavior DRY across multiple applications—with the added benefit (and responsibility) of having a self-contained package suitable for contribution to the Ruby on Rails community at large. The third solution shows the power of simple metaprogramming tricks when DRYing up fairly localized and small pieces of code.

Solution: Extract into Modules

Ruby modules are designed to centralize behavior among classes, and using them is possibly the simplest way of DRYing up your code. A module is essentially the same as a Ruby class, except that it cannot be instantiated, and it is intended to be included inside other classes or modules. When a class includes a module via `include ModuleName`, all the methods on that module become instance methods on the class. Although less commonly done, a class can also choose to add a module's methods as class-level methods by using `extend` instead of `include`: `extend ModuleName`.

Let It Ride!

Let's consider a Ruby on Rails driving game in which two models are defined: Car and Bicycle. Both of these models can accelerate, brake, and turn, and the code for these methods is identical:

```ruby
class Car << ActiveRecord::Base
  validates :direction, :presence => true
  validates :speed,     :presence => true

  def turn(new_direction)
    self.direction = new_direction
  end

  def brake
    self.speed = 0
  end

  def accelerate
    self.speed = speed + 10
  end

  # Other, car-related activities...
end

class Bicycle << ActiveRecord::Base
  validates :direction, :presence => true
  validates :speed,     :presence => true

  def turn(new_direction)
    self.direction = new_direction
  end

  def brake
    self.speed = 0
  end

  def accelerate
    self.speed = speed + 10
  end

  # Other, bike-related activities...
end
```

Clearly, this code is not DRY. There are a number of ways to extract and centralize these methods, but the most natural technique is to move them into a module that's included by both classes:

```ruby
# lib/drivable.rb
module Drivable
  def turn(new_direction)
    self.direction = new_direction
  end

  def brake
    self.speed = 0
  end

  def accelerate
    self.speed = speed + 10
  end
end

class Car << ActiveRecord::Base
  validates :direction, :presence => true
  validates :speed,     :presence => true
  include Drivable
  # Other, car-related activities...
end

class Bicycle << ActiveRecord::Base
  validates :direction, :presence => true
  validates :speed,     :presence => true
  include Drivable
  # Other, bike-related activities...
end
```

With the Drivable module, both Car and Bicycle share a common definition for the accelerate, brake, and turn methods. You place modules like this under the /lib directory and require those files inside an initializer, like this:

```ruby
#config/initializers/requires.rb
Dir[File.join(Rails.root, 'lib', '*.rb')].each do |f|
  require f
end
```

This way, all modules defined under /lib are automatically available to your Ruby classes.

The Drivable module centralizes the method implementations, but you still have duplication in the validation for direction and speed. You can push the validation into the module as well, by making use of the ActiveSupport::Concern module. This provides a method named included that will be run when the module is included in a Ruby class.

This hook lets you make use of the Active Record validation macros, which are not available for you to use when the module is defined. The included method on Drivable now opens the class that included the module and calls the validation method there:

```ruby
# lib/drivable.rb
module Drivable
  extend ActiveSupport::Concern

  included do
    validates :direction, :presence => true
    validates :speed,     :presence => true
  end

  def turn(new_direction)
    self.direction = new_direction
  end

  def brake
    self.speed = 0
  end

  def accelerate
    self.speed = speed + 10
  end
end

class Car << ActiveRecord::Base
  include Drivable
  # Other, car-related activities...
end

class Bicycle << ActiveRecord::Base
  include Drivable
  # Other, bike-related activities...
end
```

Many developers coming from other object-oriented languages will notice that this use of modules is functionally identical to using a common superclass. It's our opinion, however, that there are very few times when it's appropriate to use a common superclass instead of modules.

Modules are more flexible than superclasses because a class can include as many different modules as it needs to incorporate different sets of behavior. This is akin to multiple inheritance, but without much of the complication introduced by that model. Using superclasses also promotes proper code organization by allowing you to group related methods into well-defined sets of behavior. The `Car` model, for instance, may include a `Drivable` module for driving behavior, a `Sluggable` module to produce friendlier URLs, and a `Searchable` module to support standard advanced searches.

Because the class-level behavior inside a module isn't evaluated until the module is included, that behavior can introspect on the including model—modifying that behavior based on the class's name, database columns, other associations, and so on. Class-level behavior defined on a superclass is executed when the superclass is evaluated. Because of this, it cannot examine the characteristics of the subclass. This leads to overly complicated code that uses the Rails `read/write_inherited_variable` or `Class#inherited` methods.

Finally, a useful trait of modules is that they can be added to a class after the class is defined. You'll make use of this trait shortly, in order to add behavior to `ActiveRecord::Base`.

I Can't Drive 55!

When centralized behavior needs to be adapted somewhat for each class using it, a good technique is to make use of the template pattern from *Design Patterns: Elements of Reusable Object-Oriented Software* by Erich Gamma, Richard Helm, Ralph Johnson, and John M. Vlissides.

The template pattern was originally designed for classic object-oriented languages, and it therefore used a single superclass for the implementation. A template is simply a superclass that implements shared behavior and allows modification of that behavior through overriding of helper methods. The template may provide default behavior by implementing those methods itself, or it may require that the subclasses implement them when there is no sensible default. It's more natural to use modules than to use a common superclass to implement the template pattern in Ruby. You see what this looks like by changing the initial constraints on our driving game.

In your new version of the `Car` and `Bicycle` models, you should add a top speed. A `Car` object cannot accelerate past 100 miles per hour, and a `Bicycle` object cannot

go faster than 20 miles per hour. These two objects also accelerate at different rates—
Car at 10 miles per hour and Bicycle at 1 mile per hour. The important fact is that
the behavior is not completely identical between the two models. The initial, non-
DRY version might look like the following:

```ruby
class Car << ActiveRecord::Base
  validates :direction, :presence => true
  validates :speed,     :presence => true

  def turn(new_direction)
    self.direction = new_direction
  end

  def brake
    self.speed = 0
  end

  def accelerate
    # Cars accelerate quickly, and can go 100mph (in Los Angeles).
    self.speed = [speed + 10, 100].min
  end

  # Other, car-related activities...
end

class Bicycle << ActiveRecord::Base
  validates :direction, :presence => true
  validates :speed,     :presence => true

  def turn(new_direction)
    self.direction = new_direction
  end

  def brake
    self.speed = 0
  end

  def accelerate
    # Bikes accelerate slower, and can only go 20mph
    self.speed = [speed + 1, 20].min
  end
```

```
    # Other, bike-related activities...
end
```

The differences in the shared behavior between the `Car` and `Bicycle` models are in the rate of acceleration and the top speed. To implement this behavior using the template pattern, you extract the shared behavior as before, but you move those values into helper methods. You then define those methods on each class that includes the module:

```ruby
# lib/drivable.rb
module Drivable
  extend ActiveSupport::Concern

  included
    validates :direction, :presence => true
    validates :speed,     :presence => true
  end

  def turn(new_direction)
    self.direction = new_direction
  end

  def brake
    self.speed = 0
  end

  def accelerate
    self.speed = [speed + acceleration, top_speed].min
  end

  end
end

class Car << ActiveRecord::Base
  include Drivable

  def top_speed
    100
  end
```

```ruby
  def acceleration
    10
  end
  # Other, car-related activities...
end

class Bicycle << ActiveRecord::Base
  include Drivable

  def top_speed
    20
  end

  def acceleration
    1
  end
  # Other, bike-related activities...
end
```

Template Snags

You need to consider a few design decisions when using the pattern described in the preceding section. Why do you use methods, instead of constants, for `top_speed` and `acceleration`? The values are constant in `Car` and `Bicycle`, so a constant would be a natural first choice. However, it's better to implement a template with methods even in cases like this, because it's possible this way to dynamically modify the behavior. An amphibian vehicle class may want to return a different top speed, based on whether it is on land or in water. Using methods gives you this flexibility, with little cost in code complexity. Using methods instead of constants also eases the burden on the unit tests for the module. A test case can modify the method (or use mocking and stubbing) for each test. This is possible but much less natural when using constants.

When using the template pattern with a dynamic language like Ruby, a developer who is writing including classes needs to know to implement those methods. C++ and Java address this in their use of purely virtual and abstract methods. Classes derived from a superclass that defines an abstract method *must* implement that method before being instantiated. Ruby has no such concepts, however, and will happily allow you to define and execute a class that is missing implementations of template methods. At best, a bug like this will cause a quick runtime exception. At worst, it could go unnoticed for months.

One way to ease a programmer's confusion when such an error occurs is to define those methods on the module and have them raise exceptions with helpful explanations:

```ruby
# lib/drivable.rb
module Drivable
  extend ActiveSupport::Concern

  class TemplateError < RuntimeError; end

  included
    validates :direction, :presence => true
    validates :speed,     :presence => true
  end

  def turn(new_direction)
    self.direction = new_direction
  end

  def brake
    self.speed = 0
  end

  def accelerate
    self.speed = [speed + acceleration, top_speed].min
  end

  def top_speed
    raise TemplateError, "The Drivable module requires the " +
                         "including class to define a " +
                         "top_speed method"
  end

  def acceleration
    raise TemplateError, "The Drivable module requires the " +
                         "including class to define an " +
                         "acceleration method"
  end
end
```

A challenge, when applying the template pattern, is in determining what aspects of the shared behavior are likely candidates for change. Refactoring every method into a tangle of trivially implemented helper methods quickly leads to unreadable code. That path is never ending, as there is no way of telling how much configurability could be needed for future modifications. For example, you could have refactored the call to `Array#min` into a `limit_speed` template method. Likewise, you could have refactored the code for `speed + acceleration` into an `add_acceleration_to_current_speed` method.

Developers new to the template pattern tend to want to err on the side of flexibility. This is a form of future-proofing, and it's a mistake—especially when working in a language as geared toward agile development and the refactoring cycle as Ruby.

Modules are one of the most simple, and most powerful, of Ruby's language features. They give a developer all the benefits of using a common superclass, without the limitations that most languages enforce on that technique. Furthermore, they add to the readability of your code by grouping and partitioning off different types of behavior.

Solution: Write a Plugin

So far, we've described methods of removing code duplication in models both through using metaprogramming and by extracting into modules.

The metaprogramming technique we described is useful for reducing duplication in a single class. Modules take this a step further, allowing reduction of duplication across a number of classes in the same application. This solution introduces the use of Rails plugins, which allow you to share duplication-busting code across applications, including those of the community at large.

We present the following three sections as possible solutions, in the recommended order of application in your own refactoring. In these solutions, as in the rest of this book, we continue to embrace a theme of simplicity. Using a simple metaprogramming loop, when it suits the purpose, is better than extracting to a module. Likewise, using a module, if it gets the job done, trumps the work required to create a plugin. Only when you need to share the code across applications or when you feel the code is valuable to others should you proceed down the plugin path. Satchel Paige summed this up with his famous quote: "Never run when you can walk, never walk when you can stand, never stand when you can sit, and never sit when you can lie down." With this concept firmly in mind, let's see what is required to move the drivable behavior from the last solution into a standalone Rails plugin.

Recall the `Car` class, which contains the behavior you'd like to extract:

```
# app/models/car.rb
class Car < ActiveRecord::Base
  validates_presense_of :direction, :speed

  def turn(new_direction)
    self.direction = new_direction
  end

  def brake
    self.speed = 0
  end

  def accelerate
    self.speed = [speed + 10, 100].min
  end

  # Other, car-related activities...
end
```

By the end of this solution, you will have produced a plugin that reduces this behavior in the class to a simple call to `drivable`. The existing `Car` unit tests should still pass swimmingly, which will be your main indication of success. Later in this chapter, in the section "Gems Fightin' Words!" we'll discuss how they should be refactored and moved into the plugin itself.

Plug It In!

When you first write a plugin, it's almost always best to extract it from within an existing application. This way, you have access to the generator and a testbed through which you can experiment along the way. Only after you've gotten the plugin to a somewhat stable state should you move that code into its own source control repository.

Getting started with a plugin is fairly easy, due to the generators that come with Rails. To build the framework for your new plugin, simply run `./script/rails generate plugin drivable`:

```
# ./script/rails generate plugin drivable
      create  vendor/plugins/drivable
      create  vendor/plugins/drivable/init.rb
      create  vendor/plugins/drivable/install.rb
      create  vendor/plugins/drivable/MIT-LICENSE
```

```
create   vendor/plugins/drivable/Rakefile
create   vendor/plugins/drivable/README
create   vendor/plugins/drivable/uninstall.rb
create   vendor/plugins/drivable/lib
create   vendor/plugins/drivable/lib/drivable.rb
invoke   test_unit
inside     vendor/plugins/drivable
create       test
create       test/drivable_test.rb
create       test/test_helper.rb
```

You can see from this output that the generator produces a good number of files; you can ignore most of them for now. The README, Rakefile, install.rb, and uninstall.rb files, for example, have little bearing on this solution. You can read more about the purpose of the rest of the files produced by the generator in the "Creating Plugins" guide at http://guides.rubyonrails.org/plugins.html.

At this point, you're mainly concerned with the contents of the init.rb file and the lib directory. A typical pattern for organizing the files in a plugin involves having a file under lib named after the plugin and a subdirectory by the same name, which holds the rest of the code. This pattern is designed to nest the files for each module in parallel with the nesting of the modules themselves. To follow this pattern, you should create the following files and directories:

```
lib/drivable.rb
lib/drivable/active_record_extensions.rb
```

The lib/drivable/active_record_extensions.rb contains the bulk of the code for the drivable plugin. It holds the Drivable::ActiveRecordExtensions module, which is responsible for extending the ActiveRecord::Base class with the new behavior.

Following another pattern in Ruby module composition, the Drivable::ActiveRecordExtensions module contains two submodules, which hold class and instance methods:

```
# lib/drivable/active_record_extensions.rb
module Drivable
  module ActiveRecordExtensions
    module ClassMethods
      def drivable
        validates_presence_of :direction, :speed
```

```
        include ActiveRecordExtensions::InstanceMethods
      end
    end

    module InstanceMethods
      def turn(new_direction)
        self.direction = new_direction
      end

      def brake
        self.speed = 0
      end

      def accelerate
        self.speed = [speed + 10, 100].min
      end
    end
  end
end
```

The only class method that this extension introduces is the `drivable` method. This method is responsible for introducing the rest of the behavior. This ensures that you don't add the `turn`, `brake`, and `accelerate` methods to every Active Record model in the application.

But you still haven't hooked the extension code into `ActiveRecord::Base`. That's the job of the `drivable.rb` file:

```
# lib/drivable.rb
require "drivable/active_record_extensions"

class ActiveRecord::Base
  extend Drivable::ActiveRecordExtensions::ClassMethods
end
```

By opening the `ActiveRecord::Base` class and extending it with the `Drivable::ActiveRecordExtensions::ClassMethods` module, you've added the `drivable` method as a class method to all the models in your application.

Finally, you need to help Rails load your plugin. When Rails initializes, it evaluates the file `init.rb` in every plugin it finds. This is where you place your hook to require the drivable file:

```
# init.rb
require File.join(File.dirname(__FILE__), "lib", "drivable")
```

At this point, your plugin is basically complete. The turn, accelerate, and break methods can be removed from the Car model and replaced with the call to drivable.

Everything in Its Right Place

This chain of require statements may seems convoluted, but each separate file serves a purpose. A mistake beginning Rails developers often make when producing a new plugin is to include the majority of the code in the init.rb file. While this method may work, it promotes bad form and has an important technical drawback. Here's what the Rails plugin creation guide has to say on this issue:

> When Rails loads plugins it looks for the file named init.rb. However, when the plugin is initialized, init.rb is invoked via eval (not require) so it has slightly different behavior.
>
> Under certain circumstances if you reopen classes or modules in init.rb you may inadvertently create a new class, rather than reopening an existing class. A better alternative is to reopen the class in a different file, and require that file from init.rb....

This is why we only use the init.rb file to bootstrap the lib/drivable.rb file. In addition, all the code in lib/drivable/active_record_extensions.rb could be placed in this lib/drivable.rb file. Maintaining this separation from the offset is useful in keeping organization for future growth of the plugin. It's also such a common pattern that following it helps other Rails developers understand and contribute to your plugin.

Gems Fightin' Words!

Ruby had the RubyGems packaging system well before the Rails framework existed. In fact, Rails itself is distributed as a collection of gems. The fact that Rails decided to "reinvent" the packaging of reusable pieces of code in a new plugin format has annoyed some Ruby developers.

There are some reasons for writing a plugin instead of a gem. The most obvious is simplicity: It's easier to produce a plugin. That being said, gems have a lot of features, which we encourage you to explore. For example, you can use gems outside a Rails application, and they come with versioning support. Now with Bundler and Rails 3, and the new http://rubygems.org, gems are easier to distribute and have all the features of plugins. It's easy to get up and running with a quick plugin, but when it's time to package up and distribute your code to others, you should consider converting it to a gem.

Solution: Make Magic Happen with Metaprogramming

Metaprogramming is a wonderful tool for producing DRY code in highly dynamic languages. We use the term *metaprogramming* as a nod to cultural convention, but not without some reservation. Metaprogramming is commonly defined as "code that produces code," and it usually encompasses static code generation, runtime introspection, and other clever tricks. Metaprogramming in most languages involves the use of language facilities designed explicitly for a particular task. In a language such as Ruby, where class definitions are evaluated as regular code, there is technically nothing that makes metaprogramming distinct from regular programming.

Case in Point

To illustrate the benefits of using metaprogramming to keep your application DRY, let's take a look at the Purchase model from a storefront application. In good test-driven development (TDD) fashion, let's first examine a sample of the tests for that model.

```
class PurchaseTest < Test::Unit::TestCase
  context "Given some Purchases of each status" do
    setup do
      %w(in_progress submitted approved
          shipped received canceled).each do |s|
        Factory(:purchase, :status => s)
      end
    end

  context "Purchase.all_in_progress" do
    setup { @purchases = Purchase.all_in_progress }

    should "not be empty" do
      assert !@purchases.empty?
    end

    should "return only in progress purchases" do
      @purchases.each do |purchase|
        assert purchase.in_progress?
```

```
          end
        end

        should "return all in progress purchases" do
          expected = Purchase.all.select(&:in_progress?)
          assert_same_elements expected, @purchases
        end
      end
    end
  end
```

A `Purchase` object can have many statuses: in_progress, submitted, approved, shipped, received, and canceled. It also defines class methods to find all `Purchase` objects of a particular status, as well as predicates for each status. This is a decent API, and one that we see repeated very often.

A First Attempt

A correct but naïve implementation of the `Purchase` model would be to define each pair of methods for every status (for example, the all_submitted and submitted? methods) by hand:

```
class Purchase < ActiveRecord::Base
  validates_presence_of :status
  validates_inclusion_of :status,
                         :in => %w(in_progress submitted approved
                                   shipped received canceled)

  # Status Finders

  def self.all_in_progress
    where(:status => "in_progress")
  end

  def self.all_submitted
    where(:status => "submitted")
  end

  def self.all_approved
    where(:status => "approved")
  end
```

```
    def self.all_shipped
      where(:status => "shipped")
    end

    def self.all_received
      where(:status => "received")
    end

    def self.all_canceled
      where(:status => "canceled")
    end

    # Status Accessors

    def in_progress?
      status == "in_progress"
    end

    def submitted?
      status == "submitted"
    end

    def approved?
      status == "approved"
    end

    def shipped?
      status == "shipped"
    end

    def received?
      status == "received"
    end

    def canceled?
      status == "canceled"
    end
  end
```

It's immediately obvious that this is a code maintenance issue in the making. For now you can ignore the fact that this is a very large amount of code for this feature (more on that in a bit) because the real issue is that the code isn't DRY.

Shim Shim Shazam!

What happens when a client says to you three months down the road that she needs Purchase objects to go through "partially shipped" and "fully shipped" statuses instead of just "shipped"? You now have to edit the states in three distinct places: the validation, the finders, and the accessors. DRY encourages you to hold that type of information in a single, authoritative place. You can accomplish this with a bit of metaprogramming:

```ruby
class Purchase < ActiveRecord::Base
  STATUSES = %w(in_progress submitted approved shipped received)

  validates_presence_of :status
  validates_inclusion_of :status, :in => STATUSES

  # Status Finders

  class << self
    STATUSES.each do |status_name|
      define_method "all_#{status_name}"
        where(:status => status_name)
      end
    end
  end

  # Status Accessors

  STATUSES.each do |status_name|
    define_method "#{status_name}?"
      status == status_name
    end
  end
end
```

The issue most beginner Ruby programmers have with metaprogramming like this is the complexity introduced; this is a completely valid point, and we address it shortly. Before we get to that, let's walk through this implementation and discuss a bit of what's going on.

The most important aspect of this code is that the list of statuses is clearly held in the Purchase::STATUSES array. This is the singular, authoritative location of the statuses list, and changing the list will immediately change the code as needed.

The class then loops through the STATUSES array and uses define_method to create the finder and accessor methods. This bit of code often confuses developers coming from static languages. The key to understanding this implementation is that in Ruby, and unlike in C++ or Java, class definitions are *just code*. Local variables, loops, and all other Ruby constructs are all valid inside a class definition.

In fact, most if not all of the libraries you use every day make use of the incredibly dynamic nature of Ruby. Active Record, for example, uses this flexibility to define setters and accessors at runtime, based on an inspection of the table's columns when a class inherits from ActiveRecord::Base.

DRY Is Not Only About Lines of Code

We hinted earlier that the solution in this section would not be the shortest solution in terms of lines of code. We firmly believe that less code is good code, and we would almost definitely refactor the original implementation to use named scopes instead. If you refactored, the resulting code would look something like this:

```
class Purchase < ActiveRecord::Base
  validates :status,
    :presence => true,
    :inclusion => { :in => %w(in_progress submitted approved
                              shipped received canceled) }

  # Status Finders

  scope :all_in_progress, where(:status => "in_progress")
  scope :all_submitted,   where(:status => "submitted")
  scope :all_approved,   .where(:status => "approved")
  scope :all_shipped,     where(:status => "shipped")
  scope :all_received,    where(:status => "received")
  scope :all_canceled,    where(:status => "canceled")

  # Status Accessors
  def in_progress?
    status == "in_progress"
  end

  def submitted?
    status == "submitted"
  end
```

```
  def approved?
    status == "approved"
  end

  def shipped?
    status == "shipped"
  end

  def received?
    status == "received"
  end

  def canceled?
    status == "canceled"
  end
end
```

We show this implementation to illustrate the point that DRY is *not* only about reducing lines of code. Though the techniques used to combat the various issues tend to overlap, it's important to keep the issues clearly differentiated. This example, suffers from the same flaw of not giving the developer a single place to manage the list of statuses.

Whazawho?

The metaprogramming example in the preceding section certainly suffers from some readability issues. You can address them by extracting the loops into a macro, which in Ruby is simply a class method that's intended to be called at class definition time:

```
# lib/extensions/statuses.rb
class ActiveRecord::Base
  def self.has_statuses(*status_names)
    validates :status,
              :presence => true,
              :inclusion => { :in => status_names }

    # Status Finders
    status_names.each do |status_name|
      scope "all_#{status_name}", where(:status => status_name)
    end
```

```
      # Status Accessors
      status_names.each do |status_name|
        define_method "#{status_name}?" do
          status == status_name
        end
      end
    end
  end

  class Purchase < ActiveRecord::Base
    has_statuses :in_progress, :submitted, :approved, :shipped,
                 :received
  end
```

This example points out the power of Ruby's open classes. Unlike C++ or Java, where a class definition is a static template for the compiler, it's common behavior in Ruby to reopen a class to add new behavior. You need to do this to add the `has_statuses` method to `ActiveRecord::Base`. Doing so both simplifies and increases the readability of the `Purchase` model. It also allows the implementation of statuses to be used in other models throughout the application. Furthermore, it's a short step to move this code from `lib/statuses.rb` into a plugin so that you can use this same pattern across applications.

One of These Things Is Not Like the Other...

An often-underappreciated benefit of DRY code is that it helps in highlighting aspects of code that are exceptional. When you jump into a bit of code with 100 lines of almost identical code, it can be very difficult to figure out which one of those lines doesn't follow the pattern of the rest (if you even know you should be looking for such deviations). If you DRY up the common code, the exceptional code stands out nicely.

Consider a `Purchase` model with the `fully_shipped` and `partially_shipped` statuses. Say that you want to add a virtual status of `not_shipped`, which corresponds to records whose status is neither of the two shipped statuses. The `all_not_shipped` and `not_shipped?` methods in the naïve implementation would quickly become lost in the noise of the rest of the status methods.

The DRY version, however, makes those exceptional methods as clear as possible:

```
  class Purchase < ActiveRecord::Base
    has_statuses %w(in_progress submitted approved
                    partially_shipped fully_shipped)
```

```
    scope :all_not_shipped, where(:status => ["partially_shipped",
                                               "fully_shipped"])

    def not_shipped?
      !(partially_shipped? or fully_shipped?)
    end
  end
```

Don't Fear the Reaper

Metaprogramming is a topic that tends to intimidate beginning Ruby programmers. The advanced nature of the code, coupled with the illusion of magic that surrounds the term is daunting. Be that as it may, any Ruby developers who avoid these techniques do themselves a great disservice. Metaprogramming is a fundamental tool for writing DRY and reusable Ruby code. If it's not one that's in your toolbox now, you should make a point of adding it.

CHAPTER 2

Domain Modeling

The Active Record pattern used in the ORM built into Rails was an innovation to many in the web development community. Because of Active Record, developers no longer have to specify details of the object-relational mapping in great detail, nor do they have to duplicate them in the models and the configuration files. In short, Active Record simplified things and allows developers to work faster.

In addition, the Active Record library also introduced further conventions and innovations that influence the strategy used with domain modeling in the Ruby on Rails framework. For example, has_many :through has pretty much supplanted the more traditional has and belongs to many relationships in Rails domain modeling; it successfully extracted and simplified the complexities and deficiencies in the implicit join model present in a has, and it belongs to many relationships.

When working to effectively model an application's domain in the Rails framework, it's important to keep the Rails principle of simplicity in mind. Many domain-modeling problems merely over-engineer the simple web application you're actually building. It's also important to keep in mind the small shortcuts that the Rails framework provides. Your domain modeling decisions will become more clear as you begin to work with the framework rather than against it.

AntiPattern: Authorization Astronaut

Many applications contain user authorization code, typically represented as user roles. Oftentimes these are programmed based on a specification or in anticipation of future requirements. As a result, typical user authorization might feature a User model like the following:

```ruby
class User < ActiveRecord::Base
  has_and_belongs_to_many :roles, :uniq => true

  def has_role?(role_in_question)
    self.roles.first(:conditions => { :name => role_in_question }) ?
                    true : false
  end

  def has_roles?(roles_in_question)
    roles_in_question =
      self.roles.all(:conditions => ["name in (?)",
                                      roles_in_question])
    roles_in_question.length > 0
  end

  def can_post?
    self.has_roles?(['admin',
                     'editor',
                     'associate editor',
                     'research writer'])
  end

  def can_review_posts?
    self.has_roles?(['admin', 'editor', 'associate editor'])
  end

  def can_edit_content?
    self.has_roles?(['admin', 'editor', 'associate editor'])
  end

  def can_edit_post?(post)
    self == post.user ||
      self.has_roles?(['admin', 'editor', 'associate editor'])
  end
end
```

In this `User` model, a user has a relationship to many different roles. There are two utility methods: the singular `has_role?` that takes a single role and checks to see whether the user has that role and the plural `has_roles?` that takes multiple roles and does the same. In anticipation of the different actions that the roles need to have performed, this example provides several convenience methods for checking to see whether the user can perform specific actions.

There are a number of issues with this code. The `has_role?` method isn't used; only the `has_roles?` method is used, and not just in the `User` model but in the rest of the application as well. This method was written in anticipation of being needed.

Providing these `can_*` convenience methods is a slippery slope. At the very least there is a question about when to provide these methods, and there is a vague and inconsistent interface. At the worst, these methods are actually written ahead of any need, based on speculation about what authorization checks may be needed in the future of the application.

Finally, the `User` model is hardcoding all the strings used to identify the individual roles. If one or more of these were to change, you would need to change them throughout the application. And, most importantly, if one or more of these changes were missed, the model would essentially fail silently.

You can accompany the preceding `User` model with the following `Role` model:

```ruby
class Role < ActiveRecord::Base
  has_and_belongs_to_many :users

  validates_presence_of :name
  validates_uniqueness_of :name

  def name=(value)
    write_attribute("name", value.downcase)
  end

  def self.[](name) # Get a role quickly by using: Role[:admin]
    self.find(:first, :conditions => ["name = ?", name.id2name])
  end

  def add_user(user)
    self.users << user
  end
```

```
  def delete_user(user)
    self.users.delete(user)
  end
end
```

Like the User model before it, this Role model has several problems. In the application that this Role code is from, there is no plan to allow administrative users to add or remove roles. Therefore, the overridden setter for name is questionable.

Also questionable is the overridden getter for roles to make it work like a hash. While something like this could potentially be used to solve the problem of changing identifiers mentioned earlier, it's not written with that intention and therefore doesn't work. This method of retrieving the role isn't actually used anywhere, and it is clearly written as a convenience and in anticipation of a use that hasn't arisen.

Finally, the convenience methods add_user and delete_user, which would be used for adding and removing users from a role are not a good interface. Therefore, they aren't actually used within the application anywhere.

In short, these two models were written in a vacuum. They were written before the application really existed, in anticipation of what might be needed in the future. This seems to happen quite a bit with authorization code. Perhaps this is because while "real planning" is happening, the authorization code is perceived as something that developers can get started on ahead of time. This is a false supposition and leads to code that is over-engineered, provides a vague or inconsistent interface, and ends up being not used properly or at all.

Solution: Simplify with Simple Flags

In order to address the problems of complexity described in the preceding section, you can refactor the User and Role models as follows:

```
class User < ActiveRecord::Base
end
```

With this sweeping change, you can get rid of the Role model entirely. You have given the User model admin, editor, and writer Booleans. With these Booleans, Active Record gives you nice admin?, editor?, and writer? query methods. Finally, the user interface for giving these roles to users is a straightforward check box that sets the associated Boolean.

This simplification of the `User` roles provides all the same functionality as the previous overly complicated `User` and `Role` models, but it effectively uses the tools provided by the Ruby framework and uses the best kind of code: no code.

In the future, it may be necessary to add additional authorization roles to the application. If you need to add just one or two roles, it's not unreasonable to add the additional Booleans to the `User` model.

If you eventually need more roles, you can add a `Role` model back into the application, but without using a `has_and_belongs_to_many`. Instead, you would just add a `has_many` to the `Role` model with a denormalized `role_type` that stores the type of role the user has, as shown here:

```
class User < ActiveRecord::Base
  has_many :roles
end

class Role < ActiveRecord::Base
  TYPES = %w(admin editor writer guest)

  validates :name, :inclusion => { :in => TYPES }

  class << self
    TYPES.each do |role_type|
      define_method "#{role_type}?" do
        exists?(:name => role_type)
      end
    end
  end
end
```

To facilitate the change from individual Booleans to a `Role` model, you use `define_method` to provide a query method for each role type that allows you to call `user.roles.admin?`. It is also possible to put these defined methods right on the `User` model itself, so that `user.admin?` can be called. That would look as follows:

```
class User < ActiveRecord::Base
  has_many :roles

  Role::TYPES.each do |role_type|
    define_method "#{role_type}?" do
      roles.exists?(:name => role_type)
    end
```

```
    end
  end

  class Role < ActiveRecord::Base
    TYPES = %w(admin editor writer guest)
    validates :name, :inclusion => {:in => TYPES}
  end
```

One of the arguments for the former method is that it keeps all the Role-related code encapsulated in the Role model. While this is a legitimate point, putting the query method for roles isn't a particularly egregious violation, especially considering the fact that the roles and the methods for asking about them were previously directly on the User model. In the end, where you put the query method definitions is a matter of personal preference, and this solution is successful regardless of the choice. It's successful because it eliminates needless code, is not over-engineered, and provides a consistent interface that leaves no question about how to work with the User roles.

The concepts outlined here do not apply just to User roles. They are also applicable to many other circumstances when modeling the application domain and defining the interfaces provided by models. The following simple guidelines will stop you from over-engineering and help you provide simple interfaces that stand up in the face of both underdefined specifications and changes in an application:

- Never build beyond the application requirements at the time you are writing the code.

- If you do not have concrete requirements, don't write any code.

- Don't jump to a model prematurely; there are often simple ways, such as using Booleans and denormalization, to avoid using adding additional models.

- If there is no user interface for adding, removing, or managing data, there is no need for a model. A denormalized column populated by a hash or array of possible values is fine.

AntiPattern: The Million-Model March

While there isn't necessarily anything wrong with Active Record models, overusing them adds unnecessary complexity and overhead. Many developers don't realize the amount of new code that "just one more model" creates. You don't have just the model class itself, but also the database migrations to create the table for the model, the unit tests for the model, the factories or fixtures for those tests, and the inevitable finders and validations that go along with a model. A domain model that has individual models for each separate piece of information is known as a *normalized domain model*.

Solution: Denormalize into Text Fields

Take a look at the following `Article` model and the associated `State` and `Category` models:

```ruby
class Article < ActiveRecord::Base
  belongs_to :state
  belongs_to :category

  validates :state_id,    :presence => true
  validates :category_id, :presence => true
end

class State < ActiveRecord::Base
  has_many :articles
end

class Category < ActiveRecord::Base
  has_many :articles
end
```

Given these models, the specific set of available states and categories would be loaded into the production application's respective database tables, and code for working with these associations would be as follows:

```ruby
@article.state = State.find_by_name("published")
```

Of course, repeating the finder and the string for the published state is bad practice, so it might be wise to abstract that out into a custom finder on the `State` model:

```
@article.state = State.published
```

Checking whether an article is in a current state might look like this:

```
@article.state == State.published
```

The code for dynamically defining these custom finder methods might be as follows:

```
class State < ActiveRecord::Base
  validates :name, :presence => true

  class << self
    all.each do |state|
      define_method "#{state}" do
        first(:conditions => { :name => state })
      end
    end
  end
end
```

You could also dynamically define methods directly on `Article`; for example, to check whether an article is published, you use `@article.published?`. The API for using and querying article state doesn't matter too much; the important thing is to not hardcode the strings or foreign keys that represent the individual states.

Very often, there is quite a bit of functionality associated with these types of models (states, categories, and so on) and, therefore, it's not desirable to allow end users—or even administrators—to add or remove available states in the database. For example, if the article publication workflow changes and a new state needs to be added, it's unlikely that an administrator can simply add the state to the database and have everything as desired. Therefore, when you're building lean, agile applications, it doesn't make sense to spend time and effort programming an administrative interface for states. And if there isn't a user interface for adding and removing states, then it simply isn't worthwhile to store the states in the database. Instead, you can just store the states in the code itself. To do this, you would denormalize the data from the state and category tables into the article table itself, and you would remove the `State` and `Category` models. When you do all this, the `Article` model looks as follows:

```ruby
class Article < ActiveRecord::Base
  STATES = %w(draft review published archived)
  CATEGORIES = %w(tips faqs misc)

  validates :state,    :inclusion => {:in => STATES}
  validates :category, :inclusion => {:in => CATEGORIES}

  STATES.each do |state|
    define_method "#{state}?" do
      self.state == state
    end
  end

  CATEGORIES.each do |category|
    define_method "#{category}?" do
      self.category == category
    end
  end

  class << self
    STATES.each do |state|
      define_method "#{state}" do
        state
      end
    end

    CATEGORIES.each do |category|
      define_method "#{category}" do
        category
      end
    end
  end
end
```

As you can see, the total code shown here for the normalized version is very similar to the code for the denormalized version. The dynamic methods are still being defined, but the difference here is that the `Article` model now has `state` and `category` columns that contain a string representing the state instead of foreign key columns to hold the ID of the `State` and `Category`. The most important thing is the complexity and code that it *not* represented here. You've completely removed the possibility of a user interface to manage states and categories without refactoring. Such a refactoring would be perfectly fine if the application requirements warranted it, but it is unnecessary when they don't.

Solution: Make Use of Rails Serialization

Earlier in this chapter, we listed the following tenets, which bear repeating:

- Never build beyond the application requirements at the time you are writing the code.

- If you do not have concrete requirements, don't write any code.

- Don't jump to a model prematurely; there are often simple ways, such as using Booleans and denormalization, to avoid using adding additional models.

- If there is no user interface for adding, removing, or managing data, there is no need for a model. A denormalized column populated by a hash or array of possible values is fine.

These guidelines will help you keep your code lean and agile. This will, in turn, allow you to more easily change your application as requirements either become more defined or change completely.

Take a look at the user interface in Figure 2.1.

Figure 2.1 A form that enables a user to select multiple values for an item, including Other.

Figure 2.1 shows a registration form where the user is asked to select the one or more ways he or she heard about the organization. A user who selects Other should fill in the "other" text input field. This is a fairly common interface, and you can model it in a few different ways, using Active Record models.

"Has" and "Belongs to Many"

The first way to model the user interface shown in Figure 2.1 is to normalize the possible "heard about" values into a `Referral` model that is related to the user with a "has and belongs to many" relationship:

```
class User < ActiveRecord::Base
  has_many :referral_types
end

class Referral < ActiveRecord::Base
  has_and_belongs_to_many :users
end
```

In addition, `User` has a string attribute, `referral_other`, that stores the value typed into the "other" input field.

"Has Many"

The second way to model the user interface shown in Figure 2.1 would be to not join the `User` and `Referral` models together with a "has many" relationship and not normalize the content of the `Referral` model. The model code for this would look as follows:

```
class User < ActiveRecord::Base
  has_many :referral_types
end

class Referral < ActiveRecord::Base
  VALUES = ['Newsletter', 'School', 'Web',
            'Partners/Events', 'Media', 'Other']
  validates :value, :inclusion => {:in => VALUES}

  belongs_to :user
end
```

In addition, the `User` model would once again have a string attribute, `referral_other`, used for storing the value typed into the "other" input field.

Nothing at All

Both of the approaches just described introduce another model. Let's refer to the tenets listed earlier and evaluate these two approaches.

There is no user interface for anyone to add or remove possible `Referral` values. The "has and belongs to many" modeling makes sense if this ability is necessary. The denormalized version attempts to address the final two guidelines by denormalizing and avoiding a secondary lookup table that would be needed by the "has and belongs to many" relationships. However, is there a way to take this one step further and remove the necessity for the `Referral` model altogether?

Yes, there is! There are, in fact, two possible ways. The first would be just to have an individual Boolean column for each check box and then the `referral_other` column that the other solutions had. This would involve using six Boolean attributes on the model. Now that they are Booleans, the naming could be adjusted, so these Boolean attributes might be called `heard_through_newsletter`, `heard_through_school`, `heard_through_web`, `heard_through_partners`, `heard_through_media`, and `heard_through_other`.

This approach is perfectly valid, but it will be strained with six check boxes and an Other option. For two to three check boxes, though, this might be a good solution. The amount of code necessary is greatly reduced, the view code is incredibly straightforward, and the attributes are easy to work with.

There is another way you can do this that does not introduce a model: You can use Ruby on Rails serialization to store which one of the many check boxes is checked. The model code for this solution would look like the following:

```
class User < ActiveRecord::Base
  HEARD_THROUGH_VALUES = ['Newsletter', 'School', 'Web',
                          'Partners/Events', 'Media', 'Other']
  serialize :heard_through, Hash
end
```

The `serialize` method declares that the specified attribute. In this case, `:heard_through` stores a serialized instance of the Ruby class specified in the second argument (in this case, a `Hash`).

Now each of the check boxes will be either checked or unchecked, resulting in a `Hash` of the checked values being submitted. The view code that makes this possible looks as follows:

```
<%= fields_for :heard_through, (form.object.heard_through||{})
    do |heard_through_fields| -%>
  <% User::HEARD_THROUGH_VALUES.each do |heard_through_val| -%>
    <%= heard_through_fields.check_box "field %>
```

```
      <%= heard_through_fields.label :heard_through,
         heard_through_val %>
   <% end -%>
<% end -%>
```

Like the Boolean method, this solution results in less code, fewer database tables, and less overall complexity. However, it does have some disadvantages. Once you begin serializing data into individual attributes, you lose the ability to efficiently search and aggregate the data by using the normal find calls. You can simulate this by using partial string matching on the serialized data, but that will get you only so far. Therefore, as with many other solutions, you should serialize data only when it is the right solution.

Another scenario where serialization of data into attributes can be the correct solution is when the data you will be storing is open ended. For example, say that you have an application that takes in data from other applications and stores it, or you have a complicated series of forms or user-generated content, and the exact format and parameters of the data will not be known. In these circumstances, it may not be worthwhile to attempt to come up with a data model using Active Record models that can effectively store this data. While it can be done, the overhead and complexity introduced by these models are not necessarily worth it.

Instead of using the models just described, it may be possible to store this data in serialized attributes on the parent model. Take, for example, the plugin Acts As Revisionable (http://actsasrevisions.rubyforge.org). This plugin allows you to declare that any model in your application should be versioned. This plugin provides functionality to the ActsAsVersioned program, but it solves the same problem in a different way. The ActsAsVersioned plugin requires an additional, identical table for each model for which you have versioning functionality. So, for example, if the Document model should save each previous version, the application must have a document_versions table where the old values can be stored.

However, the Acts As Revisionable plugin provides the versioning functionality by using serialization (not the serialization provided by Ruby on Rails) to store the old values. With this technique, one table can be used to store multiple models, regardless of the attributes and associations they each contain.

Another example of open-ended data for which the format is not known is thoughtbot's web-based error catching application Hoptoad (http://hoptoadapp.com). Hoptoad receives data—typically Ruby exceptions—from client applications, saves them, identifies duplicate exceptions, and aggregates like exceptions together. Along

with an exception, Hoptoad takes in other open-ended data, including details about
the request that caused the exception, the session data of the application and the environment of the web server when the exception occurred, and the full backtrace of the
application for the exception. The request and session data, in particular, can be composed of any number of other Ruby objects (which have all been serialized for communication to Hoptoad over HTTP).

To further complicate matters, Ruby and Ruby on Rails are not the only supported platforms for Hoptoad. The service accepts any data, from any application, as
long as it's formatted as Hoptoad expects. While it would certainly be possible to normalize some of the data Hoptoad receives into associated models, the incredibly open-
ended nature of this data begs you to just keep it simple and serialize the data into the
database. This is precisely what you do. The model code for doing this is straightforward—which is one of the reasons serialization of the data is an attractive solution:

```ruby
# Notices represent the exceptions sent in from other applications
class Notice < ActiveRecord::Base
  serialize :request,     Hash
  serialize :session,     Hash
  serialize :environment, Hash
  serialize :backtrace,   Array
end
```

Because Ruby and Rails are the primary supported language and framework of
Hoptoad, and because you do want to aggregate the data and easily present some data
in the user interface, you should take the opportunity to read some of this serialized
data and store it specifically into attributes on the notice. For example, data such as
the Rails environment in which the error occurred, the controller and action from the
request, and the file and line number from the backtrace are all stored specifically in
attributes. These attributes are extracted from the serialized backtrace, request, and
environment in `before_create` callbacks on `Notice`:

```ruby
before_validation :extract_backtrace_info,   :on => :create
before_validation :extract_request_info,     :on => :create
before_validation :extract_environment_info, :on => :create

private

def extract_backtrace_info
  unless backtrace.blank?
```

```
      self.file, self.line_number = backtrace.first.split(':')
    end
  end

  def extract_request_info
    unless request.blank? or request[:params].nil?
      self.controller = request[:params][:controller]
      self.action     = request[:params][:action]
    end
  end

  def extract_environment_info
    unless environment.blank?
      self.rails_env = environment['RAILS_ENV']
    end
  end
end
```

As previously mentioned, the primary downside of serialization of data is that you lose the ability to search through the serialized data. However, in some cases, such as with versioning or simply the storage of complex, open-ended data such as in Hoptoad, searching past data is not a concern, and serialization is a valid—or even preferred—technique over attempting to normalize all the data into individual models.

CHAPTER 3

Views

The *V* in MVC—*View* in a Ruby on Rails application—is the presentation layer. The default view-rendering engine built into Ruby on Rails is ERb, and when Rails was first released, standard ERb templates were the only built-in supported type of template. As Rails has evolved, so has the capability of the View layer, expanding to include the ability to render different views based on MIME type and to include a new technology called RJS, among other changes.

Like the rest of the Rails framework, views follow convention over configuration. Rails encourages standard names and locations for view files, standard locations for helpers, conventions for common DOM elements, and so on. With this organization, everything has a place and can be easily found.

For our purposes, we consider the entire presentation stack to be the View layer of Rails. This includes the view template files and view helpers, as well as JavaScript and CSS. This holistic approach to the View layer allows you, as a developer, to keep your sights on the overall picture of the presentation layer, establishing and following conventions that address the needs of the entire presentation layer rather than just a small portion of it.

Despite the relatively straightforward nature of Rails views, developers often face challenges in using the View layer of Rails effectively. While the holistic approach just described is beneficial, the fact that the View layer is a mix of different technologies and languages living together—JavaScript, HTML, CSS, and Ruby (often in the same file)—stands in contrast to the rest of the Rails framework. This can lead to confusion, disorganization, and often completely incorrect implementations.

The views in an application may also have the added benefit of being edited by non-Ruby programmers, such as designers and HTML/CSS wranglers. Ultimately, it's just as important to practice restraint and organization in the views as in the models and controllers. Unfortunately, for many reasons, developers often overlook this practice.

Throughout this chapter, we show practical, best-practice techniques for maintaining the organization and tidiness that will ultimately lead to more straightforward code that is easier to test and maintain.

AntiPattern: PHPitis

The View layer of the MVC framework can vary widely in the technologies it contains, depending on the nature of the framework. For example, an MVC framework for desktop applications may deal in binary representations of buttons and widgets on the screen, while the Ruby on Rails framework primarily uses ERb. Regardless of the technology, the purpose of the View layer is to deal only with presentation, and while it can often be overlooked by Ruby on Rails developers more concerned with the back end, the View layer of a Rails application is ultimately just as important, if not more so, to the overall success of an application than the Model and Controller layers.

The View layer of Ruby on Rails consists of the view template files, view helpers, JavaScript, and CSS. The view templates are kept in the `/app/views` directory, which contains multiple subdirectories, one for each controller and mailer, as well as the `layouts` directory. The `layouts` directory contains the global templates that encapsulate the individual templates in the other directories and often contains other pieces of the view, such as partials, that are used across multiple controllers or mailers. In addition, view helpers are stored in `/app/helpers`, which by convention contains one file for each controller. Finally, CSS and JavaScript are stored in `/public/stylesheets` and `/public/javascripts`, respectively.

The view templates in a default Rails installation can be one of three types—an ERb template, an RJS template, or a builder template—and each template can also be used for rendering for a specific format.

While the individual components of the Rails View layer are stored in an organized fashion, the components are in different locations, and they have many permutations.

In addition, because a mix of technologies is used, it's very easy—especially as development of an application progresses—for HTML, CSS, JavaScript, and Ruby to become coupled and intermingled.

Perhaps the most egregious intermingling that can occur is pure Ruby in the view template. There are several reasons this is undesirable:

- The Ruby in the view could be domain logic instead of presentation logic. There is a difference, and following the MVC pattern, domain logic never belongs in the view.

- The Ruby could be presentation logic but could be so complex as to overly complicate the view, make it hard to maintain or change, and make it difficult to test.

- The view templates are primarily HTML (or XML or RJS). If this is not the case, and too much pure Ruby is contained in the template, then concerns regarding the template itself may be masked. For example, properly formatted, validating HTML will be harder to achieve and debug if the View template is littered with excess Ruby.

The PHP language is not, out of the box, an MVC framework and doesn't provide the rigid structure that Rails provides. Many PHP applications commingle the domain logic, complex presentation logic, and controller code all in one file. For this reason, when lots of code, including domain logic, is included in a Rails view, the view starts to look very much like PHP code. For many PHP programmers coming to Rails, this might feel comfortable, but it's a false comfort.

In the following sections, we discuss some very effective measures you can take to address the problem of excess Ruby in your view templates. Doing so will result in clean templates that are a joy to work in, are well tested, and can be easily maintained and changed.

Solution: Learn About the View Helpers That Come with Rails

Ruby on Rails provides hundreds of helper methods that are direct extractions of common view-centric tasks. From displaying alternating rows of data to building complex forms, many common tasks for a web application are already handled, or partially handled, by existing Rails helpers. While it may be impossible to learn them all, let alone the details about the individual options each helper takes, a working knowledge of the helpers available, and the ability to find new ones and the customization of each, is an important skill that will assist in the creation of svelte, maintainable view code.

In addition, Ruby on Rails continues to adapt its extractions even further, based on the traditional Rails values of convention over configuration and DRY principals. Keeping up with these changes will allow you to reduce the amount of Ruby on a view even further.

Take, for example, the following view code. This code used to be necessary to output a form to the update action of a RESTful `UsersController`:

```
<%= form_for :user,
             :url => user_path(@user),
             :html => {:method => :put} do |form| %>
```

This code outputs the following HTML:

```
<form action="/users/5" method="post">
  <div style="margin:0;padding:0">
    <input name="_method" type="hidden" value="put" />
  </div>
```

The following is the corresponding code for the new form for a user.

```
<%= form_for :user, :url => users_path do |form| %>
```

This code outputs the following HTML:

```
<form action="/users" method="post">
```

Notice that both of these methods have a lot of redundant information, and the edit form needs to specify the HTTP method to be used for editing an existing user.

In Rails 2.1, this was reduced to the simple, consistent method call:

```
<%= form_for @user do |form| %>
```

This one signature for a form_for call can be used for both the edit and new forms. When the @user is not yet saved, the code outputs the form for an unsaved user, as follows:

```
<form action="/users" method="POST" class="new_user" id="new_user">
```

And when @user contains a User record that is already saved to the database, the code outputs the form for editing that existing user as shown here:

```
<form action="/users/5" method="post" class="edit_user"
      id="edit_user_5">
  <div style="margin:0;padding:0">
    <input name="_method" type="hidden" value="put" />
  </div>
```

Notice that this leaner form_for call also adds additional class and id attributes to the form tag. The HTML required for adding these other classes made it unwieldy to do before, but now that it's done automatically, this consistency enables ease of programming in both JavaScript and CSS.

Similarly, the mechanism for rendering a collection of elements in a view has been revised. The "manual" way of rendering a collection of posts in a view would be as follows:

```
<!-- posts/index.html.erb -->
<% @posts.each do |post| %>
  <h2><%= post.title %></h2>
  <%= format_content post.body %>
  <p>
    <%= link_to 'Email author', mail_to(post.user.email) %>
  </p>
<% end %>
```

This code loops over the collection of posts and outputs the content for each post in the collection. You can clean this up in the view by moving the template code for each individual post into a post partial, as shown here:

```
<!-- posts/index.html.erb -->
<% @posts.each do |post| %>
  <%= render :partial => 'post', :object => :post %>
<% end %>

<!-- posts/_post.erb -->
<h2><%= post.title %></h2>
<%= format_content post.body %>
<p>
  <%= link_to 'Email author', mail_to(post.user.email) %>
</p>
```

Now, for each post in the loop, the partial is rendered. Fortunately, this was abstracted, and the Rails render method can handle collections of objects on its own, as follows:

```
<!-- posts/index.html.erb -->
<%= render :partial => 'post', :collection => @posts %>

<!-- posts/_post.erb -->
<h2><%= post.title %></h2>
<%= format_content post.body %>
```

```
<p>
  <%= link_to 'Email author', mail_to(post.user.email) %>
</p>
```

In this example, the manual looping through the collection is no longer needed. Instead, the Rails `render` method does this on its own, rendering the post partial for each item in the collection.

Finally, Rails developers noticed that it was incredibly common for the partial to be named the same thing all the time (that is, using the class name of the items in the collection). Therefore, a further abstraction was made, allowing for the following simplified `render` call:

```
<!-- posts/index.html.erb -->
<%= render @posts %>

<!-- posts/_post.erb -->
<h2><%= post.title %></h2>
<%= format_content post.body %>
<p>
  <%= link_to 'Email author', mail_to(post.user.email) %>
</p>
```

If the view code for an application was originally written in an earlier version of Ruby on Rails, or if the developer was simply not aware of these improvements, the result would be overly verbose view code that could be improved by these shortcuts.

An additional view helper provided by Rails but often overlooked by developers is the `content_for` helper. This helper is a powerful tool that can introduce additional organization into your view files without the need for custom methods.

You use the `content_for` method to insert content into various sections of a layout. For example, consider the following view layout:

```
<html>
  <body>
    <ul class="nav">
      <li><%= link_to "Home", root_url %></li>
      <li><%= link_to "Maps", maps_url %></li>
      <%= yield :nav %>
    </ul>
    <div class="main">
```

```
    <%= yield %>
  </div>
 </body>
</html>
```

The yield method in this application is a companion to the content_for method. Envision a website where the content of the nav can change, depending on the view being rendered to the visitor. An accompanying view would call content_for and give it the content for the nav. Any view content not handed to a specific named section is given to the default, unnamed yield. For example, a view that populates the nav and the main section of the view would appear as follows:

```
<% content_for :nav do %>
  <li>
    <%= link_to "Your Account", account_url %>
  </li>
  <li>
    <%= link_to "Your Maps", user_maps_url(current_user) %>
  </li>
<% end %>


This is the content for the main section of the website.  Go <%=
link_to "Home", root_url %>
```

When this view is rendered, the call will render the additional content for the nav to yield :nav.

Many developers who are not familiar with content_for will accomplish this functionality by assigning the content for various sections to instance variables, either in the controller or the view itself, using the render_to_string or render :inline methods. It's almost never necessary to assign for use in the view instance variables that are content and not specific Ruby objects and collections. Any time you find yourself doing so, you should reevaluate your approach to the problem you're attempting to solve.

Developers seem to overlook using content_for for smaller pieces of content. For example, it's a fairly common user interface design technique to place an id or class attribute on the BODY tag of an HTML page. It's possible to use the content_for helper for this as well. For example, the BODY tag in the layout would be as follows:

```
<body class="<%= yield :body_class %>">
```

And the view would contain a call to content_for:

```
<% content_for :body_class, "home" %>
```

In addition, using content_for to populate page titles and breadcrumbs is a convenient technique:

```
<head>
  <title>Acme Widgets : <%= yield :title %></title>
</head>
```

Finally, it's possible to only conditionality yield content if that content is supplied. This has two common use cases: to provide default content and to not include surrounding tags if there is no content. For example, if you want a default page title if no title is supplied in the view, you would use the title tag and yield as follows:

```
<head>
  <title>
    Acme Widgets : <%= yield(:title) || "Home" %>
  </title>
</head>
```

In this example, if no title is supplied by the view, and therefore, yield(:title) returns nil, the default title "Home" will be used.

This same technique can be used to conditionally include surrounding tags only if content is supplied. For example, given a layout with a sidebar, if a view does not provide content for the sidebar, the sidebar should not be included in the view, and because the style for the page is flexible, this would cause the main content to extend the full width of the page. It's possible to accomplish this by including the entire content of the sidebar, including the sidebar itself, in the call to content_for, as shown here:

```
<% content_for :sidebar do %>
  <div class="sidebar">
    This is content for the sidebar.
    <%= link_to "Your Account", account_url %></li>
  </div>
<% end %>
```

However, `<div class="sidebar">` is repeated in each view with a sidebar. This can lead to errors, and if the class or markup needs to change for the sidebar, then it must be changed in every view where it appears. `<div class="sidebar">` should be in the layout, and it should be conditionally rendered only if the view is providing content for the sidebar. This is accomplished as follows:

```
<% if content_for?(:sidebar) %>
  <div class="sidebar">
    <%= yield :sidebar %>
  </div>
<% end %>
```

Solution: Add Useful Accessors to Your Models

When refactoring your view code to remove Ruby, or when creating view helpers right off the bat, it's important to keep in mind that not all Ruby code that's in the views may belong in a helper method. Instead, it's possible that this code is actual domain logic and belongs in the model instead. You shouldn't move code into a helper, and you shouldn't create helpers for logic that doesn't really have anything to do with the view at all and instead has to do with the model itself. For example, if a link to edit a post is conditional, based on several circumstances, the non-ideal view code might look something like the following:

```
<% if current_user &&
      (current_user == @post.user ||
       @post.editors.include?(current_user)) &&
       @post.editable? &&
       @post.user.active? %>
  <%= link_to 'Edit this post', edit_post_url(@post) %>
<% end %>
```

It might be tempting to move all this conditional logic into a view helper, like `post_editable_by?`. However, this logic actually should be on the post model itself, in a method called `editable_by?`, so your view would then contain the following:

```
<% if @post.editable_by?(current_user) %>
  <%= link_to 'Edit this post', edit_post_url(@post) %>
<% end %>
```

Generally, whether a method belongs in a view helper or in the model is decided by where the method will be used. The `editable_by?` method will be used both in the view to conditionally present an edit link and also in the controller edit and update actions to enforce the post editing permissions. Because this method is used both in the view and the controller, and it relates specifically to permissions to take action on a model, these are indicators that this method belongs on the model itself.

On the other hand, methods that are used only in the view for presentation concerns, even though they directly relate to the model, are best kept as view helper methods. Take, for example, a web-based job board application with a `Job` model that has a title attribute. Frequently, the available jobs are listed in the sidebar of the application, which is of limited width. One day, a bug report is filed, reporting that when a `Job` is entered where the title contains slashes (for example, `"Software Developer/Ruby/Washington, D.C."`), the text wrapping in the limited-width sidebar is not broken on the slashes, causing the content to overrun the width of the box, throwing off the look of the page. After attempting various CSS and HTML solutions to get the text to wrap properly, you determine that no cross-browser solution is available to cause the job title to be wrapped on the slashes, and the only solution is to add a space on either side of each slash, so that the title become `"Software Developer / Ruby / Washington, D.C."`

In the preceding scenario, there are a few different ways to solve this problem. First, it would be possible to transform the data being input into the title field to ensure that slashes are surrounded by spaces. One major downside to this is that the original data the user entered is not preserved. It's not possible to know what the user originally typed in, and you lose the flexibility to deal with future requirements changes regarding the `title` attribute. In addition, this solution works only for newly entered job titles. A data migration would need to be performed to transform existing job titles in this same way.

Another solution would be to override the getter method for the title attribute on the model so that when the title is requested, it is modified in the desired way. While this addresses most of the problems with the first proposed solution, it does not address the additional issue that this concern is strictly limited to view presentation of the data entered by the user. An excellent place to deal with this requirement is in a view helper used for the presentation of job titles:

```
def display_title(job)
  job.title.split(/\s*\/\s*/).join(" / ")
end
```

As you approach view helpers, it's important that you keep in mind MVC concerns and ensure that your methods are in the appropriate places.

Solution: Extract into Custom Helpers

The most obvious way to deal with excess Ruby code in your views is to remove it. Rails provides the facility to do this by enabling you to move this code into methods called helpers. You can then call the helper methods from the view. Helpers increase readability and maintainability of your views, and because helpers are methods on a `Helper` class, it's possible to unit test your helper methods, which is typically much easier than doing more complex functional tests in order to test logic that's contained within a view.

For example, the following is an example of view code in the index view of an `AlertsController`:

```
<div class="feed">
  <% if @project %>
    <%= link_to "Subscribe to #{@project.name} alerts.",
          project_alerts_url(@project, :format => :rss),
          :class => "feed_link" %>
  <% else %>
    <%= link_to "Subscribe to these alerts.",
            alerts_url(format => :rss),
            :class => "feed_link" %>
  <% end %>
</div>
```

In this application, `AlertsController` can either show all alerts across all projects, or it can be limited to show just the alerts of one project. If it's showing alerts for all projects, the text of the link will be "Subscribe to these alerts"; otherwise, the link text will include the specific project name.

Deprecation of Formatted URL Helpers

In Rails 2.0 through 2.2, to output the URL of a "formatted" route—that is, one with an extension, such as /projects/alerts.rss—you would use the formatted URL helpers (for example, `formatted_project_alerts_url(@project, :rss)`). Starting with Rails 2.3, these methods were deprecated in favor of the `:format` option to the regular URL helpers (for example, project_alerts_url(@project, :format => :rss)). These extra helpers were taking up a lot of extra memory in Rails applications and served minimal purpose.

The view code above can be moved into a helper named rss_link, as shown here:

```
def rss_link(project = nil)
  if project
    link_to "Subscribe to #{project.name} alerts.",
            project_alerts_url(project, :format => :rss),
            :class => "feed_link"
  else
    link_to "Subscribe to these alerts.",
            alerts_url(:format => :rss),
            :class => "feed_link"
  end
end
```

The rss_link method shown here is essentially the view code moved into a helper method. You can continue to improve this method. There are two reasons you need a conditional in this method: you need to include the project name in the text of the link, and you need a different URL helper. By creating a second helper method for the determination of the URL helper, you can simplify the rss_link method. You can call this method alerts_rss_url:

```
def alerts_rss_url(project = nil)
  if project
    project_alerts_url(project, :format => :rss)
  else
    alerts_url(:rss)
  end
end
```

With this new helper method in place, you can simplify the rss_link method:

```
def rss_link(project = nil)
  link_to "Subscribe to these #{project.name if project} alerts.",
          alerts_rss_url(project),
          :class => "feed_link"
end
```

You have cleaned up the view by using this method. It's now as simple as the following:

```
<div class="feed">
  <%= rss_link(@project) %>
</div>
```

Markup Helpers

Helpers are used for more than just cleaning up Ruby code in your views. You can also include the markup surrounding your code in the helpers. Because the div surrounding the link will always be present and is an implementation detail that distracts from the view code as a whole, it's an ideal candidate for inclusion in the helper. Also, to further structure the markup produced by a helper, and to facilitate inclusion of additional markup in helper methods, you should use the content_tag method.

The content_tag method takes an HTML tag as its first argument and a hash as its second argument (with the keys and values used as the attributes of the resulting HTML tag). In addition, content_tag takes an optional block, which is then used to provide further subtags. By using content_tag and including the surrounding div in rss_link, the helper now looks as follows:

```
def rss_link(project = nil)
  content_tag :div, :class => "feed" do
    link_to "Subscribe to these #{project.name if project} alerts.",
            alerts_rss_url(project),
            :class => "feed_link"
  end
end
```

It's worth considering consistent use of the content_tag method as an alternative to the link_to helper. This can lead to a more readable structure when you have more complex markup. For more information on this technique, see the section "AntiPattern: Markup Mayhem," later in this chapter. If you change to using the content_tag method instead of the link_to helper, the rss_link method appears as follows:

```
def rss_link(project = nil)
  content_tag :div, :class => "feed" do
    content_tag :a,
                "Subscribe to these
```

```
                    #{project.name if project} alerts.",
                    :href => alerts_rss_url(project),
                    :class => "feed_link"
        end
    end
```

By making effective use of helpers that are self-contained (in that they include the surrounding markup), your views will be significantly easier to read. However, as with any other technique, it's good only in moderation. If you need to include a lot of markup, you should probably just use a view partial instead.

Everything in Its Place

When using view helpers effectively, it's important not to just put all your helper methods in `application_helper.rb`. While this is "easy" because they are then automatically available in all your controllers and views, `ApplicationHelper` quickly becomes a dumping ground for everything, resulting is a confusing mess of unconnected code. In this scenario, it's not unsurprising to find old helpers in `ApplicationHelper` that aren't even used in the application anymore.

You should provide structure to your helpers by putting them in the helper files of the resource they are related to. You should even feel free to abandon the convention of strictly sticking to a helper file for each resource (controller) and instead create new helper files, organized by functional area. Your helpers are available throughout your entire application, and you can focus on keeping them organized logically, without worrying about how to call them appropriately.

Test Rails View Helpers

Traditionally, unlike the rest of the framework, the view helper portion of Rails lacked built-in support for testing. Therefore, at worst, many helper methods written by Rails developers would go completely untested, and at best, the strategy for testing helper methods was inconsistent from application to application, or even within a single application.

Fortunately, Rails 2.1 introduced a built-in mechanism for testing view helpers that incorporates many of the setup conventions that have made helper testing particularly challenging in the past. Now, there is no reason your helper methods should remain untested.

The class `ActionView::TestCase` provides the setup harnesses for effectively testing helper methods, but it is not included in your tests by default, so you need to require it when your tests are run. You do this by including `require 'action_view/test_case'` in your `test/test_helper.rb` file.

`ActionView::TestCase` provides a `TestController`, with test request (`ActionController::TestRequest`), test response (`ActionController::TestResponse`), and empty `params`. `ActionView::TestCase` also sets up your helper tests so that when they run and you call one of your helper methods in your tests, the helper is executed within the `TestController`. In this way, your helpers have access to the test request, response, and `params` from your helper tests.

Finally, the standard location for helper tests is in `test/unit/helpers`, and the filenames follow the standard Rails unit test naming conventions. For example, if you have `PlansHelper`, its unit tests would live in `test/unit/helpers/plans_helper_test.rb`.

Now that you have the relevant background and setup information, you can run the following tests for the `rss_link` and `alerts_rss_url` methods:

```
require 'test_helper'

class ProjectsHelperTest < ActionView::TestCase

  context "the rss_link method" do
    setup do
      @result = rss_link(@project)
    end

    should "include a link to the alerts_rss_url" do
      assert_match /href="#{alerts_rss_url}"/, @result
    end

    should "include a div with the class feed" do
      assert_match /div class="feed"/, @result
    end

    should "include an A tag with the class feed_link" do
      assert_match /a class="feed_link"/, @result
    end
  end
```

```
context "with a project" do
  setup do
    @project = Factory(:project)
  end

  context "the rss_link method" do
    setup do
      @result = rss_link(@project)
    end

    should "have the project name in the rss link" do
      assert_match /Subscribe to these #{@project.name} alerts/,
                   @result
    end

    should "include a link to the rss for the project" do
      assert_match /href="#{alerts_rss_url(@project)}"/,
                   @result
    end
  end
end

context "the alerts_rss_url method" do
  setup do
    @result = alerts_rss_url
  end

  should "return the rss alerts url" do
    assert_equal alerts_url(:rss), @result
  end
end

context "with a project" do
  setup do
    @project = Factory(:project)
  end

  context "the alerts_rss_url method" do
    setup do
      @result = alerts_rss_url(@project)
    end
```

```
        should "return the rss project alerts url" do
          assert_equal project_alerts_url(@project,
                                              :format => :rss),
                    @result
        end
      end
    end
  end
```

AntiPattern: Markup Mayhem

As all good designers know (and are more than willing to expound upon at length over a beer), semantic markup is king.

Semantic markup is a fancy term for separating content and presentation in your HTML. From a practical point of view, this means three things:

- Every element in the page that wraps specific content should have a `class` or `id` attribute applied to it that identifies that content.

- The right tags should be used for the right content.

- Styling should be done at the CSS level and never on the element directly.

Some tags have intrinsic semantic meaning. A `<p>` tag represents a paragraph, an `<h1>` the main header, and so on. Some other common tags, such as `<div>` and `<span>`, do not have intrinsic semantic meaning.

The following is an example of HTML markup that's likely to get you into a bar fight with a designer (they're a rough crowd):

```
<div>
  <div>
    <span style="font-size: 2em;">
      I love kittens!
    </span>
  </div>
  <div>
    I love kittens because they're
    <span style="font-style: italic">
      soft and fluffy!
    </span>
  </div>
</div>
```

This is the epitome of non-semantic markup. The `<div>` and `<span>` tags have no meaning and are unadorned with `class` or `id` attributes. And the styles are applied directly on the elements. The following is a much better example:

```
<div id="posts">
  <div id="post_1" class="post">
    <h2>
```

```
      I love kittens!
    </h2>
    <div class="body">
      I love kittens because they're
      <em>
        soft and fluffy!
      </em>
    </div>
  </div>
</div>
```

Isn't this better? This example uses the <h2> and <em> tags correctly, and it tags the various divs to identify the content they represent. Another way of evaluating the semantic nature of a page is by considering how much sense the page makes when the content is stripped out and only the tags are left. Consider the following:

```
<div>
  <div>
    <span style="font-size: 2em;" />
  </div>
  <div>
    <span style="font-style: italic" />
  </div>
</div>
```

Now look at the more semantic version:

```
<div id="posts">
  <div id="post_1" class="post">
    <h2/>
    <div class="body">
      <em/>
    </div>
  </div>
</div>
```

It's clear what the general form of the content would be in the second version, even without seeing it.

The holy grail of web design is a site that can be completely restyled without modifying any HTML content; only CSS changes would be allowed. While this is a lofty goal, sites such as http://csszengarden.com have shown that it is possible. Keeping your HTML semantic is a major step toward this goal. Not only are you no longer required to find and modify every `<span style="color: blue">`, but you can target your elements in your CSS files as `.posts .post .body`, which makes the CSS much more maintainable.

Another hallmark of modern web development is the concept of unobtrusive JavaScript. A full treatise on this concept is beyond the scope of this solution, but the basic concept is simple: JavaScript should not be included inline in a page, but should be separated into external JavaScript files and attached to the relevant pieces of the DOM at runtime. Targeting the DOM is much easier when the proper `id` and `class` attributes are used.

The next two solutions describe ways of keeping the views in your Rails application semantic and well structured, without adding extra programmer overhead.

Solution: Make Use of the Rails Helpers

Say that you are a fearless Ruby on Rails developer who believes in progress, quality, and the importance of keeping current on best practices. You have bought into the importance of semantic markup, and you want to keep your designer as happy as possible. To that end, you've been trying to keep all the views in your latest Ruby on Rails project semantically correct. You've been making use of all the right tags and adding `id` and `class` attributes wherever they make sense. This is one of your ERb views:

```
<div class="post" id="post_<%= @post.id %>">
  <h2 class="title">Title</h2>
  <div class="body">
    Lorem ipsum dolor sit amet, consectetur...
  </div>
  <ol class="comments">
    <% @post.comments.each do |comment| %>
      <li class="comment" id="comment_<%= comment.id %>">
        <%= comment.body %>
      </li>
    <% end %>
  </ol>
</div>
```

After spending the last few hours going through your views, though, you're starting to lose faith. The outcome of semantic HTML is a definite win for your project, but the maintenance costs of having all this Ruby code littering your views is starting to out-weigh all those benefits.

You can remove some of this complexity if you've used the built-in semantic view helpers included in Rails. Specifically, you can get rid of the terribly ugly <div class= "post" id="post_<%= @post.id %>"> and <li class="comment" id="comment_ <%= comment.id %>"> lines by making use of the div_for and content_tag_for helpers:

```erb
<%= div_for @post do %>
  <h2 class="title">Title</h2>
  <div class="body">
    Lorem ipsum dolor sit amet, consectetur...
  </div>
  <ol class="comments">
    <% @post.comments.each do |comment| %>
      <%= content_tag_for :li, comment do %>
        <%= comment.body %>
      <% end %>
    <% end %>
  </ol>
<% end %>
```

This not only helps with keeping the ERb readable, but it also enforces consis-tency in the class and id scheme. This helps avoid CSS cruft as the project matures. div_for and content_tag_for helpers both use dom_class and dom_id internally. Therefore, using these helpers also gives you a single place to make changes if you need to change the CSS class for all posts.

Money for Nothin'

While you must explicitly use the div_for and content_tag_for helpers, some other parts of Rails automatically produce semantic HTML. For example, form_for and related helpers produce forms with semantically correct class and id attributes:

```erb
<%= form_for @user do |f| %>
  <%= f.label      :first_name %>
  <%= f.text_field :first_name %>
  <%= f.label      :last_name %>
  <%= f.text_field :last_name %>
```

```
    <%= submit_tag 'Create' %>
<% end %>

<form action="/users/4" method="post" class="edit_user"
id="edit_user_4">
    ...
    <label for="user_first_name">First Name</label>
    <input id="user_first_name" name="user[first_name]" type="text" />
    <label for="user_last_name">Last Name</label>
    <input id="user_last_name"  name="user[last_name]"  type="text" />
    <input name="commit" type="submit" value="Create" />
</form>
```

CSS authors and JavaScript developers can now target selectors such as `form.edit_`
`user` or `input#user_first_name`, resulting in a much more clear and maintainable
front end.

Using the freely available Rails helpers in your ERb views is a great step toward
creating semantic and maintainable code, but you can take it a major leap further. The
next solution shows how using Haml in your application can make it even easier to
produce semantic HTML and also to create well-structured HTML in general.

Solution: Use Haml

We discussed in the last solution how to make use of the built-in Rails helpers to produce
semantic HTML. They make semantic HTML easier to produce from an ERb template, but they don't remove all the pain. Take this example from the preceding solution:

```
<div id="blawg">
  <%= div_for @post do %>
    <h2 class="title">
      <%= @post.title %>
    </h2>
    <div class="body">
      Lorem ipsum dolor sit amet, consectetur...
    </div>
    <ol class="comments">
      <% @post.comments.each do |comment| %>
        <%= content_tag_for :li, comment do %>
          <%= comment.body %>
        <% end %>
```

```
      <% end %>
    </ol>
  <% end %>>
</div>
```

While this code is quite familiar to anyone comfortable with HTML and ERb, if you look at this snippet with a fresh eye, you can see some issues. The very nature of XML-based syntax means there is a good amount of gibberish going on. If you distill this to just the pertinent information, you begin to realize just how much boilerplate you've been writing. Here's a fanciful version that would convey exactly the same information in roughly half the lines:

```
div#blawg
  div for @post
    h2.title
      output @post.title
    div.body
      "Lorem ipsum dolor sit amet, consectetur..."
    ol.comments
      for each @post.comments as comment
        li for comment
          output comment.body
```

Thanks to the work of Hampton Catlin and his Haml gem, this made-up syntax isn't too far off the mark of what you can do today. In many ways, because of some basic assumptions that Haml makes, you can make this example even more concise:

```
#blawg
  %div[@post]
    %h2.title= @post.title
    .body
      Lorem ipsum dolor sit amet, consectetur...
    %ol.comments
      - @post.comments.each do |comment|
        %li[comment]
          = comment.body
```

Install Haml

Haml is packaged as a Ruby gem, so installing it in your application is as simple as adding a `gem 'haml'` line to your gemfile. Haml can live side-by-side with ERb templates. In fact, just installing Haml should not change the behavior of your application at all.

To make use of the Haml format, you simply name your view template with a `.haml` extension instead of `.erb`. For example, the `UsersController#show` template would be named `app/views/users/show.html.haml` instead of `app/views/users/show.html.erb`. Remember not to leave the old `.erb` file in place, as Rails will give it precedence over the `.html` file.

Anything in a Haml template follows the rules described in the following section.

Whitespace Sensitivity

Haml, much like Python, is known as a "whitespace-sensitive" language. This means that indentation is syntactically important. In other words, the snippets below will result in very different results:

```
#parent-tag
  #child-tag
    #grandchild-tag
```

This Haml example will output the following HTML, with each `div` nested inside the next:

```
<div id="parent-tag">
  <div id="child-tag">
    <div id="grandchild-tag"/>
  </div>
</div>
```

On the other hand, the following Haml snippet will produce HTML with the two divs side-by-side:

```
#brother-tag
#sister-tag
```

Here is the HTML produced by the Haml above:

```
<div id="brother-tag"/>
<div id="sister-tag"/>
```

HTML, being a highly hierarchical language, is well suited to Haml's whitespace-sensitive syntax. Not only does this remove the necessity for closing tags, but it enforces correct indentation, for which good designers are already sticklers.

Haml achieves its refreshing brevity through the use of some special shorthand characters. While these can be a bit overwhelming when you first encounter them, it won't be long until you're reading Haml faster than HTML.

Classes, IDs, Elements, and Embedded Ruby

Haml borrows the use of the . and # characters from CSS to represent `id` and `class` attributes. Specifying an element in Haml as `#foo.biz.baz`, for example, results in `<div id="foo" class="biz baz">`.

Notice that, by default, Haml assumes that a bare `id` or `class` attribute is being applied to a `<div>` element. While this is definitely the most common case, you can override it by using the `%` character to specify an element type. For example, you can easily specify an `<h1 id="title">` element as `%h1#title`.

Haml was written to replace ERb and has the same Ruby constructs. A Ruby snippet can be included silently with the – operator or printed inline with the rest of the output, using =. For example, the following loops through a `status_updates` of a `@user` rendering each one in turn and then rendering a footer partial:

```
- @user.status_updates.each do |status_update|
  = render status_update
= render :partial => "footer"
```

You may have noticed a subtle point, here: In Haml, even the Ruby code is whitespace aware. Haml recognizes the fact that you have nested the first call to `render` under the start of the block, and it adds an implicit `end` statement to close off the block.

Another shortcut that Haml gives you is inline text. If you follow an element definition with any text, that text is assumed to be the text for that element. Similarly, putting a = after the element tells Haml to interpret the rest of the line as Ruby code:

```
#page-title This is my blawg.
%p
  There are
  %span#post-count= Post.count
  posts.
```

Semantic Sugar

One of the best and most underused features of Haml is the [ ] operator. When given an object, such as [record], [ ] acts as a combination of div_for and content_for, outputting a tag with the id and class attributes set by that record. Here's an example:

```
%div[bike]
  %ul.wheels
    - bike.wheels.each do |wheel|
      %li[wheel]
        = wheel.position
```

This will produce the following semantic and cleanly formatted HTML:

```
<div class="bike" id="bike_3">
  <ul class="wheels">
    <li class="wheel" id="wheel_1">
      Front
    </li>
    <li class="wheel" id="wheel_2">
      Rear
    </li>
  </ul>
</div>
```

Sass and CSS

Haml comes with a sister library named Sass, which does for your CSS files what Haml does for HTML. While we won't go too far into the details of Sass, it's worth a quick preview to whet your appetite. A Sass snippet looks something like this:

```
#footer
  :border-top 3px solid black
  :color = $primary_color
  :font-size .8em
  :font-weight bold
  .citation
    :text-align right
  *
    :padding-left 1px
```

Like Haml, Sass is whitespace sensitive. Sass allows nesting of CSS selectors, use of variables (such as `$primary_color`), and many other conveniences. If you're using Haml, you'll almost definitely want to use Sass as well. Sass is part of the Haml gem, so once you've installed Haml in your application, you can start using Sass as well.

The Haml Takeover

Haml is quickly gaining converts in the Ruby on Rails world. The concise syntax, enforced indentation, and focus on making semantic output as easy as possible makes it a clear winner. That being said, there are some issues to be aware of. For one, it can be difficult and time-consuming to convert an existing code base to Haml (or back again). Haml comes with some tools to assist with migration, but they are really 80% solutions. Also, while the Haml syntax can be learned very quickly, adoption can be thwarted when orthodox designers are uninterested in learning a new technology. This is especially true of designers who are used to using their favorite HTML generation tools, such as Dreamweaver. However, the benefits of Haml are well worth a developer's perseverance when trying to gain Haml adoption among a team.

CHAPTER 4

Controllers

Controllers put the *C* in *MVC* and are a fundamental part of the Rails framework. However, the relationship that many Rails programmers have with controllers is complex.

On one hand, controllers are categorically loathed, with most Rails programmers having the goals that as little code as possible should go into controllers and that controllers should all be pretty much the same auto-generated scaffolding.

On the other hand, there is an intense focus on controllers—so much so that the aforementioned goals have been an immense source of abstraction and innovation in Rails, allowing programmers to write more functionality with less code.

In fact, in the 2.x Rails releases, the most fundamental changes came to controllers and things they touch, such as routes and rendering. Whether the motivation for this focus is loathing or love doesn't really matter, as you can hardly say that Rails isn't a better framework for the improvements that have been made to the Controller layer.

Of course, with improvements come challenges. The need to stay up to date with controller best practices as they change from Rails version to Rails version and the need to deliver continuing business value and improvements in applications while keeping them maintainable and agile can put a significant burden on Rails developers.

In the following AntiPatterns, we explore several pitfalls that you may face in your application controllers. The solutions range from the well-known "skinny controller, fat model" approach to the application of RESTful principles to non-RESTful applications.

AntiPattern: Homemade Keys

Many applications contain user authentication code. *Authentication* is the management of the user session (sign-in and sign-out) and the existence of users in the system (sign-up). This is different from user *authorization*, which defines what users can and cannot do in a system once they log in.

Because the great majority of applications require user authentication, this has been an area of collaboration on open-source plugins for some time in the Rails community. Unfortunately, many of the user authentication plugins in the past have had a few problems. Having been around for some time, they often contain old, outdated code that is not up to current best practices and may be difficult to understand. In addition, plugins tend to try to be all things to all people. They frequently have configuration options for various ways of doing things, such as password encryption, optional user parameters, different login or user creation flows, and so on. Unfortunately, this results in an overly complex login system that can be confusing to a developer. You can sometimes overlook such downsides when your authentication system needs to look and behave exactly like what is provided by the plugin. However, if you need to customize or improve something, it can be very difficult to do so in the context of the framework provided by the plugin.

What are you to do when faced with the need to add user authentication to an application? You may think that your only options are to use a plugin and have potential pain down the road or to take the time upfront to write your own, thereby potentially reinventing the wheel and potentially ending up with a system just as poorly written as the plugin, if not more so.

First, you should *not* write your own plugin. Rolling your own authentication system requires time and effort for something that is now effectively a solved problem. There are simply too many pitfalls involved in writing your own. Consider the additional functionality that will inevitably be part of any production authentication system: password resets, "remember me," email confirmations, and so on. What might start off as a simple task eventually turns into custom written code that is inevitably a liability.

Fortunately, there are now several newer gems that take new, cleaner approaches to user authentication, are written using current best practices, and have limited scope in order to provide a solid basic authentication system without providing so much that it becomes a burden.

In the following solutions to this AntiPattern, we present the two of these newer gems, Clearance and Authlogic. Which gem you should use depends on the exact needs of the application. However, the choice to write your own authentication code should no longer be considered an option except in the most extreme circumstances. The gems described in this chapter have been used successfully in many different types of applications.

Solution: Use Clearance

One of the gems that has emerged as an antidote to overly complex authentication plugins is Clearance. It includes sign-up, sign-in, sign-out, and password reset functionality—and nothing more.

It seeks to provide a clean, straightforward authentication system while providing a test suite that can be integrated into your own application's test suite to ensure that its functionality, as well as any functionality you have customized, is well tested.

You can obtain the Clearance source code from http://github.com/thoughtbot/clearance. While you can install Clearance into an existing application, it's usually better to have user authentication added as one of the first things in your new application. It's easier to understand what's going on and manage the changes that way.

Clearance is a Rails engine. Rails engines, in contrast to generators, enable plugins to provide actual functionality to an application without copying the source code for models, controllers, and views directly within the application's source code. Engines stay inside the gem. The benefit to this is that you can upgrade a gem and get the new functionality, such as bug and security fixes, in a relatively straightforward manner.

View the README for Clearance for the full, up-to-date installation instructions, as well as more information on specific advanced Clearance topics. Here we highlight a few important topics that will hopefully give you an idea of the strategy that Clearance takes, contrast it with the other gem presented in this AntiPattern, and allow you to get started with it.

To install the Clearance gem, bundle the `clearance` gem into your Rails application. Next, from within your Rails application, you run `script/generate clearance` to configure your application for Clearance. You need to insert Clearance into the appropriate places in your controllers and routes, and you need to generate the migrations for your database. After running the generator and following any additional instructions given, Clearance is ready to go in your application. You should now have `/sign_in`, `/sign_up`, `/sign_out`, shortcut URLs, and a functioning authentication system.

If you want to require users to be logged in to access a specific controller or controller action, you accomplish this with the `:authenticate` before filter:

```
class class WidgetsController < ApplicationController
  before_filter :authenticate
  def index
    @widgets = Widget.all
  end
end
```

To change any of the actions provided by Clearance, you simply subclass the controller provided by Clearance. For example, to change the behavior of the new action of the sign-in controller, you redefine it in your subclass as shown here:

```
class SessionsController < Clearance::SessionsController
  def new
    # your special new behavior
  end
end
```

Then you add the route for your new controller before the Clearance routes in config/routes.rb, as shown here:

```
map.resource :session, :controller => 'sessions'
```

You can override actions that redirect (create, update, and destroy) in Clearance controllers by redefining url_after_(action) methods as shown here:

```
class SessionsController < Clearance::SessionsController
  def url_after_create
    your_special_path
  end
end
```

One of the features that sets Clearance apart from other gems is that it provides complete Cucumber integration tests for your application to use as base tests for the authentication logic Clearance provides. A generator put these in place, and they run along with the rest of your integration tests. To generate the Cucumber features, you simply run the following command:

```
script/rails generate clearance_features
```

If you modify existing functionality, you can modify the Cucumber features accordingly. This should make adding or customizing functionality easier, without introducing regressions to the authentication logic.

Solution: Use Authlogic

Another gem that was specifically created to address the perceived deficiencies in the older, more complex, and messy authentication libraries is Authlogic. Authlogic takes an entirely different approach than any previous authentication library. It pushes the majority of authentication functionality down into the Model layer, using additional model types and callbacks to existing models. This approach leads to a very clean and unobtrusive implementation for an application.

You can obtain Authlogic source code from http://github.com/binarylogic/authlogic. Then you bundle the `authlogic` gem into your Rails application.

View the README for Authlogic for the full, up-to-date installation instructions, as well as more information on specific advanced Authlogic topics. Here we highlight a few important topics that will hopefully give you an idea of the strategy that Authlogic takes, contrast it with the other gem presented in this AntiPattern, and allow you to get started with it.

To perform authentication, Authlogic introduces a new type of model, `Authlogic::Session::Base`. You can have as many `Session` models as you want, and you can name them whatever you want, just as you can your other models. Say that you want to authenticate with the `User` model, which is inferred by the name:

```
class UserSession < Authlogic::Session::Base
  # specify configuration here
end
```

Any of the following examples log in the specified user:

```
UserSession.create(:login       => "bjohnson",
                   :password     => "my password",
                   :remember_me => true)

session = UserSession.new(:login       => "bjohnson",
                         :password     => "my password",
                         :remember_me => true)
session.save
```

```
# requires the authlogic-oid "add on" gem
UserSession.create(:openid_identifier => "identifier",
                    :remember_me       => true)

# skip authentication and log the user in directly,
# the true means "remember me"
UserSession.create(my_user_object, true)
```

For most applications, you will create a `UserSessionsController` that uses the `UserSession` model, just like a normal model.

In contrast to Clearance, Authlogic doesn't provide controllers and views in its standard distribution. You have to create them by hand or copy them from the sample application provided by Authlogic. Because Authlogic provides no application-specific functionality, it also doesn't provide integration tests for your application to use.

You can mix in the authentication functionality directly into your `User` model:

```
class User < ActiveRecord::Base
  acts_as_authentic
end
```

This provides validations as well as additional functionality for password and user creation.

The Choice Is Yours

The implementation strategies that Clearance and Authlogic use may be different, but their goals are the same: to have a cleanly written, well-architected authentication gem that limits its scope in order to stay focused on those goals. As long as you use one of these well-written gems as a base for your authentication system, rather than using one of the older, outdated plugins or rolling your own, your application will be well served. Which one you choose to use is up to you.

AntiPattern: Fat Controller

The concept of the fat controller is one of the most popularized AntiPatterns in the Rails community. It's a fundamental problem that affects many Rails applications, and frankly, it's likely popular because fixing it is not only an extremely effective improvement, it's also typically a straightforward one to make.

A fat controller typically includes business logic that properly belongs in the model. In addition, by moving code to the model, you can unit test the code. Many Rails developers agree that writing unit tests is often easier than writing functional tests.

Faced with the concept of cleaner code that is easier to test (and, therefore, likely better tested), the choice is clear: The fat controller is out, and the skinny controller is in.

The following solutions provide extensive examples of how to refactor your fat controllers to remove the business logic and place it properly in the model. Features provided by Active Record, such as callbacks, setters, and database defaults, make an important set of tools for this task. In addition, there are other patterns, such as the Presenter Pattern, that we can call on to provide effective measures for encapsulating complex behavior when our normal models aren't enough.

Solution: Use Active Record Callbacks and Setters

One of the core organizational structures of Rails is the Model-View-Controller (MVC) pattern. The blurring of the lines between these three components is a common mistake that takes place for many reasons, including inexperience, confusion, coping with complex or changing requirements, and mere laziness. Let's take a look at an offending controller action:

```ruby
class ArticlesController < ApplicationController
  def create
    @article = Article.new(params[:article])
    @article.reporter_id = current_user.id

    begin
      Article.transaction do
        @version = @article.create_version!(params[:version],
                                            current_user)
      end
    rescue ActiveRecord::RecordNotSaved,
           ActiveRecord::RecordInvalid
      render :action => :index and return false
```

```
    end
    redirect_to article_path(@article)
  end
```

The code for this `ArticlesController#create` action was taken from an actual production application. To be clear, this code *works*. However, it's poorly structured, has minor MVC violations, and makes use of several techniques that are either incorrect or are not Rails best practices.

Next, we walk through a complex refactoring of this controller action, in an attempt to rectify each of the problems. Before we begin, there are a few things to note.

It's simply not effective to perform refactoring on a production application without having an adequate test suite in place. Very often, you are not the original author of code you're working on. The test suite will assist you in understanding the intention of the code, and it will help you prevent regressions as you dramatically alter the code. For these reasons, you will have the added benefit of being able to perform refactorings such as the ones outlined here more quickly than you would otherwise.

The next thing to note is that at 14 lines, this controller action is too long. While a 14-line controller action may not seem very long to you, it's very important to keep your guard up against doing too much in your controller. Doing too much is a sign that you are performing logic that would be better done in the Model layer of your application. If you're not careful to keep your guard up against this, your applications will end up with controller actions that are hundreds of lines long. We know. We've seen several Rails applications where this is the case.

Now, let's take a look at the `create` action again, paying particular attention to the elements that are bold:

```
class ArticlesController < ApplicationController
  def create
    @article = Article.new(params[:article])
    @article.reporter_id = current_user.id

    begin
      Article.transaction do
        @version = @article.create_version!(params[:version],
                                            current_user)
      end
    rescue ActiveRecord::RecordNotSaved, ActiveRecord::RecordInvalid
      render :action => :new and return false
    end
```

```
    redirect_to article_path(@article)
  end
```

The first bold item is `Article.transaction do`, a statement that starts a database transaction. Database transactions are used to ensure that all the statements executed within them are reverted, or rolled back, if any one of them fails. For a few reasons, it's very unlikely that a database transaction needs to be started in the controller. The first of these reasons is that you should never be doing so much in a controller that you have multiple statements that depend on each other. The second is that the normal Active Record lifecycle methods are wrapped in transactions themselves. As you can see in this controller, and as highlighted by the second bold item, a standard Active Record lifecycle method, such as `save`, is never called.

Without a doubt, there are times when multiple actions that are dependent on each other must occur. Clearly, because the `save` method is wrapped in a transaction, simply calling `save` in the controller without any other model methods surrounding it would be ideal. But how should multiple actions then be accomplished? The answer is through callbacks and setters on the model itself—in this case the `Article` and the `Version` models.

Finally, the third bold statement is rescuing the `ActiveRecord::RecordNotSaved` and `ActiveRecord::RecordInvalid` exceptions. It's preferable to not use exceptions as flow control because exceptions should be used only in exceptional circumstances. A record not being found, or a record being invalid because of user input, in most web applications, is not an exceptional circumstance and therefore should be handled a little more gracefully. Used as flow control, these exceptions are little more than glorified GOTO statements.

Here is a conceptualization of how this `create` action might ideally look:

```
class ArticlesController < ApplicationController
  def create
    @article = Article.new(params[:article])
    @article.reporter_id = current_user.id

    if @article.save
      redirect_to article_path(@article)
    else
      render :action => :new
    end
  end
end
```

In this ideal `create` action, you can see that the normal Active Record `save` method is now being used to save the article. This method returns `true` when the save has been successful, which causes the user to be redirected to the article show page. However, if `save` returns `false` because the save has not been successful, the page to create a new article is rendered to the user again. The only additional step that is occurring in the controller action is the assignment of the ID of the user who is creating the article. Generally, for security purposes, these types of actions should occur in the controller rather than in hidden form fields. Doing this guards against users tampering with the form values to create an article as if it were created by another user. We'll discuss the nature of these assignments later in this chapter, but you should keep them as is for now.

The First Step

Let's explore how to achieve the ideal controller described in the preceding section. The change from calling a `create_version!` method to calling the `save` method on `Article` is the biggest conceptual difference, so let's take a look at the `create_version!` method:

```
def create_version!(attributes, user)
  if self.versions.empty?
    return create_first_version!(attributes, user)
  end
  # mark old related links as not current
  if self.current_version.relateds.any?
    self.current_version.relateds.each { |rel|
      rel.update_attribute(:current, false) }
  end

  version = self.versions.build(attributes)
  version.article_id = self.id
  version.written_at = Time.now
  version.writer_id = user.id
  version.version = self.current_verison.version + 1
  self.save!
  self.update_attribute(:current_version_id, version.id)
  version
end
```

The first thing that occurs in this method is that `create_first_version!` is called with the same parameters that were passed in if `self.versions.empty?` is true. Before taking a look any further, let's review the `create_first_version!` method:

```
def create_first_version!(attributes, user)
  version = self.versions.build(attributes)
  version.written_at = Time.now
  version.writer_id = user.id
  version.state ||= "Raw"
  version.version = 1
  self.save!
  self.update_attribute(:current_version_id, version.id)
  version
end
```

As you can see, `create_first_version!` is strikingly similar to the eight closing lines of the `create_version!` method. Therefore, your first refactoring task will be to remove the `create_first_version!` method altogether. You want to do this because the less custom things that can happen, the more likely it is that you'll be able to just call the `save` method on the article.

Built-in Rails Functionality

The two bolded lines in the following code, which are identical in the two methods, are assigning the current time to the `written_at` attribute of the version:

```
def create_version!(attributes, user)
  if self.versions.empty?
    return create_first_version!(attributes, user)
  end

  # mark old related links as not current
  if self.current_version.relateds.any?
    self.current_version.relateds.each { |rel|
      rel.update_attribute(:current, false) }
  end

  version = self.versions.build(attributes)
  version.article_id = self.id
  version.written_at = Time.now
  version.writer_id = user.id
```

```
      version.version = self.current_verison.version + 1
      self.save!
      self.update_attribute(:current_version_id, version.id)
      version
   end

   def create_first_version!(attributes, user)
      version = self.versions.build(attributes)
      version.written_at = Time.now
      version.writer_id = user.id
      version.state ||= "Raw"
      version.version = 1
      self.save!
      self.update_attribute(:current_version_id, version.id)
      version
   end
```

Upon inspection, you see that the `Version` model does not have either an
`updated_at` or `created_at` attribute. Therefore, the `written_at` attribute should be
renamed `created_at`, and Active Record will automatically populate it with the current time when the record is saved to the database. After that attribute is renamed,
these two lines of code can be removed.

Default Values

The bold code below is causing the version state to be set to `"Raw"` if the state is not
already set. This occurs only for the first version and not in any other versions.
However, in all other versions after the first, the state is set via the forms in the view to
the state of the version before it. Therefore, this effectively amounts to a default value
for all versions.

```
   def create_version!(attributes, user)
      if self.versions.empty?
         return create_first_version!(attributes, user)
      end

      # mark old related links as not current
      if self.current_version.relateds.any?
         self.current_version.relateds.each { |rel|
            rel.update_attribute(:current, false) }
      end
```

```
    version = self.versions.build(attributes)
    version.article_id = self.id
    version.writer_id = user.id
    version.version = self.current_verison.version + 1
    self.save!
    self.update_attribute(:current_version_id, version.id)
    version
  end

  def create_first_version!(attributes, user)
    version = self.versions.build(attributes)
    version.writer_id = user.id
    version.state ||= "Raw"
    version.version = 1
    self.save!
    self.update_attribute(:current_version_id, version.id)
    version
  end
```

The recommended way to set default values on Active Record models is by using a database default. Note that this does not apply to constraints, which are best handled by validations. Rails introspects on the schema when returning a new, unsaved record, and it populates the attributes with any default values set in the database. This type of integration isn't supported for validations.

You change the default value of the state column by using a migration like the following:

```
class AddRawDefaultToState < ActiveRecord::Migration
  def self.up
    change_column_default :article_versions, :state, "Raw"
  end

  def self.down
    change_column_default :article_versions, :state, nil
  end
end
```

Effective Callback Use

Once your migration is in place and has been run, the code looks as follows:

```
def create_version!(attributes, user)
  if self.versions.empty?
    return create_first_version!(attributes, user)
  end

  # mark old related links as not current
  if self.current_version.relateds.any?
    self.current_version.relateds.each { |rel|
      rel.update_attribute(:current, false) }
  end

  version = self.versions.build(attributes)
  version.article_id = self.id
  version.writer_id = user.id
  version.version = self.current_verison.version + 1
  self.save!
  self.update_attribute(:current_version_id, version.id)
  version
end

def create_first_version!(attributes, user)
  version = self.versions.build(attributes)
  version.writer_id = user.id
  version.version = 1
  self.save!
  self.update_attribute(:current_version_id, version.id)
  version
end
```

The two bold lines here set the version number. The first version of an article is assigned the version number 1, and all other versions are assigned the version number of the current version incremented by 1.

The best way to accomplish this functionality is in a callback method on the Version model, as shown here:

```
class Version < ActiveRecord::Base
  before_validation :set_version_number, :on => :create
  validates :version, :presence => true

  private
```

```
def set_version_number
  self.version =
   (article.current_version ?
     article.current_version.version : 0) + 1
end
```

This callback occurs before validation, every time a version is created, so that a validation can ensure that a version always has a version number. This callback, named set_version_number, takes the current version number, or 0 if there is no current version number, and increments it by 1.

Identification of Unnecessary Code

Once the set_version_number callback is in place on your Version model, your create_version! and create_first_version! methods are as follows:

```
def create_version!(attributes, user)
  if self.versions.empty?
    return create_first_version!(attributes, user)
  end

  # mark old related links as not current
  if self.current_version.relateds.any?
    self.current_version.relateds.each { |rel|
      rel.update_attribute(:current, false) }
  end

  version = self.versions.build(attributes)
  version.article_id = self.id
  version.writer_id = user.id
  self.save!
  self.update_attribute(:current_version_id, version.id)
  version
end

def create_first_version!(attributes, user)
  version = self.versions.build(attributes)
  version.writer_id = user.id
  self.save!
  self.update_attribute(:current_version_id, version.id)
  version
end
```

The bold code is the only difference now between the final lines of the `create_version!` method and the `create_first_version!` method. Fortunately, this line of code is completely unnecessary because calling `versions.build` on the article already populates the `article_id` on the version. Therefore, this is redundant and can be removed. Therefore, the two code blocks are identical.

Another Callback

Now the only difference between the `create_version!` and `create_first_version!` methods is the code that is marking all related links to an article as no longer current:

```
def create_version!(attributes, user)
  if self.versions.empty?
    return create_first_version!(attributes, user)
  end

  # mark old related links as not current
  if self.current_version.relateds.any?
    self.current_version.relateds.each { |rel|
      rel.update_attribute(:current, false) }
  end

  version = self.versions.build(attributes)
  version.writer_id = user.id
  self.save!
  self.update_attribute(:current_version_id, version.id)
  version
end

def create_first_version!(attributes, user)
  version = self.versions.build(attributes)
  version.writer_id = user.id
  self.save!
  self.update_attribute(:current_version_id, version.id)
  version
end
```

As a programmer who is new to this code base, you're probably thankful for this comment, as you'd otherwise have no idea of the purpose of this code in the context of the domain. That being said, this code happens only if you're not creating the first version of an article, so you can wrap it in a conditional that will be executed only if you're not creating the first version so that you can remove the create_first_version! method entirely, as follows:

```ruby
def create_version!(attributes, user)
  unless self.versions.empty?
    # mark old related links as not current
    if self.current_version.relateds.any?
      self.current_version.relateds.each { |rel|
        rel.update_attribute(:current, false) }
    end
  end

  version = self.versions.build(attributes)
  version.writer_id = user.id
  self.save!
  self.update_attribute(:current_version_id, version.id)
  version
end
```

Now it's clear that this logic can be moved to another callback on the Version model, as shown here:

```ruby
class Version < ActiveRecord::Base
  before_validation_on_create :set_version_number
  before_create :mark_related_links_not_current

  private

  def set_version_number
    self.version = (article.current_version ?
                    article.current_version.version : 0) + 1
  end

  def mark_related_links_not_current
    unless article.versions.empty?
      # mark old related links as not current
      if article.current_version.relateds.any?
        article.current_version.relateds.each do |rel|
          rel.update_attribute(:current, false)
```

```
        end
      end
    end
  end
```

Notice that the callback has been named mark_related_links_not_current. This method name is detailed in the same way as the comment. Therefore, you can now remove the comment. Descriptive method naming is always important, especially for callbacks, because it ensures that the intention and function of what can eventually be many callbacks on a model is always clear.

Simplified Callbacks

The bold code below is unnecessary because the loop below it will just be skipped if there are no elements:

```
class Version < ActiveRecord::Base
  before_validation_on_create :set_version_number
  before_create :mark_related_links_not_current

  private

  def set_version_number
    self.version = (article.current_version ?
                     article.current_version.version : 0) + 1
  end

  def mark_related_links_not_current
    unless article.versions.empty?
      if article.current_version.relateds.any?
        article.current_version.relateds.each do |rel|
          rel.update_attribute(:current, false)
        end
      end
    end
  end
end
```

Active Record relationship collections on models never return nil if there are no records found. Instead, they return an empty collection. You can simply remove this code.

You can now focus on the bold line below:

```
class Version < ActiveRecord::Base
  before_validation_on_create :set_version_number
  before_create :mark_related_links_not_current

  private

  def set_version_number
    self.version = (article.current_version ?
                        article.current_version.version : 0) + 1
  end

  def mark_related_links_not_current
    unless article.versions.empty?
      article.current_version.relateds.each do |rel|
        rel.update_attribute(:current, false)
      end
    end
  end
end
```

The `unless` conditional keyword tends to be confusing, especially to developers looking at code for the first time. In addition, what this code is checking is whether the article has any previous versions. However, it then doesn't use the versions collection at all to perform the action of this callback. The developer's intention is actually to check whether there is a current_version, to ensure that it's not nil. It's always best to do the simplest, most straightforward, and intentionally revealing check as possible, so you can now change this conditional to look like this:

```
class Version < ActiveRecord::Base
  before_validation_on_create :set_version_number
  before_create :mark_related_links_not_current

  private

  def set_version_number
    self.version =
      (article.current_version ?
      article.current_version.version : 0) + 1
  end
```

```
def mark_related_links_not_current
  if article.current_version
    article.current_version.relateds.each do |rel|
      rel.update_attribute(:current, false)
    end
  end
end
```

The four occurrences of `article.current_version` in bold above bring attention to the fact that within a version, you're calling `article.current_version` several times. This duplication alone should prompt you to refactor it, so that the concept of what a current version is to a `Version` is encapsulated. This allows for ease of maintenance down the road. One of the principles behind this refactoring is the Law of Demeter. (To read more about the Law of Demeter and how it can be applied in Rails applications, see Chapter 1.)

To perform this refactoring, you create a new method on `Version` that returns the current version. You can name this method `current_version`, as shown here:

```
class Version < ActiveRecord::Base
  before_validation_on_create :set_version_number
  before_create :mark_related_links_not_current

  private

  def current_version
    article.current_version
  end

  def set_version_number
    self.version = (current_version ? current_version.version : 0) + 1
  end

  def mark_related_links_not_current
    if current_version
      current_version.relateds.each do |rel|
        rel.update_attribute(:current, false)
      end
    end
  end
```

The bold line of code above is fairly typical once you begin to abstract common behavior into callbacks on your models, as you are doing here. What is actually being conveyed by a callback that is entirely wrapped in a conditional statement is that there are times when the callback shouldn't be executed at all. This was so common, in fact, that in Rails 2.1 this concept was integrated directly into Active Record, with the addition of conditional callbacks. Here the callback has been refactored to use conditional callbacks:

```
class Version < ActiveRecord::Base
  before_validation :set_version_number, :on => :create
  before_create :mark_related_links_not_current,
                :if => :current_version

  private

  def current_version
    article.current_version
  end

  def set_version_number
    self.version = (current_version ? current_version.version : 0) + 1
  end

  def mark_related_links_not_current
    current_version.relateds.each do |rel|
      rel.update_attribute(:current, false)
    end
  end
end
```

This new callback definition, denoted with bold, says "Before create, mark related links not current if there is a current version," and now the callback method performs exactly the action stated in its method name, unconditionally.

Yet Another Callback

You've successfully moved the functionality for marking related links not current into a callback, and you've also reduced the number of lines for the method from eight to three. Now you can go back and take a look at where the create_version! method stands:

```
def create_version!(attributes, user)
  version = self.versions.build(attributes)
  version.writer_id = user.id

  self.save!
  self.update_attribute(:current_version_id, version.id)
  version
end
```

Notice (see the bold above) that after each new version is successfully created, it replaces the current version on the article. This, too, can be a callback on the Version model, as shown here:

```
class Version < ActiveRecord::Base
  before_validation :set_version_number, :on => :create
  before_create :mark_related_links_not_current,
                :if => :current_version
  after_create :set_current_version_on_article

  private

  def set_current_version_on_article
    article.update_attribute :current_version_id, self.id
  end
end
```

This callback occurs after the creation of an article, and it uses exactly the same logic as the code in the create_version! method.

Cleaned-up Code

Now that you've created the additional callback, you can return to the create_version! method again, as you've eliminated nearly everything from it:

```
def create_version!(attributes, user)
  version = self.versions.build(attributes)
  version.writer_id = user.id

  self.save!
  version
end
```

Aside from the two lines at the top of the method, in bold, this `create_version!` method is only a call to `save!`. Notice that these two lines use the two arguments that are passed into this method from the controller. Given those facts, you can actually move these two lines back up into the controller itself, to eliminate this additional argument passing, and to reach the goal of making the `create_version!` method a simple call to `save!`:

```ruby
class ArticlesController < ApplicationController
  def create
    @article = Article.new(params[:article])
    @article.reporter_id = current_user.id
    @version = @article.versions.build(params[:version])
    @version.writer_id = current_user.id

    begin
      Article.transaction do
        @version = @article.create_version!(params[:version],
                                            current_user)
      end
    rescue ActiveRecord::RecordNotSaved, ActiveRecord::RecordInvalid
      render :action => :index and return false
    end
    redirect_to article_path(@article)
  end
```

With the two bold lines moved into the controller (adjusted to use the instance variables and `params` available in the controller), the `create_version!` method is now just a call to `save!`, so it can be eliminated and replaced with the call to `save!`, as shown here:

```ruby
class ArticlesController < ApplicationController
  def create
    @article = Article.new(params[:article])
    @article.reporter_id = current_user.id
    @version = @article.versions.build(params[:version])
    @version.writer_id = current_user.id

    begin
      Article.transaction do
        @article.save!
      end
```

```
  rescue ActiveRecord::RecordNotSaved,
         ActiveRecord::RecordInvalid
    render :action => :index and return false
  end
  redirect_to article_path(@article)
end
```

Now that the Active Record save! method is the only thing inside the transaction block, a transaction does not need to be manually started at all. The transaction, in bold above, can now be removed:

```
class ArticlesController < ApplicationController
  def create
    @article = Article.new(params[:article])
    @article.reporter_id = current_user.id
    @version = @article.versions.build(params[:version])
    @version.writer_id = current_user.id

    begin
      @article.save!
    rescue ActiveRecord::RecordNotSaved,
           ActiveRecord::RecordInvalid
      render :action => :index and return false
    end
    redirect_to article_path(@article)
  end
```

Recall that the use of save is preferable to the use of save! when the action being performed is based on user input. Therefore, exceptions for not found and invalid records wouldn't be considered exceptional circumstances. Rewritten to use the normal save method, which returns true or false, the controller action is as follows:

```
class ArticlesController < ApplicationController
  def create
    @article = Article.new(params[:article])
    @article.reporter_id = current_user.id
    @version = @article.versions.build(params[:version])
    @version.writer_id = current_user.id

    if @article.save
      render :action => :index
```

```
    else
      redirect_to article_path(@article)
    end
  end
```

It's accepted best practice to set the actual association proxy of an Active Record relationship than the _id method, as highlighted above. The following example shows this change:

```
class ArticlesController < ApplicationController
  def create
    @article = Article.new(params[:article])
    @article.reporter = current_user
    @version = @article.versions.build(params[:version])
    @version.writer = current_user

    if @article.save
      render :action => :index
    else
      redirect_to article_path(@article)
    end
  end
```

This new create action, which is very close to the ideal presented earlier in this chapter, performs exactly the same functionality as the old one, but now it's cleaner, shorter, and more precise.

As you can see, this controller is still explicitly referencing the params[:version] hash and building a new version. This functionality can be pushed into the Article model, making it responsible for creating a new version. You can accomplish this by creating a new_version getter and setter on the Article model. You can then nest the form inputs for a version underneath the form elements for an article so that they appear in the params as params[:article][:new_version] instead of params[:version]. If you name the nested params in this way, the params values will be passed directly to the new_version setter by the call to Article.new. This new setter is as follows:

```
class Article < ActiveRecord::Base
  def new_version=(version_attributes)
    @new_version = versions.build(version_attributes)
  end
```

```
  def new_version
    @new_version
  end
end
```

With these two new methods in place, you can now revise the
`ArticlesController#create` controller action to the following:

```
class ArticlesController < ApplicationController
  def create
    @article = Article.new(params[:article])
    @article.reporter = current_user
    @article.new_version.writer = current_user

    if @article.save
      render :action => :index
    else
      redirect_to article_path(@article)
    end
  end
end
```

The technique of using callbacks and setters on models to perform complex operations while keeping your controllers skinny and clean is very powerful. However, it can
be overused as well. Complex callbacks can be a source of confusion or bugs when used
in inappropriate ways. While adding additional setters is a great and straightforward
solution to the problem at hand, it can become overkill when you've created several of
them. Therefore, moderation is a good principle when using this technique. The
Presenter Pattern can also be used with similar effectiveness when the interactions
become overly complex, as outlined in the next section.

Solution: Move to a Presenter

While staying within the confines of the RESTful model when developing Rails applications can make life much easier for a programmer, there may be times when it seems
impossible to do so. Often, it seems that a controller action must perform more tasks
than just what's necessary to create or update a single record. As we've discussed, such
an increase in responsibilities increases the overall complication of a controller.

We discussed earlier how to move some of that extra logic into callbacks on the
primary model. That is a fine solution when the extra functionality is simple and is

part of a primary model's responsibility. Once the complexity increases, however, the complication in the callbacks can quickly get out of hand.

Sign Me Up!

One basic example of the type of complexity just discussed is when a controller must create multiple models at the same time. Consider an application with accounts and users. When a new user signs up, you must create both an account with a subdomain and a user with an email address and a password.

A naïve approach to this requirement would be to just modify the #new and #create methods in the controller to deal with both an @account and a @user record simultaneously. The functional test for such a controller might be as follows:

```ruby
# test/functionals/account_controller_test.rb
class AccountsControllerTest < ActionController::TestCase
  context "on GET to #new" do
    setup { get :new }
    should assign_to(:account)
    should assign_to(:user)
    should render_template(:new)

    should "render form for account and user" do
      assert_select "form[action$=?]", accounts_path do
        assert_select "input[name=?]", "account[subdomain]"
        assert_select "input[name=?]", "user[email]"
        assert_select "input[name=?]", "user[password]"
      end
    end
  end

  context "on POST to #create with good values" do
    setup do
      post :create,
        :account => {:subdomain => "foo"},
        :user => {:email    => "foo@bar.com",
                  :password => "issekrit?"}
    end

    should set_the_flash.to(/created/i)

    should_change "User.count",    :by => 1
    should_change "Account.count", :by => 1
```

```
    should "assign the user to the account" do
      assert_equal assigns(:account).id, assigns(:user).account_id
    end
  end

  context "on POST to #create with bad account values" do
    setup do
      post :create,
        :account => { },
        :user => {:email => "foo@bar.com", :password => "issekrit?"}
    end

    should assign_to(:account)
    should assign_to(:user)
    should render_template(:new)
  end

  context "on POST to #create with bad user values" do
    setup do
      post :create,
        :account => { :subdomain => "foo" },
        :user => { }
    end

    should assign_to(:account)
    should assign_to(:user)
    should render_template(:new)
  end
end
```

Implementing the controller and view for this functional test is fairly easy. For the controller, you simply instantiate and save both an account and a user record in the two actions. In addition, you make sure to assign the new user to the account before saving both of them:

```
# app/controllers/account_controller.rb
class AccountsController < ApplicationController
  def new
    @account = Account.new
    @user = User.new
  end
```

```ruby
def create
  @account = Account.new(params[:account])
  @user    = User.new(params[:user])
  @user.account = @account

  if @account.save and @user.save
    flash[:notice] = 'Account was successfully created.'
    redirect_to(@account)
  else
    render :action => "new"
  end
end
end
```

The form within new.html.erb below must deal with sending two sets of parameters to the controller—one for the account and one for the user. You use form_for's cousin, the fields_for helper, to accomplish this.

```erb
# app/views/accounts/new.html.erb
<h1>New account</h1>

<%= form_for(@account) do |f| %>
  <%= f.error_messages %>

  <p>
    <%= f.label :subdomain %><br />
    <%= f.text_field :subdomain %>
  </p>

  <%= fields_for(@user) do |u| %>
    <%= u.error_messages %>

    <p>
      <%= u.label :email %><br />
      <%= u.text_field :email %>
    </p>

    <p>
      <%= u.label :password %><br />
      <%= u.text_field :password %>
    </p>
  <% end %>
```

```
  <p>
    <%= f.submit "Create" %>
  </p>
<% end %>
```

A Subtle Bug

The implementation in the preceding section contains a somewhat subtle bug. The #create action first tries to save the account record. If that succeeds, it then tries to save the user record. If the client sends in valid account parameters and invalid user parameters, the system will be left with a saved account record without an associated user—an undesirable situation. Obviously, reordering the calls to #save won't help here, as that would only allow the client to create an orphaned user record instead.

The following example shows a modified functional test to illustrate this bug:

```
# test/functionals/account_controller_test.rb
class AccountsControllerTest < ActionController::TestCase
  # ...
  context "on POST to #create with good values" do
    setup do
      post :create,
        :account => {:subdomain => "foo"},
        :user => {:email => "foo@bar.com", :password => "issekrit?"}
    end

    should set_the_flash.to(/created/i)

    should_change "User.count",    :by => 1
    should_change "Account.count", :by => 1

    should "assign the user to the account" do
      assert_equal assigns(:account).id, assigns(:user).account_id
    end
  end

  context "on POST to #create with bad account values" do
    setup do
      post :create,
        :account => { },
        :user => {:email => "foo@bar.com", :password => "issekrit?"}
    end
```

```
      should_not_change "User.count"
      should_not_change "Account.count"
      should assign_to(:account)
      should assign_to(:user)
      should render_template(:new)
    end

    context "on POST to #create with bad user values" do
      setup do
        post :create,
          :account => { :subdomain => "foo" },
          :user => { }
      end

      should_not_change "User.count"
      should_not_change "Account.count"
      should assign_to(:account)
      should assign_to(:user)
      should render_template(:new)
    end
    # ...
  end
```

In Rails 2.2 and Rails 2.3, when dealing with transactions in an application, it's important to turn off transactional fixtures. In these releases, Active Record does not handle nested transactions correctly. Rails 3 has fixed this problem. In Rails 2.2 and Rails 2.3, however, you need to ensure that use_transactional_fixtures is set to false in your test_helper.rb file:

```
# test/test_helper.rb
class Test::Unit::TestCase
  self.use_transactional_fixtures = false
end
```

Running this functional test will reveal that posting to #create with valid account parameters and invalid user parameters will still create an account record. The only way to deal with this situation correctly is to make use of database transactions. By wrapping your database statements in a call to ActiveRecord::Base.transaction, you can ensure that either both of the two #save operations happen or neither happens. If an exception is raised inside the transaction block, the whole transaction is rolled back. The exception is also raised again in order to allow the application to grab it and act accordingly.

Modifying the #create action to use transactions requires touching most of that code. You need to use #save! to ensure that the failed save operations will trigger an exception, thus rolling back the transaction. Also, you must use the frowned-upon begin ... rescue ... end pattern instead of simple conditionals because you're using exceptions on failed saves:

```ruby
# app/controllers/account_controller.rb
class AccountsController < ApplicationController
  def new
    @account = Account.new
    @user = User.new
  end

  def create
    @account = Account.new(params[:account])
    @user    = User.new(params[:user])
    @user.account = @account

    ActiveRecord::Base.transaction do
      @account.save!
      @user.save!
    end
    flash[:notice] = 'Account was successfully created.'
    redirect_to(@account)
  rescue ActiveRecord::RecordInvalid, ActiveRecord::RecordNotSaved
    render :action => "new"
  end
end
```

You're Doing It Wrong

At this point, we've introduced enough code smells into the #create action that we should step back and reevaluate the path we're taking.

One of the general guidelines we're breaking is "Exceptions should be exceptional." We're now using exceptions to handle validation failures—a common and expected situation for a web application.

Another guideline we're breaking is that we've introduced transactions, a low-level database concept, into the Controller layer. Typically, anytime a controller is making explicit use of transactions, you've gone down the wrong path.

Finally, a less pungent smell is introduced by the very fact that your actions aren't identical to those in the rest of your RESTful controllers. While small changes can be unavoidable at times, you should approach any large deviation with caution.

Presenting...

In the example from the preceding section, you can preserve the RESTful nature of the controller by making use of the Presenter Pattern.

The Model-View-Presenter (MVP) pattern was originally developed by Taligent and used extensively in some Smalltalk variants. One thing to keep in mind is that no two descriptions of MVP seem to be able to agree on exactly what the presenter's role is. We will be adhering closely to the version of the MVP pattern made recently popular by Jay Fields, who wrote about it extensively at `http://blog.jayfields.com`. In this merger of MVC and MVP, the presenter sits between the Model layer and the View and Controller layers.

A *presenter* is simply a plain old Ruby class that orchestrates the creation of multiple models. It can also take on the responsibility of sending emails or triggering other events that would normally be shoehorned into a controller action.

As much as possible, a presenter should mimic a single Active Record model. While people were experimenting with presenters in Rails applications, they wrote about a variety of ways of doing this. It seemed that building a good presenter was replacing building a new data structure library as the yak shaving hobby of choice. Luckily, James Golick released a fantastic gem, Active Presenter, which we discuss in this section. You can find Active Presenter, with installation instructions, at `http://github.com/jamesgolick/active_presenter`.

A presenter named `Signup` encapsulates the creation and association of the `Account` and `User` models. You should start with the unit test to describe how you expect it to behave:

```
# test/unit/signup_test.rb
class SignupTest < ActiveSupport::TestCase
  should validate_presence_of :account_subdomain
  should validate_presence_of :user_email
  should validate_presence_of :user_password

  should "be a presenter for account and user" do
    assert_contains Signup.new.presented.keys, :account
    assert_contains Signup.new.presented.keys, :user
  end
```

```
    should "assign the user to the account on save" do
      signup = Signup.new(:account_subdomain => "subdomain",
                          :user_email       => "e@mail.com",
                          :user_password    => "passw0rd")
      assert signup.save
      assert user    = signup.user
      assert account = signup.account
      assert_equal account.id, user.account_id
    end
  end
```

The first few macros here ensure that the Signup presenter is sending validations correctly and that the fields are named as you expect them to be named. Active Presenter maps the fields on the models to the presenter by prepending the model name to each field. User#email becomes Signup#user_email, and Account#subdomain becomes Signup#account_subdomain.

The first should statement ensures that the Signup class is an Active Presenter class and that it is responsible for the User and Account classes. You don't want to retest the library itself (Active Presenter is well tested in its own right), but you do need to ensure that you are using it correctly. Finally, a test ensures that the Signup presenter associates the user and the account with each other on save.

The following class definition is all that's necessary to make these tests pass:

```
# app/models/signup.rb
class Signup < ActivePresenter::Base
  before_save :assign_user_to_account
  presents :user, :account

  private

  def assign_user_to_account
    user.account = account
  end
end
```

The simplicity of this class is possible because it descends from ActivePresenter::Base. Active Presenter takes care of all the details, including running the before_save callback.

Now that you have what looks like a single Active Record model, the rest of the code is much simpler. For example, the view now looks like a normal single-model view:

```
# app/views/signups/new.html.erb
<h1>Signup!</h1>

<%= form_for(@signup) do |f| %>
  <%= f.error_messages %>

  <p>
    <%= f.label :account_subdomain %><br />
    <%= f.text_field :account_subdomain %>
  </p>

  <p>
    <%= f.label :user_email %><br />
    <%= f.text_field :user_email %>
  </p>

  <p>
    <%= f.label :user_password %><br />
    <%= f.text_field :user_password %>
  </p>

  <p>
    <%= f.submit "Create" %>
  </p>
<% end %>
```

Our functional test is also almost boilerplate. You leave in the tests for ensuring that neither record is created if either is invalid just to verify that everything is working as expected:

```
# test/functional/signup_controller_test.rb
class SignupsControllerTest < ActionController::TestCase
  context "on GET to #new" do
    setup { get :new }
    should assign_to(:signup)
    should render_template(:new)

    should "render form for signup" do
      assert_select "form[action$=?]", signups_path do
        assert_select "input[name=?]", "signup[account_subdomain]"
        assert_select "input[name=?]", "signup[user_email]"
        assert_select "input[name=?]", "signup[user_password]"
```

```
          end
      end
  end

  context "on POST to #create with good values" do
    setup do
      post :create,
            :signup => {:account_subdomain => "foo",
                         :user_email         => "foo@bar.com",
                         :user_password      => "issekrit?"}
    end

    should set_the_flash.to(/thank you/i)

    should_change "User.count",    :by => 1
    should_change "Account.count", :by => 1
  end

  context "on POST to #create with bad account values" do
    setup do
      post :create,
            :signup => {:user_email    => "foo@bar.com",
                         :user_password => "issekrit?"}
    end

    should_not_change "User.count"
    should_not_change "Account.count"
    should assign_to(:signup)
    should render_template(:new)
  end

  context "on POST to #create with bad user values" do
    setup do
      post :create, :signup => {:account_subdomain => "foo"}
    end

    should_not_change "User.count"
    should_not_change "Account.count"
    should assign_to(:signup)
    should render_template(:new)
  end
end
```

Finally, the moment you've been waiting for. The controller itself no longer contains any domain-specific logic, but it looks like a normal RESTful controller:

```ruby
# app/controllers/signup_controller.rb
class SignupsController < ApplicationController
  def new
    @signup = Signup.new
  end

  def create
    @signup = Signup.new(params[:signup])

    if @signup.save
      flash[:notice] = 'Thank you for signing up!'
      redirect_to root_url
    else
      render :action => "new"
    end
  end
end
```

And Remember to Tip Your Waitress

While you can move extra logic from your controllers into setters and callbacks on the primary model, there are times when that's not the right path to take. Doing too much work in Active Record setters and callbacks can lead to unexpected behavior and convoluted callback chains between different models. At times like these, it's useful to introduce a third-party object whose job is to manage the complexity on behalf of your controller and models. The beauty of the Presenter Pattern is that it mimics and Active Record model while fulfilling that role, requiring little or no change in the RESTful controller.

AntiPattern: Bloated Sessions

The general philosophy for the Rails framework and Rails applications is that each request to the application should be relatively stateless. This means that each request is independent of prior and future requests and contains all the information needed to perform that request.

For example, if an application features a multistep wizard, the server doesn't record internally which step a user is on as he or she moves through the wizard. Instead, the client itself communicates which step it's on and provides all the information necessary to process the request.

This stateless methodology is the Rails ideal, and following it helps to produce clean, straightforward applications that are easier to maintain. That being said, there are times when storing something in a stateful manner greatly improves either the ease of implementation or the end-user experience. One such example is storing the user the client is currently signed in as. Rails provides the concept of the session store, a place where information can be placed so it can persist between requests by the same client.

Strictly speaking, a default Ruby on Rails session is now mostly stateless as well, as all the data in the session is stored on the client side, in cookies. This fact has only exacerbated a problem that has been present in many Rails applications that have forgone the stateless methodology and instead stored a lot of information in the session.

The default Rails session store, the cookie store, stores a maximum of 4K of data. In a typical application, this will be just the current user id and any flash messages that are being presented to the user. Attempting to store more than 4K of data in the session store will result in an exception.

Other session stores allow you to store more than 4K of data. However, if your application needs one of them, it's likely that it is suffering from too much information being stored in the session, most of which is likely unnecessary.

Fortunately, unless there have been fundamental flaws in application design, transitioning an existing application that is abusing the session into one that is barely using it at all is a relatively straightforward exercise. Even better, you can avoid getting into that situation in the first place by following a few simple rules.

Solution: Store References Instead of Instances

You should never put entire models into a session. Instead, if you absolutely must keep track of an entity across requests, you should place a *reference* to that entity, such as the id, into the session. Then, when the entity is needed again, it can be reinstantiated for the request. Take, for example, the following controller actions for multistep wizard:

```ruby
class OrdersController < ApplicationController
  def new
    session[:order] = Order.new
  end

  def billing
    session[:order].attributes = params[:order]
    if !session[:order].valid?
      render :action => :new
    end
  end

  def shipping
    session[:order].attributes = params[:order]
    if !session[:order].valid?
      render :action => :billing
    end
  end

  def payment
    session[:order].attributes = params[:order]
    if !session[:order].valid?
      render :action => :shipping
    end
  end

  def create
    if session[:order].save
      flash[:success] = "Order placed successfully"
      redirect_to order_path(session[:order])
    else
      render :action => :payment
    end
  end

  def show
    @order = Order.find params[:id]
  end
end
```

In this OrderController class, the order being worked on is stored in the session and used in each step of the wizard. At each step, the in-progress order is validated to ensure that it's being filled out correctly. After the order is submitted in the final step, it is saved to the database. It's then retrievable as a normal object, as illustrated in the show action. There is no order id passed to each step of the wizard, so the routes for this controller appear as follows:

```
resources :posts do
  collection do
    post :shipping
    post :billing
    posft :payment
  end
end
```

The URLs as a user moves through this process appear as follows:

```
/orders/new
/orders/shipping
/orders/billing
/orders/payment
/orders/1
```

While this method works, it's an abuse of the session object. It would not work in the default Rails session store and is a poor design. Instead, you can store the order in the database in each step, as shown in the following OrdersController example:

```
class OrdersController < ApplicationController
  def new
    @order = Order.new
  end

  def billing
    @order = Order.find(params[:id])
    if !@order.update_attributes(params[:order])
      render :action => :new
    end
  end
end
```

```
def shipping
  @order = Order.find(params[:id])
  if !@order.update_attributes(params[:order])
    render :action => :billing
  end
end

def payment
  @order = Order.find(params[:id])
  if !@order.update_attributes(params[:order])
    render :action => :shipping
  end
end

def create
  @order = Order.find(params[:id])
  if @order.update_attributes(params[:order])
    flash[:success] = "Order placed successfully"
    redirect_to order_path(session[:order])
  else
    render :action => :payment
  end
end

def show
  @order = Order.find params[:id]
  end
end
```

In this example, the in-progress order is stored in the database instead of the session. Because a specific Order instance is being operated on in this example, the steps for the wizard are member actions, as follows:

```
resources :posts do
  member do
    post :shipping
    post :billing
    post :payment
  end
end
```

The order wizard steps now have the following URLs:

```
/orders/new
/orders/1/shipping
/orders/1/billing
/orders/1/payment
/orders/1
```

One of the main reasons a developer might choose to store the in-progress order in the session rather than in the database is that once in-progress and incomplete orders are stored in the database, they must be distinguished from orders that completed the wizard in all future database queries across the system. This can be tedious as well as a source for bugs. Therefore, it might be attractive to attempt to address this by storing an in-progress order in a session before saving it to the database.

A better way to address this is to store the information about the Order entirely on the client side. It can then be transmitted to the server with each request; at the server, it is processed, and action is taken accordingly. With each step of the wizard, the order details can be written to the client. The order details can be represented to the client in different ways, the most straightforward of which is perhaps in hidden form fields on each step of the wizard. For example, the following controller implements this strategy:

```
class OrdersController < ApplicationController
  def new
    @order = Order.new
  end

  def billing
    @order = Order.new(params[:order])
    if !@order.valid?
      render :action => :new
    end
  end

  def shipping
    @order = Order.new(params[:order])
    if !@order.valid?
      render :action => :billing
    end
  end
```

```ruby
  def payment
    @order = Order.new(params[:order])
    if !@order.valid?
      render :action => :shipping
    end
  end

  def create
    @order = Order.new(params[:order])
    if @order.save
      flash[:success] = "Order placed successfully"
      redirect_to order_path(session[:order])
    else
      render :action => :payment
    end
  end

  def show
    @order = Order.find params[:id]
  end
end
```

This controller is very similar to the original session-based `OrdersController`, and the routes are the same. However, instead of storing the order in the session, it places the order in an instance variable that will be available to the view.

Next, let's take a look at the order billing entry view:

```erb
<h2>Shipping Address</h2>
<%= form_for @order,
             :url => shipping_order_path,
             :html => { :method => :post } do  |form| %>
  <%= form.label :shipping_address %>
  <%= form.text_field :shipping_address %>
  <%= form.label :shipping_city %>
  <%= form.text_field :shipping_city %>
  <%= form.label :shipping_state %>
  <%= form.text_field :shipping_state %>
  <%= form.label :shipping_zip %>
  <%= form.text_field :shipping_zip %>

  <%= submit_tag %>
```

```
    <%= form.hidden_field :billing_address %>
    <%= form.hidden_field :billing_city %>
    <%= form.hidden_field :billing_state %>
    <%= form.hidden_field :billing_zip %>
  <% end %>
```

In this view code, the fields that the user is filling out in the current step are presented to the user, and the fields that the user has already filled out are hidden on the form for the current step.

The strategy you choose depends on the needs of your application. Storing everything on the client typically works best for smaller flows, typically not exceeding two or three steps, or for applications where it is absolutely critical that in-progress and incomplete orders not be stored to the database. Persisting everything to the database is usually the best solution for more complex sequences involving multiple objects or many steps.

AntiPattern: Monolithic Controllers

Ruby on Rails 2.0 embraced a RESTful structure and never looked back. In the context of Rails, a RESTful structure simply means mapping the "standard" controller actions index, new, create, edit, update, show, and destroy to the HTTP verbs POST, PUT, GET, and DELETE rather than strictly adhering to all the ideas in REST (REpresentation State Transfer, a term coined by Roy Fielding).

There are two telltale signs of an application that doesn't use RESTful practices. One is extra parameters in URLs used to identify what additional actions are performed by the controller action. The other is nonstandard controller actions (actions that are not one of index, new, create, edit, update, show, and destroy).

The seven Rails actions have been fairly standard in Rails for some time, but there are still applications that don't use them, let alone worry about mapping them to the HTTP verbs. This may be because of developer inexperience with Rails, the age of the application, or determination to do something the wrong way. Fortunately, the course of action for fixing this flaw is the same, regardless of the cause.

Solution: Embrace REST

RESTful controllers have only recently been introduced, and as a result, we still see many examples of non-RESTful, monolithic controllers in the wild. Take, for example, the following snippet of code from an AdminController object:

```
def users
  per_page = Variable::default_pagination_value
  @users = User.find(:all)
  # First, check to see if there
  # was an operation performed
  if not params[:operation].nil? then
    if (params[:operation] == "reset_password") then
      user = User.find(params[:id])
      user.generate_password_reset_access_key
      user.password_confirmation = user.password
      user.email_confirmation = user.email
      user.save!
      flash[:notice] = user.first_name + " " +
        user.last_name + "'s password has been reset."
    end
```

This `AdminController` object has a users action. The users action expects an additional parameter, `operation`, which takes values that determine what functionality occurs within the action.

Controller naming is very important, and the name of the controller in this case may indicate a problem. In a RESTful structure, the controller is named for the resource that is being operated on. An `AdminController` object, then, would be expected to operate on `Admins`. This is not the case.

The following code is the remainder of the controller action, for the sake of clarity and thoroughness:

```
if (params[:operation] == "delete_user") then
  user = User.find(params[:id])
  user.item_status = ItemStatus.find_deleted()
  user.password_confirmation = user.password
  user.email_confirmation = user.email
  user.save!
  flash[:notice] = user.first_name + " " +
    user.last_name + " has been deleted"
end
if (params[:operation] == "activate_user") then
  user = User.find(params[:id])
  user.item_status = ItemStatus.find_active()
  user.password_confirmation = user.password
  user.email_confirmation = user.email
  user.save!
  flash[:notice] = user.first_name + " " +
    user.last_name + " has been activated"
end
if (params[:operation] == "show_user") then
  @user = User.find(params[:id])
  render :template => show_user
  return true
end
end
user_order = 'username'
if not params[:user_sort_field].nil? then
  user_order = params[:user_sort_field]
  if !session[:user_sort_field].nil? &&
    user_order == session[:user_sort_field] then
    user_order += " DESC"
  end
```

```
      session[:user_sort_field] = user_order
  end

  @user_pages, @users = paginate(:users,
    :order => user_order,
    :conditions => ['item_status_id <> ?',
                    ItemStatus.find_deleted().id],
    :per_page  => per_page)
end
```

As you can see, this one action is using the `operation` parameter to provide the same functionality that would normally be present within the `index`, `show`, and `destroy` actions of a `UsersController`, as well as additional actions for resetting a user's password and activating a user, with URLs that looked something like the following:

```
/admin/users?operation=reset_password?id=x
/admin/users?operation=delete_user?id=x
/admin/users?operation=activate_user?id=x
/admin/users?operation=show_user?id=x
/admin/users
```

Before we go any further in identifying the changes and solutions to this problem, we need to note the importance of using an automated test suite when making large refactorings like this. If this application didn't have a test suite (it probably wouldn't), then it's recommended that one be written. The most appropriate types of tests would be integration tests using a tool such as Cucumber. These tests allow you to prevent regressions because it should be possible to write the integration tests such that they don't fail if you haven't broken anything. This is because integration tests operate on the links that are clicked, the fields that are typed in, and so on, rather than on the internal controller organization of the application.

When your integration tests have been addressed, you can refactor the monolithic controller into one or more RESTful controllers. Fortunately, non-RESTful controller actions are very often given the name that your controllers should have. Let's start by mapping out what the new URLs will be:

```
POST    /admin/users/:id/password
DELETE  /admin/users/:id
POST    /admin/users/:id/activation
GET     /admin/users/:id
GET     /admin/users
```

You need to rename `AdminController` to `UsersController` (or create a new one) and create new `PasswordsController` and `ActivationsController` objects. Next, you simply take the existing code from the `if` statements in the existing controller and move it into the corresponding new controller actions:

```
class UsersController < ApplicationController
  def index
    per_page = Variable::default_pagination_value
    user_order = 'username'
    if not params[:user_sort_field].nil? then
      user_order = params[:user_sort_field]
      if !session[:user_sort_field].nil? &&
        user_order == session[:user_sort_field] then
        user_order += " DESC"
      end
      session[:user_sort_field] = user_order
    end

    @user_pages, @users = paginate(:users,
      :order => user_order,
      :conditions => ['item_status_id <> ?',
                      ItemStatus.find_deleted().id],
      :per_page  => per_page)
  end

  def destroy
    user = User.find(params[:id])
    user.item_status = ItemStatus.find_deleted()
    user.password_confirmation = user.password
    user.email_confirmation = user.email
    user.save!
    flash[:notice] = user.first_name + " " +
      user.last_name + " has been deleted"
  end

  def show
    @user = User.find(params[:id])
    render :template => show_user
  end
end
```

```ruby
class PasswordsController < ApplicationController
  def create
    user = User.find(params[:id])
    user.generate_password_reset_access_key
    user.password_confirmation = user.password
    user.email_confirmation = user.email
    user.save!
    flash[:notice] = user.first_name + " " +
      user.last_name + "'s password has been reset."
  end
end

class ActivationsController < ApplicationController
  def create
    user = User.find(params[:id])
    user.item_status = ItemStatus.find_active()
    user.password_confirmation = user.password
    user.email_confirmation = user.email
    user.save!
    flash[:notice] = user.first_name + " " +
        user.last_name + " has been activated"
    end
  end
end
```

Now, with functionality organized into these new controllers, the routes for these controllers would be as follows:

```ruby
namespace :admin do
  resources :users do
    resource :passwords
    resource :activations
  end
end
```

As you review this code in more detail, you're likely to see many other things that could be improved in it. While fixing this example is fairly straightforward, it's important that you tackle only one issue at a time. You should refactor to a RESTful controller *first* and then continue improving the code from there. Making a controller RESTful often exposes better improvements and keeps things easier to organize. In addition, by tackling one item at a time, you lessen the risk of getting lost or overwhelmed.

Finally, monolithic controllers often have many non-RESTful actions. Suppose that instead of the `operation` parameter and `if` statements, the monolithic controller above had `index`, `reset_password`, `delete_user`, `activate_user`, and `show_user` actions. The changes outlined would be the same: Rename the `delete_user` and `show_user` actions and break the `reset_password` and `activate_user` actions into their own RESTful controllers. For more related details, read see the next section.

AntiPattern: Controller of Many Faces

As applications grow, RESTful controllers often take on some non-RESTful trappings. This situation should be avoided whenever possible, and it often make sense to extract these extra, non-RESTful actions into their own RESTful resource.

Solution: Refactor Non-RESTful Actions into a Separate Controller

A common example of a RESTful controller taking on too much responsibility is in authentication. Far too often, we see authentication shoehorned into the UsersController, like this:

```ruby
class UsersController < ApplicationController
  def login
    if request.post?
      if session[:user_id] = User.authenticate(params[:user][:login],
                                                params[:user][:password])
        flash[:message]  = "Login successful"
        redirect_to root_url
      else
        flash[:warning] = "Login unsuccessful"
      end
    end
  end

  def logout
    session[:user_id] = nil
    flash[:message] = 'Logged out'
    redirect_to :action => 'login'
  end

  ... RESTful actions ...
end
```

What Is a Resource?

It may seem at first glance that authentication is under the mandate of the UsersController, but with authentication, you're really managing the concept of a user's session. Once you begin to view a controller for a representation of a resource, you realize that the resource doesn't have to correspond directly to an Active Record model.

Let's look at what happens when you extract the `UsersController#login` and `UsersController#logout` methods into their own resource. First, you must add the route to your `config/routes.rb` file. You can also add a couple named URL helpers for convenience and the sake of using prettier URLs:

```
resource :sessions, :only => [:new, :create, :destroy]
match "/login"  => "user_sessions#new",     :as => :login
match "/logout" => "user_sessions#destroy", :as => :logout
```

Note that you should use the singular version, `resource`. A session is a great example of a singular resource, as it makes no sense to ask for a listing of sessions, and sessions have no concept of a unique identifier.

You're going to implement three actions on your `SessionsController`: new, create, and destroy:

```
class SessionsController < ApplicationController
  def new
    # Just render the sessions/new.html.erb template
  end

  def create
    if session[:user_id] = User.authenticate(params[:user][:login],
                                              params[:user][:password])
      flash[:message]  = "Login successful"
      redirect_to root_url
    else
      flash.now[:warning] = "Login unsuccessful"
      render :action => "new"
    end
  end

  def destroy
    session[:user_id] = nil
    flash[:message] = 'Logged out'
    redirect_to login_url
  end
end
```

This is a much cleaner design than the original. It separates the concerns of session management from the concerns of user profile management; the consistent set of RESTful actions will help with overall maintainability; and, as an added bonus, it removes the ugly `if request.post?` call.

When RESTful Actions Aren't RESTful

While this solution is about identifying and extracting non-RESTful actions in a RESTful controller, there are some exceptions to this solution to be aware of. If asked to list the RESTful actions on a Rails controller, most developers would be able to recite them from memory: `index`, `new`, `create`, `show`, `edit`, `update`, and `destroy`. This is almost correct, but it's also useful when trying to really understand the philosophy of REST. You see, `new` and `edit` are not really RESTful actions. At its core, REST asks for only the `index`, `create`, `show`, `update`, and `destroy` actions. The `new` and `edit` actions are really just different ways of representing the `show` action.

A good way of thinking about this is "What actions would you implement when writing an XML-only controller?" Clearly, when consuming an API, there is no reason to request the `edit` action. It simply serves as a user interface enhancement for us lowly humans.

You can decide for yourself whether a `preview` action belongs on a RESTful `PostsController`.

Simply Strong OOP

Viewing each controller as a class is really just an application of the Single Responsibility Principle discussed in Chapter 1. Each controller should contain only the logic that pertains to the resource it represents. Failing to abide by this principle will lead you down the slippery slope that ends in the monolithic controller problem we discussed earlier in this chapter, in the section "AntiPattern: Monolithic Controllers." Furthermore, this type of refactoring can reveal code smells at the Model layer. In fact, the Authlogic gem was written precisely because of this pattern of using a `SessionsController` object. We discussed Authlogic in more detail in this chapter, in the section "AntiPattern: Homemade Keys."

AntiPattern: A Lost Child Controller

RESTful resources generally parallel the models they represent, which is part of the reason you're able to gain such a fantastic productivity increase when developing applications in an entirely RESTful fashion. You no longer need to imagine different ways of dividing your problem space for the Model, View, and Controller layers. Once you've determined the division of responsibilities in the underlying domain, the Controller and View layers follow along nicely.

That being said, mapping controllers and the URL paradigm on top of the complex and powerful capabilities of the Model layer is sometimes a challenge. Take, for example, representing one-to-many associations in a RESTful manner. Consider an application that manages Songs and Albums. As a modern Rails developer, you want to represent this system RESTfully. With that in mind, you can create Song and Album resources:

```
$ rails generate scaffold Album title:string artist:string
   invoke   active_record
   create      db/migrate/20100522002832_create_albums.rb
   create      app/models/album.rb
   invoke      test_unit
   create        test/unit/album_test.rb
   create        test/fixtures/albums.yml
    route    resources :albums
   invoke   scaffold_controller
   create      app/controllers/albums_controller.rb
   invoke      erb
   create        app/views/albums
   create        app/views/albums/index.html.erb
   create        app/views/albums/edit.html.erb
   create        app/views/albums/show.html.erb
   create        app/views/albums/new.html.erb
   create        app/views/albums/_form.html.erb
   invoke      test_unit
   create        test/functional/albums_controller_test.rb
   invoke      helper
   create        app/helpers/albums_helper.rb
   invoke        test_unit
   create          test/unit/helpers/albums_helper_test.rb
   invoke   stylesheets
   create      public/stylesheets/scaffold.css
```

```
$ rails generate scaffold Song title:string genre:string
      invoke  active_record
      create     db/migrate/20100522003017_create_songs.rb
      create     app/models/song.rb
      invoke     test_unit
      create        test/unit/song_test.rb
      create        test/fixtures/songs.yml
       route   resources :songs
      invoke  scaffold_controller
      create     app/controllers/songs_controller.rb
      invoke     erb
      create        app/views/songs
      create        app/views/songs/index.html.erb
      create        app/views/songs/edit.html.erb
      create        app/views/songs/show.html.erb
      create        app/views/songs/new.html.erb
      create        app/views/songs/_form.html.erb
      invoke     test_unit
      create        test/functional/songs_controller_test.rb
      invoke     helper
      create        app/helpers/songs_helper.rb
      invoke        test_unit
      create           test/unit/helpers/songs_helper_test.rb
      invoke  stylesheets
   identical     public/stylesheets/scaffold.css
```

Clearly, an `Album` object can have many `Song` objects, and a `Song` object can belong to an `Album` object. You can add the `album_id` attribute to the `Song` model and set up the associations as follows:

```
$ rails generate migration add_album_id_to_songs album_id:integer
   invoke  active_record
   create     db/migrate/20100522003327_add_album_id_to_songs.rb
```

```
class Album < ActiveRecord::Base
  has_many :songs
end
```

```
class Song < ActiveRecord::Base
  belongs_to :album
end
```

Now that you have the basic Model layer associations set up, you have to present the album and its songs to the user. The `AlbumsController#show` view, which is mapped to `/albums/123`, might look something like the following:

```
<h2> <%= @album.title %> </h2>
<p> By: <%= @album.artist %> </p>

<ul>
  <% @album.songs.each do |song| %>
    <li><%= link_to song.title, song %></li>
  <% end %>
</ul>

<%= link_to "Add song", new_song_url(:album_id => @album.id) %>
```

The interesting bit in this view is the `:album_id` parameter passed to the "Add song" link. You'd like the user to be able to add songs for this album without having to choose the album from a dropdown. The other components for making this work lie in catching the value of `params[:album_id]` as it comes into the `SongsController#new` action:

```
class SongsController < ApplicationController
  def new
    @song = Song.new(:album_id => params[:album_id])
```

Then, you add an `album_id` hidden field to the songs form in app/views/songs/ _form.html.erb:

```
<%= form_for(@song) do |f| %>
  <%= f.hidden_field :album_id %>
  ...
```

While this works, it's not ideal. Passing the parent ID around like a hot potato is a definite code smell. Furthermore, the "Add song" link takes the user to the new song form with a URL like `/songs/new?album_id=123`. While it might seem somewhat nitpicky to worry about the quality of the URL, these small details can erode the confidence users have in an application.

To make matters worse, your ideal `SongsController` object would be able to handle the addition of an `album_id` for all the actions. When given an `album_id`, the index action would list only songs for that album, the show action would show the song only if it exists for that album, and so on. This can quickly get out of hand.

Solution: Make Use of Nested Resources

Rails provides an answer to the problem of having to explicitly pass around parent IDs in the form of nested resources. Since Rails 2, it's been possible to specify in a routes file that one resource should be accessible as a nested URL under another resource. For your application, that routes declaration would be as simple as this:

```
MyApp::Application.routes.draw do
  resources :albums do
    resources :songs
  end
  ...
```

To see how this affects the URLs your application now responds to, take a look at the output of the rake routes task:

```
$ rake routes | grep song
...
                  GET    /albums/:album_id/songs(.:format)
   album_songs POST     /albums/:album_id/songs(.:format)
 new_album_song GET     /albums/:album_id/songs/new(.:format)
                  GET    /albums/:album_id/songs/:id(.:format)
                  PUT    /albums/:album_id/songs/:id(.:format)
     album_song DELETE  /albums/:album_id/songs/:id(.:format)
edit_album_song GET     /albums/:album_id/songs/:id/edit(.:format)
...
```

As you can see, all access to your songs controller is now scoped under /albums/:album_id. This means it's no longer possible to access a song directly, which may or may not be the desired behavior. For now, let's assume that's fine, and we'll look at a more complex alternative later.

SongsController will now always have access to params[:album_id]. Keep in mind that this does not necessarily have to be a valid album_id; it's your job to ensure that it's valid. You can use before_filter to grab the album from this parameter before each action. And you can place that album in the @album instance variable to make it available to all actions:

```ruby
class SongsController < ApplicationController
  before_filter :grab_album_from_album_id
  ...
  private

  def grab_album_from_album_id
    @album = Album.find(params[:album_id])
  end
end
```

Now that you have the parent album to work with, you need to ensure that all your actions make use of it. There are two fundamental changes that you have to make. The first is to replace all references to the Song class in SongsController with @album.songs. The second is to make sure you're generating the correct URLs with the new album_song_url helpers. It's cleaner to just pass the instance variables into redirect_to or link_to instead of using the helpers whenever possible. Here's the full controller after these changes are made:

```ruby
class SongsController < ApplicationController
  before_filter :grab_album_from_album_id

  def index
    @songs = @album.songs.all
  end

  def show
    @song = @album.songs.find(params[:id])
  end

  def new
    @song = @album.songs.new
  end

  def edit
    @song = @album.songs.find(params[:id])
  end

  def create
    @song = @album.songs.new(params[:song])
```

```
    if @song.save
      redirect_to([@album, @song],
                  :notice => 'Song was successfully created.')
    else
      render :action => "new"
    end
  end

  def update
    @song = @album.songs.find(params[:id])

    if @song.update_attributes(params[:song])
      redirect_to([@album, @song],
                  :notice => 'Song was successfully updated.')
    else
      render :action => "edit"
    end
  end

  def destroy
    Song.find(params[:id]).destroy
    redirect_to(album_songs_url(@album))
  end

  private

  def grab_album_from_album_id
    @album = Album.find(params[:album_id])
  end
end
```

You have to make similar changes to the views. The new _form.html.erb partial is shown next. Note that you use [@album, @song] as the argument to form_for so that it knows to post the results to the fully nested URL:

```
<%= form_for([@album, @song]) do |f| %>
  ...
<% end %>
```

Similarly, the new edit.html.erb view is shown next. You have to modify the 'Show' and 'Back' links to account for the nesting under /albums/:album_id:

```
<h1>Editing song</h1>
<%= render 'form' %>

<%= link_to 'Show', [@album, @song] %> |
<%= link_to 'Back', @album %>
```

Nested and Un-nested

Allowing a controller to be accessed as a nested *and* an un-nested resource can be complicated. Your main challenge is to get the controller to respond appropriately to both /albums/:album_id/songs/... and /songs/.... The first step is to tell the router that you want to be able to access the songs controller via either route. You do this by duplicating the :songs resources definition—once nested under :albums and once by itself:

```
MyApp::Application.routes.draw do
  resources :albums do
    resources :songs
  end
  resources :songs
```

To simplify the problem a bit, you can assume that a song does not require an album and that the un-nested URL is the canonical version. You can therefore redirect the user to the same place (/songs/:id) after creating or updating the song. If you were not able to make this assumption, you would need to override the songs_url and song_url(song) helpers to detect whether the song has an album and return the correct URL string.

The first main change to the controller is that you're calling Album.find only if the :album_id parameter is available. The second, subtler, change is that you're adding a songs private method, which returns either @album.songs or Song, depending on whether @album is set. You use this helper wherever you would have accessed the Song class by itself:

```
class SongsController < ApplicationController
  before_filter :grab_album_from_album_id

  def index
    @songs = songs.all
  end
```

```
def show
  @song = songs.find(params[:id])
end

def new
  @song = songs.new
end

def edit
  @song = songs.find(params[:id])
end

def create
  @song = songs.new(params[:song])

  if @song.save
    redirect_to(@song,
                :notice => 'Song was successfully created.')
  else
    render :action => "new"
  end
end

def update
  @song = songs.find(params[:id])

  if @song.update_attributes(params[:song])
    redirect_to(@song,
                :notice => 'Song was successfully updated.')
  else
    render :action => "edit"
  end
end

def destroy
  Song.find(params[:id]).destroy
  redirect_to(songs_url)
end

private
```

```
    def songs
      @album ? @album.songs : Song
    end

    def grab_album_from_album_id
      @album = Album.find(params[:album_id]) if params[:album_id]
    end
  end
```

Now that you're done with the controller, you need to face the easier task of making the views work. Because you're considering the un-nested /songs/:id routes to be canonical, you remove all links to the nested versions. For example, the edit.html.erb template looks like the following:

```
<h1>Editing song</h1>

<%= render 'form' %>

<%= link_to 'Show', @song %> |
<%= link_to 'Back', :back %>
```

Notice the use of link_to with the :back option, a convenient Rails helper that uses JavaScript to return the user to the referring page.

Finally, the _form.html.erb partial now includes a new conditional to determine whether to show the albums dropdown when editing a song:

```
<%= form_for([@album, @song]) do |f| %>
  ...
  <% unless @album %>
    <div class="field">
      <%= f.label :album %><br />
      <%= f.select(:album_id,
            options_from_collection_for_select(Album.all,
                                                :id,
                                                :title,
                                                @song.album_id),
                   { :include_blank => true }) %>
    </div>
  <% end %>
  ...
```

Cleanup

From the example in the preceding section, you can see that correctly creating a resource that responds to both the nested and un-nested URLs can be a challenge, and it can add a bit of complication to an application. The complication becomes worse when the user interface differs significantly between the two situations. In that case, you should use two completely separate controllers for the different types of access. While this introduces duplication between the controllers, the savings in simplicity is well worth it. We discuss that refactoring in the next AntiPattern.

Models that have a distinct parent/child relationship are best represented by using the nested resource feature introduced in Rails 2. Doing so gives you very readable and predicable URLs, as well as all the same forms of syntactic sugar that RESTful resources give you above regular controllers. Being able to use `link_to "new song",` `new_album_song_url(album)` instead of the `messier link_to "new song", song_` `url(song, :album_id => album.id)` is a big improvement in making an application predictable and maintainable.

AntiPattern: Rat's Nest Resources

Nesting controllers so that the parameters to the controllers are managed and understood by the application routes is a powerful technique. However, imagine that a website lists all messages posted by all users and has the ability to list all the messages posted by a single user. If the controllers for these two lists were the same controller, the index action of that controller would look something like the following:

```ruby
class MessagesController < ApplicationController
  def index
    if params[:user_id]
      @user = User.find(params[:user_id])
      @messages = @user.messages
    else
      @messages = Message.all
    end
  end
end
```

And the routes for the above controller would be as shown here:

```ruby
resources :messages
resources :users do
  resources :messages
end
```

Finally, the view for this `MessagesController#index` action might be something like the following:

```erb
<h1>Messages<% if @user %> for <%= @user.name %><% end %></h1>

<ul>
  <% @messages.each do |message| %>
    <%= content_tag_for :li, @message do %>
      <span class="subject"><%= message.subject %></span>
      <% if !@user %>
        <span class="poster">Posted by <%= message.user.name
%></span>
      <% end %>
      <span class="body"><%= message.body %></span>
```

```
    <% end %>
  <% end %>
</ul>
```

In this example, you can see that the view is altered based on whether the instance variable @user is defined. If it is not, then you know the view is showing all messages. When the view is showing messages for a specific user, the header of the page is different, and the author of each message is not shown because it would be redundant.

In this example, the existence of two possible nestings with minor difference between the views is somewhat manageable. However, imagine if this system actually grouped Messages into Projects as well. A user might have this global view of all messages across all projects, the messages of just one project, the messages of just one user across all projects, or the messages of just one user in one project. The conditional logic in the controller and views would be overwhelming.

Or, imagine if the differences between the views for nested and un-nested versions of this controller were drastic. It would become tedious and error prone to maintain one view with so much conditional logic.

Solution: Use Separate Controllers for Each Nesting

At some point—a point that comes more quickly than you might think—it becomes beneficial not to try to keep the same controller for each different resource path but to instead create a new controller for each nesting.

You store each of these individual controllers in a directory with the same name as its parent controller. The new controllers for the earlier messages controller would be laid out like this:

```
controllers/messages_controller.rb
controllers/users/messages_controller.rb
```

And the accompanying routes would be as shown here:

```
resources :messages
resources :users do
  resources :messages, :controller => 'users/messages'
end
```

Now, each version of the messages path would have its own controller and views, as shown here:

```ruby
# controllers/messages_controller.rb
class MessagesController < ApplicationController
  def index
    @messages = Message.all
  end
end


# controllers/users/messages_controller.rb
class MessagesController < ApplicationController
  def index
    @user = User.find(params[:user_id])
    @messages = @user.messages
  end
end


<!-- views/messages/index.html.erb -->
<h1>Messages</h1>

<ul>
  <% @messages.each do |message| %>
    <%= content_tag_for :li, @message do %>
      <span class="subject"><%= message.subject %></span>
      <span class="poster">Posted by <%= message.user.name %></span>
      <span class="body"><%= message.body %></span>
    <% end %>
  <% end %>
</ul>


<!-- views/users/messages/index.html.erb -->
<h1>Messages for <%= @user.name %></h1>

<ul>
  <% @messages.each do |message| %>
    <%= content_tag_for :li, @message do %>
      <span class="subject"><%= message.subject %></span>
      <span class="body"><%= message.body %></span>
    <% end %>
  <% end %>
</ul>
```

Using this strategy, you might find that there is some confusion if some nested controllers are not in subdirectories and others are. Therefore, you might find it helpful to keep all your nested controllers in subdirectories that match their nested URLs so that the locations of the controllers are consistent.

The technique of using separate controllers for these nested routes is less DRY, but in the right situations, it will ultimately lead to cleaner and easier-to-maintain code. If you find yourself swimming in conditional logic based on alternate nested versions of the same controller, give it a try.

AntiPattern: Evil Twin Controllers

As an application grows and matures, the number of things that occur in its controllers increases. Even if you remain diligent and move as much functionality from the controllers into the models as possible, there will inevitably be functionality that remains in the controllers, such as alternative formats available for APIs (JSON, XML, and so on). For example, examine the following controller for Songs, which exposes an XML API:

```ruby
class SongsController < ApplicationController
  before_filter :grab_album_from_album_id

  def index
    @songs = songs.all
    respond_to do |format|
      format.html
      format.xml { render :xml => @songs }
    end
  end

  def show
    @song = songs.find(params[:id])
    respond_to do |format|
      format.html
      format.xml { render :xml => @song }
    end
  end

  def new
    @song = songs.new
    respond_to do |format|
      format.html
      format.xml { render :xml => @song }
    end
  end

  def edit
    @song = songs.find(params[:id])
  end
```

```
def create
  @song = songs.new(params[:song])

  respond_to do |format|
    if @song.save
      format.html do
        redirect_to(@song,
                    :notice => 'Song was successfully created.')
      end
      format.xml do
        render :xml => @song,
               :status => :created,
               :location => @song
      end
    else
      format.html { render :action => "new" }
      format.xml do
        render :xml => @song.errors,
               :status => :unprocessable_entity
      end
    end
  end
end

def update
  @song = songs.find(params[:id])

  respond_to do |format|
    if @song.update_attributes(params[:song])
      format.html do
        redirect_to(@song,
                    :notice => 'Song was successfully updated.')
      end
      format.xml { head :ok }
    else
      format.html { render :action => "edit" }
      format.xml do
        render :xml => @song.errors,
               :status => :unprocessable_entity
      end
    end
  end
end
```

```
def destroy
  Song.find(params[:id]).destroy
  respond_to do |format|
    format.html { redirect_to(songs_url) }
    format.xml { head :ok }
  end
end

private

def songs
  @album ? @album.songs : Song
end

def grab_album_from_album_id
  @album = Album.find(params[:album_id]) if params[:album_id]
end
end
```

This Songs controller actually isn't doing much more than the normal controller, generated by the Rails scaffold, would do. However, it is already much longer than a normal controller without the XML API. In addition, imagine if one of the actions had extra functionality. There is so much other code that it might not be apparent.

The primary issue here is that this controller is not DRY. Another controller in the application doing everything the same only with a different model will have just as much code. Then, when differences are introduced between the controllers, those important differences are harder to spot because the "unimportant" code gets in the way.

Solution: Use Rails 3 Responders

Rails 3 introduced a new set of methods called *responders* that abstract the boilerplate responding code so that the controller becomes much simpler. In the following example, the preceding Songs controller is rewritten using responders:

```
class SongsController < ApplicationController
  respond_to :html, :xml
  before_filter :grab_album_from_album_id

  def index
    @songs = songs.all
```

```ruby
    respond_with(@songs)
  end

  def show
    @song = songs.find(params[:id])
    respond_with(@song)
  end

  def new
    @song = songs.new
    respond_with(@song)
  end

  def edit
    @song = songs.find(params[:id])
    respond_with(@song)
  end

  def create
    @song = songs.new(params[:song])
    if @song.save
      flash[:notice] = 'Song was successfully created.'
    end
    respond_with(@song)
  end

  def update
    @song = songs.find(params[:id])
    if @song.update_attributes(params[:song])
      flash[:notice] = 'Song was successfully updated.'
    end
    respond_with(@song)
  end

  def destroy
    @song = Song.find(params[:id])
    @song.destroy
    respond_with(@song)
  end

  private
```

188 Chapter 4. Controllers

```
  def songs
    @album ? @album.songs : Song
  end

  def grab_album_from_album_id
    @album = Album.find(params[:album_id]) if params[:album_id]
  end
end
```

The entire `respond_to` block is now gone, abstracted away in the `respond_with` method, which does the right response behavior, depending on the state of the object given to it and the action in which it is called. This new controller is smaller and easier to read. The ways that it differs from other controllers in the application will now be more obvious because they will not be hidden away. You can therefore focus on the true business logic of the application rather than the repetitive "scaffolding."

CHAPTER 5

Services

Services are an incredibly important part of the Internet now, and their importance, as well as our dependence on them—with the rise of software as a service (SaaS) and the cloud—is only increasing.

More services are being launched that can be used to both run a business and to offload many of the pieces of an application that are not core business logic, such as billing, logging, performance, and user messaging. These functions would traditionally have been built for an application and resided within the application's code base. Now, they are external components, run by disparate service providers. Furthermore, most applications now expose APIs. And in today's Internet-dependent world, essentially everything can be considered a service. As an author of a website, you may need to provide numerous APIs and services that are exposed to either partner websites or the Internet at large.

Both consuming and publishing services have common pitfalls and issues. This chapter covers both sides of the equation, ensuring that your interactions with services—both those that you consume and those that you build—are clean, reliable, and enjoyable.

AntiPattern: Fire and Forget

When dealing with external services, there are three main response strategies:

- Check the response, catching any and all errors, and gracefully handle each potential case.

- Check the response for simple success or failure and don't gracefully handle anything else.

- Don't check the response at all; either assume that the request always succeeds or simply don't care if it fails.

The third strategy, which we call "fire and forget," may be valid in rare circumstances, but in most cases, it's insufficient. For example, if you're providing status updates to a noncritical service such as Facebook, it may simply not matter if the update never makes it to Facebook. The following code sample is an illustration of this strategy. It uses the Facebooker library to post to the Facebook feed:

```
def post_to_facebook_feed(message, action_links)
  facebook_session.user.publish_to(facebook_session.user,
                                   :message => message,
                                   :action_links => action_links)
end
```

Unfortunately, the publish_to method can raise a number of exceptions. Even if you don't care if this feed item was successfully posted, if you don't rescue those exceptions, an uncaught exception is thrown, resulting in a 500 error being presented to the user.

Solution: Know What Exceptions to Look Out For

You could solve the problem of exceptions being thrown by using a heavy hand and rescuing all exceptions as shown in the following rewritten method:

```
def post_to_facebook_feed(message, action_links)
  facebook_session.user.publish_to(facebook_session.user,
                                   :message => message,
                                   :action_links => action_links)
rescue
end
```

Unfortunately, rescuing all errors is a very bad practice to get into; frankly, you should never do it. When you rescue all errors, you run the risk of squelching potentially important information. For a more in-depth discussion of handling failure, see Chapter 10.

The proper solution here is to understand the actual exceptions that will be raised by the Facebook communication and rescue those, even if you decide not to do anything with them. This can be difficult to do if you're using a poorly documented library, but it's worth it in the long run.

It turns out that Facebooker can potentially raise 17 different individual errors. These can be stored in an array and splatted on the rescue in order to increase readability and reusability:

```
def post_to_facebook_feed(message, action_links)
  facebook_session.user.publish_to(facebook_session.user,
                                    :message => message,
                                    :action_links => action_links)
rescue *FACEBOOK_ERRORS => facebook_error
  HoptoadNotifier.notify facebook_error
end
```

The FACEBOOK_ERRORS constant contains the following exceptions:

```
FACEBOOK_ERRORS = [Facebooker::NonSessionUser,
                   Facebooker::Session::SessionExpired,
                   Facebooker::Session::UnknownError,
                   Facebooker::Session::ServiceUnavailable,
                   Facebooker::Session::MaxRequestsDepleted,
                   Facebooker::Session::HostNotAllowed,
                   Facebooker::Session::MissingOrInvalidParameter,
                   Facebooker::Session::InvalidAPIKey,
                   Facebooker::Session::CallOutOfOrder,
                   Facebooker::Session::IncorrectSignature,
                   Facebooker::Session::SignatureTooOld,
                   Facebooker::Session::TooManyUserCalls,
                   Facebooker::Session::TooManyUserActionCalls,
                   Facebooker::Session::InvalidFeedTitleLink,
                   Facebooker::Session::InvalidFeedTitleLength,
                   Facebooker::Session::InvalidFeedTitleName,
                   Facebooker::Session::BlankFeedTitle,
                   Facebooker::Session::FeedBodyLengthTooLong]
```

In this code, you manually send the error to the error service Hoptoad. You do this so that potential problems, even if you don't really care about them, can be logged and bigger problems can be identified. Again, for a more in-depth discussion of handling failures, see Chapter 10.

The preceding examples are third-party libraries, but what happens with normal HTTP requests? It turns out that a number of errors could potentially be raised when making an HTTP request using the standard Net::HTTP library:

```
HTTP_ERRORS = [Timeout::Error,
               Errno::EINVAL,
               Errno::ECONNRESET,
               EOFError,
               Net::HTTPBadResponse,
               Net::HTTPHeaderSyntaxError,
               Net::ProtocolError]
```

You would then use the following:

```
begin
  req = Net::HTTP::Post.new(url.path)
  req.set_form_data({'xml' => xml})
  http = Net::HTTP.new(url.host, url.port).start
  response = http.request(req)
rescue *HTTP_ERRORS => e
  HoptoadNotifier.notify e
end
```

Note that you shouldn't rescue all errors with rescue => e, and there is a gotcha if you try to. Timeout::Error doesn't descend from StandardError, and rescue with no exception classes specified rescues only exceptions that descend from StandardError. Therefore, timeouts aren't caught, and they result in total failure.

Message in a Bottle

In a very common scenario—email sending—most Rails applications are using a "fire and forget strategy" and don't even realize it. Most applications specify the following in their environment:

```
config.action_mailer.raise_delivery_errors = false
```

With this setting, no errors can be raised, including those for both connection errors and bad email addresses.

But when sending an email with `ActionMailer` via SMTP, two possible types of exceptions can occur. The first type can be considered server errors: exceptions caused because of network problems or incorrect SMTP configuration. The second class of exceptions are user errors, such as the user typing in an invalid email address.

The user can do nothing about server errors. Therefore, you could silently rescue these errors if you'd like to fire and forget email sending. The following array shows all these errors:

```
SMTP_SERVER_ERRORS = [TimeoutError,
                      IOError,
                      Net::SMTPUnknownError,
                      Net::SMTPServerBusy,
                      Net::SMTPAuthenticationError]
```

Client-side errors are issues that a user sending an email message could potentially correct. You wouldn't want to fire and forget these errors because they shouldn't fail silently. The client errors are shown in the following array:

```
SMTP_CLIENT_ERRORS = [Net::SMTPFatalError,
                      Net::SMTPSyntaxError]
```

Take, for example, a system in which when a user performs some action, an email alert is sent to a list the user has specified. If one of those email addresses is incorrect, it might be nice if the user were told to correct it. However, if there is some communication issue, you don't want to do anything. Here's how this would look:

```
def notify_of_action(user, action)
  begin
    Mailer.action_notification(user, action).deliver
  rescue *SMTP_CLIENT_EXCEPTIONS
    flash[:warning] = "There was an issue delivering your
                       notification. Please check the
                       notification list settings."
  rescue *SMTP_SERVER_EXCEPTIONS => e
    HoptoadNotifier.notify e
  end
end
```

You Don't Know What You Don't Know

Knowing what exceptions you need to rescue can be difficult, particularly when you're working with third-party libraries and unknown systems. Oftentimes, you simply don't know you should have been rescuing an exception until it occurs. The exceptions in the preceding section were identified over time or through close investigation of the libraries used.

The strategy you should use is to under-rescue in the beginning rather than rescue too much and risk hiding legitimate issues. When new exceptions that should be rescued are discovered, you can add them to the rescue list. An important part of this strategy is to have an effective error logging mechanism. The preceding examples use Hoptoad, a popular error logging service for Rails applications. However, there are a number of other services and plugins, including exception_notification (http://github.com/rails/exception_notification), Exceptional (www.getexceptional.com), and New Relic (www.newrelic.com).

Once again, for more information about strategies for handling failures, including exceptions, see Chapter 10.

AntiPattern: Sluggish Services

A big concern in interacting with remote services is how they might affect application performance. If a network connection is slow or has issues, or even if the remote service itself is slow or is currently having issues, the performance of an application may be severely affected.

Solution: Set Your Timeouts

The problem of unreliable or unavailable remote services is often exacerbated by the fact that the default timeout of the standard Net::HTTP library is 60 seconds.

If you have a remote service and you ultimately don't want to wait for it, and you don't care if the communication goes through (because you'll retry it or it's not important enough), setting the timeout to a lower value may be a simple fix that solves the problem. The following example shows how to change the timeout from the default of 60 seconds down to 3:

```
request = Net::HTTP::Post.new(url.path)
request.set_form_data({'xml' => xml})
http = Net::HTTP.new(url.host, url.port).start
http.read_timeout = 3
response = http.request(req)
```

In this case, you set read_timeout on the http object. read_timeout takes a value that is the number of seconds for the timeout.

Solution: Move the Task to the Background

There may be times when simply decreasing the timeout is not an option. For example, if the remote service is simply too slow to respond within a shorter time period, or if it's so critical that it must be retried if the initial interaction with the remote service fails, then a more robust solution must be used.

In such cases, the proper solution may be to move the interaction with the remote service into a background task. Of course, this works only if the user doesn't need immediate feedback from the action. If the user doesn't need immediate feedback, most remote tasks can be put into the background.

> **Note**
>
> We recommend delayed_job and Resque for background
> queue systems. For full instruction and things to consider
> when implementing background processing, read the section
> "AntiPattern: Painful Performance" in Chapter 8.

If you're using delayed_job for your background needs, you'll likely want to move all your interaction with the third-party service into job objects. The following is an example of a job class that submits an order record to a remote service:

```
class SendOrderJob < Struct.new(:message, :action_links)
  def perform(order)
    OrderSender.send_order(order)
  end
end
```

Note that the only aspect of this class that makes it compatible with delayed_job is the perform method, which will be triggered by a worker process after it's been submitted to the job queue. You can add the job object to the job queue with the following:

```
def create
  Delayed::Job.enqueue SendOrderJob.new(order)
end
```

Keep Things Quick

When interacting with remote services, your system becomes intimately intertwined with them, and the performance of a remote service can adversely affect your own application. By decreasing timeouts and/or moving communication into background tasks, you should be able to build an application that integrates with remote systems and performs well.

AntiPattern: Pitiful Page Parsing

Sometimes the remote systems that your application must interact with simply don't expose a nice API. Instead, you must manually parse the web page to get the data you want. Take the following web page, for example:

```
<html>
  <body>
    <p>Welcome to the Awesome Hosting Company, Inc. website.</p>
    <div class="sidebar">
      All systems are currently
      <span class="status"><img
src="/images/normal.png">normal</span>
    </div>
  </body>
</html>
```

Say that you want to parse the status text normal out of that web page, so you turn to your trusted friend the regular expression and write some code that looks something like the following:

```
require 'uri'
require 'open-uri'

url = 'http://theurlofthewebpage.com'

html = open(url).read

if html =~ /class="status"><img
src="\/images\/.*\.png">(.*)<\/span/
  status = $1
end
```

This works and gets the string "normal" in the status variable.

Say that the remote site makes seemingly innocuous changes to its markup, as shown here:

```
<html>
  <body>
    <p>Welcome to the Awesome Hosting Company, Inc. website.</p>
```

```
    <div class="sidebar">
      All systems are currently
      <span class="status">
        <img src="/images/normal.png">
        normal
      </span>
    </div>
  </body>
</html>
```

The change here is only to add additional newlines and spacing to the HTML. Unfortunately, you didn't take this into account in your regular expression, and now the status can't be read, even though the site didn't change any of the actual markup.

You can fix this problem by modifying the regular expression and making it more robust and flexible. In the somewhat trivial example above, this may seem relatively straightforward. With more complicated examples in the real world, that's less feasible. Even if you decide to take on the task, you then essentially enter into an arms race with the developers of the remote site. When the *actual markup* of the page changes, you'll need to completely rewrite your very resilient (and probably very large) regular expressions to match the new markup.

Solution: Use a Gem

The proper solution for parsing web pages is to use one of the available gems that are made for just that purpose.

Using a gem that actually parses the HTML ensures that small changes such as adding or removing new lines won't break your parsing. Using a gem also makes it easier to change your parsing script when actual markup changes occur.

We recommend two gems for doing this type of work. If you need to parse a single web page, as in the preceding example, you can use Nokogiri (http://nokogiri.org). Nokogiri is an HTML and XML parser that, among other things, features the ability to search documents via XPath or CSS3 selectors. If you actually need to scrape multiple pages on the same site, following links, preserving cookies, and so on, you can use Mechanize (http://mechanize.rubyforge.org) to automate interaction with websites. Mechanize can automatically store and send cookies, follow redirects, follow links, and submit forms. It can also populate and submit form fields. Mechanize also keeps track of the sites you have visited. Mechanize uses Nokogiri as its actual parsing engine.

Here's what you need in order to parse a status web page with Nokogiri:

```
require 'rubygems'
require 'nokogiri'
require 'open-uri'

url = 'http://theurlofthewebpage.com'

doc = Nokogiri::HTML(open(url))

status = doc.css('.status').first.content
```

In this example, Nokogiri actually parses the HTML of the web page and allows you to select the appropriate container, based on its CSS class. If the spacing or the markup changes in several small ways (for example, changing a span to a div), it won't break the parsing. Nokogiri also gives you the content method, which provides the text content of any node. You can use content to reliably get the text from the status container, even though it also contains an image tag.

And Now for Something a Little More RESTful

What if an application is parsing or interacting with more structured data from a remote service such as XML? In many cases, Nokogiri is also the best tool for this type of job. You can just tell it to parse XML, not HTML, and the same selectors and methods are available to you:

```
doc = Nokogiri::XML(open(url))
```

However, if the XML is coming from a RESTful remote system and you need to perform multiple actions, such as GET and POST, then RestClient (http://github.com/archiloque/rest-client) is a better choice than Mechanize. RestClient is a simple HTTP and REST client for Ruby. It allows you to perform RESTful actions such as the following more easily:

```
require 'rest_client'

RestClient.get 'http://example.com/resource'
```

```
RestClient.post 'http://example.com/resource',
                :param1 => 'one',
                :nested => { :param2 => 'two' }

RestClient.delete 'http://example.com/resource'
```

AntiPattern: Successful Failure

Using RESTful URLs is only part of the practice you should be using to build a RESTful service. Consider the following RESTful API:

```ruby
class SongsController < ApplicationController
  before_filter :grab_album_from_album_id

  def index
    @songs = songs.all
    respond_to do |format|
      format.xml { render :xml => @songs }
    end
  end

  def show
    @song = songs.find(params[:id])
    respond_to do |format|
      format.xml { render :xml => @song }
    end
  end

  def new
    @song = songs.new
    respond_to do |format|
      format.xml { render :xml => @song }
    end
  end

  def create
    @song = songs.new(params[:song])

    respond_to do |format|
      if @song.save
        format.xml { render :xml => @song,
                            :location => @song }
      else
        format.xml { render :xml => @song.errors }
      end
    end
  end
```

```
def update
  @song = songs.find(params[:id])

  respond_to do |format|
    if @song.update_attributes(params[:song])
      format.xml { head :ok }
    else
      format.xml { render :xml => @song.errors }
    end
  end
end

def destroy
  respond_to do |format|
    format.xml { head :ok }
  end
end

private

def songs
  @album ? @album.songs : Song
end

def grab_album_from_album_id
  @album = Album.find_by_id(params[:album_id])
end
end
```

This API for songs is RESTful because it exposes a song resource and responds to the
normal RESTful actions.

Now take a closer look at the create action:

```
def create
  @song = songs.new(params[:song])

  respond_to do |format|
    if @song.save
      format.xml { render :xml => @song,
                          :location => @song }
    else
      format.xml { render :xml => @song.errors }
```

```
        end
      end
    end
```

In this create action, if the saving of the record fails, the error details are returned to the client as XML. The client would then check for the presence of the errors element in the response to see if the save was successful. Parsing the response to determine failure is less than ideal because it is more work and is potentially more error prone than if the client could essentially just check a flag to see if the response was successful.

In a truly RESTful API, clients would never have to rely on parsing the response body to determine success or failure. HTTP, upon which the REST concept is based, provides a built-in mechanism for this, one that essentially provides that flag for the client to check: HTTP status codes.

Solution: Obey the HTTP Codes

Fortunately, Rails has built-in support for HTTP status codes. Here is the same API controller as in the preceding section, modified here to return proper status codes:

```
class SongsController < ApplicationController
  before_filter :grab_album_from_album_id

  def index
    @songs = songs.all
    respond_to do |format|
      format.xml { render :xml => @songs }
    end
  end

  def show
    @song = songs.find(params[:id])
    respond_to do |format|
      format.xml { render :xml => @song }
    end
  end

  def new
    @song = songs.new
    respond_to do |format|
```

```ruby
      format.xml { render :xml => @song }
    end
  end

  def create
    @song = songs.new(params[:song])

    respond_to do |format|
      if @song.save
        format.xml { render :xml => @song,
                             :status => :created,
                             :location => @song }
      else
        format.xml {
          render :xml => @song.errors,
                 :status => :unprocessable_entity
        }
      end
    end
  end

  def update
    @song = songs.find(params[:id])

    respond_to do |format|
      if @song.update_attributes(params[:song])
        format.xml { head :ok }
      else
        format.xml {
          render :xml => @song.errors,
                 :status => :unprocessable_entity
        }
      end
    end
  end

  def destroy
    respond_to do |format|
      format.xml { head :ok }
    end
  end
```

```
    private

    def songs
      @album ? @album.songs : Song
    end

    def grab_album_from_album_id
      @album = Album.find_by_id(params[:album_id])
    end
  end
```

Rails provides several symbols for common HTTP statuses, including `:created` and `:unprocessable_entity`, which should be used for `create` and `update` actions, respectively. Rails also allows you to provide a number for the `:status` option that is any of the HTTP status codes.

The HTTP status codes are a fun and interesting playground of potential responses for an API. When designing and programming an API, very often there will be an HTTP status code that meets your needs that you didn't realize existed. You can find a list of these codes at www.w3.org/Protocols/rfc2616/rfc2616-sec10.html.

By using the HTTP status codes, you'll be a friendlier web citizen, and your consumers will thank you for making their code cleaner and more reliable.

Go the Distance

It's entirely possible to take the concept of HTTP status codes and extend it to non-API services. After all, in today's Internet-dependent world, everything is a service. Applying this concept to non-API-only actions will have the same effect as for API actions: cleaning up and standardizing your responses to be more straightforward and predictable.

For example, consider the HTTP status code 401, Unauthorized. The HTTP spec says this code is used for "when authentication is possible but has failed or not yet been provided." If your application provides a sign-in page, you can render it when a user is not allowed to perform an action with the appropriate 401 status, as follows:

```
class UsersController < ApplicationController
  before_filter :ensure_user_is_admin

  def create
    @user = User.new(params[:user])
```

```
  if @user.save
    flash[:success] = "User successfully created."
    redirect_to users_path
  else
    render :action => :new
  end
end


protected


def ensure_user_is_admin
  if !current_user.admin?
    flash.now[:failure] = "You do not have permission to perform
                            this action"
    render :template => 'sessions/new', :status => :unauthorized
  end
end
```

In this example, a user who is not an administrator will be presented with a sign-in page. The bonus here is that the sign-in page is rendered with the proper unauthorized status.

Clarity Is King

The goal with using HTTP status codes to communicate status is to make your systems and services as clear as possible. That way, consumers and users can expect your system to behave in a reliable, expected way. This is not the case when you use ad hoc methods that are custom to your particular service. HTTP gives you these status codes, and you should use them.

AntiPattern: Kraken Code Base

Even if you're part of a conscientious development team that tirelessly pushes back on profitless features, it's inevitable that you'll find yourself working on the dreaded behemoth code base.

A good rule of thumb for measuring application size and complexity is the number of models it contains. We've seen applications from 2 to 200 models, and we've learned from experience that the maintenance costs never scale linearly with the size of the application. Instead, developers end up drudging through 20-minute test runs, thousand-line models, and other issues as an application grows.

Solution: Divide into Confederated Applications

Reducing the size of the code base is a crucial goal during development. Doing so without reducing the feature set can be a difficult task. One solution that can often work quite well is to split the code into entirely separate applications.

Low-Hanging Fruit

On some applications, where some functional concerns are clearly disconnected from the others, the decision to chop out those pieces of the code base into separate applications is easy to make.

Consider a time-tracking application that also contains a blog and a shiny brochure section to attract new users. The blog and brochure sections require little to no interaction with the rest of the application. There are no user accounts to worry about, so splitting those into separate applications is a relatively simple task.

Once the applications have been extracted, you can make changes to them without needing to run the full test suite for the main application. In addition, you can deploy and scale the applications separately, saving on costs. Finally, downtime for the blog or brochure will have no effect on the primary time-tracking application.

We recommend going with a hosted, packaged solution for these type of sections whenever possible. There are thousands of high-quality hosted blog solutions out there, and there's very little reason to actually develop one yourself.

Higher Fruit

More complicated extractions, where the separate applications must interact with each other, are also feasible. Consider a simple ticket-tracking application. This application allows users to create and manage tickets such as in Lighthouse (http://lighthouseapp.com) or Pivotal Tracker (http://pivotaltracker.com). Each ticket has a unique email address that allows users to comment on the ticket via email.

Figure 5.1 shows the main parts of the ticket-tracking application.

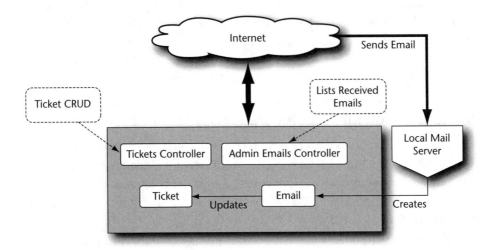

Figure 5.1 A monolithic application.

You have a `Ticket` model, a `TicketsController` model for managing tickets, an `Email` model for accepting incoming emails via SMTP, and an `EmailsController` model for the administrator to inspect those email messages. You can accept incoming emails because you've configured a local SMTP server to "deliver" the emails to a Ruby script, which, in turn, creates `Email` records in the application. The `Email` model then finds and updates the `Ticket` record, possibly adding the body as a new comment.

Even though the email functionality must be able to trigger an update of the `Ticket` model, it's possible to extract this area of the application into a separate application altogether. Figure 5.2 shows this new system.

Here, `EmailsController`, the `Email` model, and the SMTP mechanism are moved into another application. This application could reside on another server altogether, allowing it to be maintained and scaled separately from the main application.

The major difference in this new system is that instead of accessing the database to find and modify the ticket associated with that email message, the `Email` model does an HTTP `Post` to the main application. (A likely entry point would be `/tickets/`

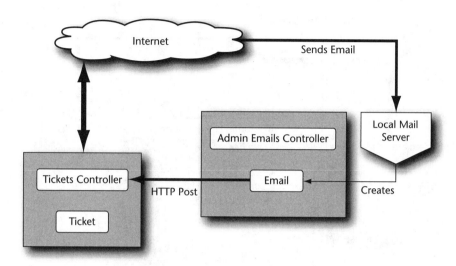

Figure 5.2 Confederated applications.

update_via_email.) The main application then finds and updates the ticket on its own. All the logic for receiving, parsing, and monitoring email deliveries would be contained in that separate application, significantly reducing the complexity of the ticket tracker.

Decouple for Resiliency

There is a small drawback to the system outlined in the preceding section. When the ticket tracking application is down for some reason (whether regular scheduled maintenance or simple error on your part), the email catching application will simply drop incoming emails. This is considered a small drawback because it is likely what would have happened before the extraction as well. However, as you move toward a loose confederation of applications, this sort of inter-application reliance can cause serious uptime issues. Just as we discussed in the section "AntiPattern: Sluggish Services," earlier in this chapter, if every application is using HTTP to connect to every other application, downtime in any one of them can cause the whole engine to grind to a halt.

To protect against this grinding to a halt, it's necessary to decouple the various applications from each other via queues and buffers. For the application we've been discussing, you can use a queue system (possibly using Resque) to solve the problem nicely. Figure 5.3 illustrates this set of loosely coupled confederated applications.

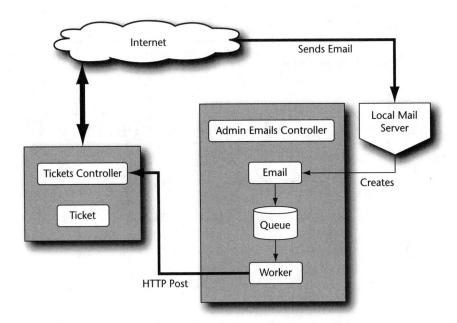

Figure 5.3 Loosely coupled confederated applications.

Now, instead of immediately doing an HTTP Post to the main application, the
Email model shoves the email into the queue and finishes execution. Another worker
process, possibly spawned every few minutes via cron, examines the queue and
attempts to post any of the emails there to the main application. If a post fails, the
email is left in the queue until the worker is spawned again.

You have now decoupled the email processing side of things from the primary
ticket tracker. Now, either side can incur downtime without affecting the other. This
gives you a graceful degradation curve and a much more maintainable system as a
whole.

Can't We All Just Get Along?

It's not always easy to pinpoint isolated parts of an application that can be extracted
entirely. However, when it's possible, isolating parts can greatly improve an application. Not only does it reduce the code size and overall complexity of each application,
it also helps reduce downtime and provide gracefully degrading services for larger
systems.

CHAPTER 6

Using Third-Party Code

The Ruby on Rails gem and plugin ecosystem is a vibrant and ever-changing community of innovation and collaboration. Indeed, this is probably one of the main contributing factors to the success and popularity of Rails. In addition, the rise of GitHub has accelerated this pace of innovation and collaboration even further and ushered in a new era of "social coding." This environment is to be embraced not shunned. This chapter discusses how to situate yourself in this ecosystem by using GitHub effectively.

> **Note**
> The Rails community has been moving to a preference for gems over Rails plugins. Especially since the release of Rails 3, it is now possible to do with a gem everything you could do with a plugin—and more. Therefore, we now recommend that all new third-party addons be written as gems and that existing ones be converted. Throughout this chapter, we refer to gems instead of plugins, but everything noted applies to both.

Gems are an extremely powerful tool for Rails developers. They allow you to get up and running with applications more quickly, and they allow you to accomplish more complex functionality in a shorter period of time than would otherwise be possible.

However, sometimes the sheer number of gems can be overwhelming. How do you know which one to choose? How do you know if there is a gem that already solves your problem? Also, is it always worth using an existing gem to solve problems? Once you choose to use a gem, what recourse do you have when you need to make changes to how it works?

The AntiPatterns in this chapter answer these questions for you, ensuring that your application code stays clean and well tested as you incorporate third-party code.

AntiPattern: Recutting the Gem

If you work on several Rails applications, at once or in sequence, or even if you work on one sufficiently large Rails application, you may find yourself repeating a common pattern or functionality.

This functionality could be anything, at any level of the Rails stack. If you've done it more than once, you've repeated yourself. And you're probably not the only one in the world to need a solution to that particular problem.

Solution: Look for a Gem First

You'll generally want to identify whether there is an existing gem that provides the functionality you need before you get started. It's not good to spend a bunch of time writing code, only to discover that there is an existing plugin that does exactly what you need. The following are some useful guidelines for when to look for an existing plugin:

- You begin to write or plan a piece of functionality and think "hey, this could be useful to other people." Someone might have thought the same thing and already written it.

- You begin to write or plan any piece of functionality that you've seen on the Internet before.

- You do the same thing twice in two consecutive applications or within the same application. Note that this doesn't mean you should make the gem yourself after you've repeated yourself; it's just a flag that you should look to see if someone else has already made it.

Once you find that an existing gem does what you need, how do you know that you *should* use it? Read the next section, "AntiPattern: Amateur Gemologist," for a solution for evaluating third-party code.

AntiPattern: Amateur Gemologist

You should not assume that just because an existing gem appears to provide the functionality you need, you will automatically use it. If it actually does what you need with minimal configuration, you still need to consider some important factors before deciding to use third-party code.

Solution: Follow TAM

There are three guidelines to use when evaluating third-party tools: tests, activity, and maturity (which we refer to as *TAM*).

Check for Tests

The most important thing to look for when evaluating a gem is that it comes with an automated test suite. Without one, there is little guarantee that it works at all or won't repeatedly break down the road.

If a gem seems truly valuable and doesn't have tests, then you should write tests for the code and contribute them to the project.

Check for Activity

It's not enough to know that a gem just exists. You also want the comfort of knowing that it is actively being used by the community. If there is very little activity in a gem's source code, trouble tickets, and mailing list, this could be a red flag that the code is out of date or not well supported. You don't want to start using inactive code unless you're prepared to make an investment in supporting it yourself.

Check for Maturity

The preceding two guidelines are closely tied to the maturity of the third-party code. However, tests and activity are not the only measures of maturity. In fact, it's entirely possible for a very new, unstable gem to have both tests and a lot of interest and activity. Time and usage are the real measures of maturity. If a gem has been around for a while, is well maintained, and has many users, it can be considered mature.

There can be consequences associated with using immature code. It's likely that your application will break or have bugs in the current release or future releases. As with inactive code, you'll want to shy away from immature code unless you're willing to make an investment in contributing to supporting it yourself.

Something Wicked This Way Comes

We don't want to discount the benefits of the wide array of third-party code available, much of it incredibly useful and good. However, using third-party code in an application is not something to take lightly. Relying on third-party code involves the same sort of liability as writing custom code yourself. You need to stay up to date with the software and be aware of discovered bugs and fixes. In addition, there may come a time where the needs of your application may differ slightly from the precise functionality provided by the gem. In that case, you will either need to work with the plugin or replace it. This is not an insurmountable task, but you also shouldn't take it lightly.

AntiPattern: Vendor Junk Drawer

When first encountering the wide selection of gems and plugins available, it's common for new Rails developers to grab any and all of these third-party tools that will help reduce the amount of code they have to write by hand.

In general, this is a good habit, and erring too far in the opposite direction results in the clearly unwanted "not invented here" syndrome. However, the open nature of Ruby means that any one of the gems and plugins you use could modify the base Ruby or Rails classes, resulting in unpredictable code. Clearly, care must be taken when adding gems, and unused gems must be removed aggressively.

The "vendor junk drawer" AntiPattern results when this care is not taken to keep the number of gems and plugins in an application manageable.

Solution: Prune Irrelevant or Unused Gems

When the number of gems and plugins an application uses becomes unmanageable, it's time to reevaluate the worth of each one. Each gem and plugin *may* be actively used within the application, but this is unlikely to be the case. When someone adds a gem to an application and writes code that can use it, the code may later be refactored, with the code that used the gem removed. It can be difficult to identify when all of the code that uses an installed gem gets removed and that gem is no longer needed.

Aside from judicious use of gems in the first place, it's best to not allow your third-party code (the `lib` and `vendor` dirs, and your application's `Gemfile`) to become an overgrown garden. You should constantly tend this garden to ensure that it stays tidy.

AntiPattern: Miscreant Modification

When using third-party code, it's incredibly important that you know what version you are using. Traditionally, Rails plugins had no versioning mechanism built in and were installed within the application in the vendor/plugins directory. Gems that have versioning built in are unpacked into vendor/gems, though with bundler and Rails 3.0, it is now considered best practice not to vendor gems at all.

There may come a time when a gem or plugin you're using either has a bug or doesn't work the way you need it to work for your application. In such a case, you need to modify the gem or plugin.

Solution: Consider Vendored Code Sacrosanct

You should never modify the files for a gem or plugin directly within your application's vendor directory. If you were to do so, your code would not match the released version of the third-party code, and there would be no readily apparent record of the fact that it doesn't match. It's incredibly easy to forget that such an in-place modification has happened, especially on teams with multiple developers. Furthermore, when you upgrade the gem or plugin, the in-place changes you've made will be lost.

Monkey patching and forking are two techniques for making necessary modifications to third-party code.

Monkey Patching

Monkey patching is a programming technique you can use in dynamic languages. With monkey patching, you modify or extend existing code at runtime, without modifying the original source code. In Ruby, you typically do this by reopening a class or module and providing an alternate definition for some or all original code.

You should place a monkey patch in an application's lib directory and name the file something that makes it clear what is being patched. For example, a monkey patch for the Validatable plugin might be located in lib/validatable_extensions.rb.

For example, the following code for validating the numericality of an attribute was originally located within vendor/gems/durran-validatable-2.0.1:

```
module Validatable
  class ValidatesNumericalityOf < ValidationBase #:nodoc:
    option :only_integer

    def valid?(instance)
      value = value_for(instance)
```

```
      return true if allow_nil && value.nil?
      return true if allow_blank && value.blank?

      value = value.to_s
      regex = self.only_integer ? /\A[+-]?\d+\Z/ : /^\d*\.{0,1}\d+$/
      not (value =~ regex).nil?
    end

    def message(instance)
      super || "must be a number"
    end

    private
      def value_for(instance)
        before_typecast_method = "#{self.attribute}_before_typecast"
        value_method =
instance.respond_to?(before_typecast_method.intern) ?
before_typecast_method : self.attribute
          instance.send(value_method)
      end
  end
end
```

This code has a problem: The regular expression in the valid? method does not work for negative floating-point numbers.

You can monkey patch this problem in the lib/validatable_extensions.rb file with the following code:

```
module Validatable
  class ValidatesNumericalityOf < ValidationBase

    def valid?(instance)
      value = value_for(instance)
      return true if allow_nil && value.nil?
      return true if allow_blank && value.blank?

      value = value.to_s
      regex = self.only_integer ? /\A[+-]?\d+\Z/ : /\A[+-
]?\d*\.{0,1}\d+$/
      not (value =~ regex).nil?
    end
```

```
        end
    end
```

Notice that the module definition is exactly the same as it was earlier. This way, you can effectively reopen the existing module and redefine it. When monkey patching, you only need to specify the actual code you want to override; there is no need to duplicate all the other code in the original module because it will remain defined.

In addition, you should attempt to override as little as you possibly can when monkey patching. This will make your patches less brittle.

Forking

When monkey patching existing open source code as outlined in the preceding section, especially if you're fixing bugs, you should contribute your changes back to the open source project to be incorporated into the official release. This used to be a relatively tedious process, but GitHub has become a well-organized and efficient mechanism for sharing and contributing code with other developers. Therefore, you can fork the original code on GitHub, make your patch (with tests), and submit it back to the original author by using a GitHub pull request.

You don't have to wait for your modifications to be accepted by the original author, however. Bundler now has the ability to point directly to a `git` repository instead of requiring an actual gem, as shown in the following:

```
gem 'gemname', :git => "git://github.com/githubuser/gemname.git"
```

Using this technique, you can then maintain a separate `git` repository that tracks your changes in detail. You can also either contribute to this `git` repository or track the original repository.

Share and Share Alike

When you don't modify original third-party source code in place, your changes are more clearly defined and less likely to be lost. You also gain the added benefit of being able to more easily contribute your changes to the original author of the third-party code. By taking this one step further and hosting your fork on a public `git` repository, you can dramatically increase the visibility of your modifications and help improve the Rails gem community even further.

CHAPTER 7

Testing

One of the strengths of the Ruby on Rails platform is that it gives you a solid testing infrastructure as part of your base project. Because of this, and because of the agile nature of most Ruby on Rails development shops, the community has rallied behind test-driven development (TDD) and behavior-driven development (BDD) with a passion unheard of in other programming circles.

TDD and BDD didn't actually begin with the Rails culture; they were around long before Ruby on Rails emerged. TDD and BDD arguably started with Kent Beck's publication "Simple Smalltalk Testing: With Patterns," and in general they have their roots in the test-first philosophy espoused by the Extreme Programming movement.

Ruby on Rails projects come preconfigured with the `Test::Unit` framework, which is the second Ruby testing framework and possibly still the most popular. `Test::Unit` follows the xUnit Pattern outlined by Kent Beck. Tests are methods that are grouped into classes called *test cases*. Any method whose name starts with `test_` and that is defined in a subclass of `Test::Unit::TestCase` will be run as a test method. A test case can have a setup method that is run before each test method and does the job of initializing instance variables and preparing other states on which the tests depend. Each test method is composed of `assert` statements that compare the output of the code to be tested against the expected state.

Ruby is a highly dynamic language and is therefore highly adaptable to any given task. This has been a great benefit to the testing community, as it has allowed the creation of much more readable and powerful testing frameworks. These new frameworks—such as RSpec, Shoulda, Dust, and Test::Spec, to name a few—all attempt to make it easier to produce and understand an application's tests. Most of the new frameworks do this by allowing tests to have names that are full, readable sentences and by introducing the concept of contexts as a way of grouping similar tests.

Throughout this book, we use the Shoulda library to illustrate the power of these next-generation testing frameworks. The techniques are almost identical between the various frameworks, and the Shoulda syntax should be easy to pick up from the examples in this book. We encourage you to explore the framework further at http://github.com/thoughtbot/shoulda.

AntiPattern: Fixture Blues

Fixtures, as a concept, have been a part of unit testing since its inception, and their analog stems from pre-computing days. When building something as complex and error prone as a car, it's important to test each piece in isolation in addition to taking the finished car for a test drive.

So that they don't need an engine in order to test a car's tires, the technicians build a physical fixture to simulate the rest of the car and road—for example, an arm to hold the tire and a high-speed treadmill for the road. Building fixtures with different arm resistances and treadmill surfaces allows the technicians to test a tire against every combination of chassis and road conditions. This exposes the tire design to a much wider range of conditions and saves days of the test driver's time.

At the time that unit testing was becoming a focus of software engineering, it was borrowing a lot from industrial techniques like this. These fixtures were translated to the software world as a set of predefined object scenarios against which to test other classes. An application that deals with calendar dates, for example, might have an event fixture with a date range that spans February 29, one that lasts only a day, one that lasts more than a year, a repeating event, and so on.

In the Ruby on Rails world, fixtures are kept in the `/test/fixtures` directory. You specify which fixtures you want preloaded into the database for all the tests in a test class by calling the `fixtures` class method:

```
class UserTest < ActiveSupport::TestCase
  fixtures :users, :teams, :challenges
  # tests using the records defined in the users fixtures
end
```

The files under the `fixtures` directory can be YAML or Ruby files, with YAML being by far the most common. Each entry in a YAML file represents one of the records to load. For example, the `/test/fixtures/users.yml` file might look something like this:

```
bonnie:
  name: Bonnie Jones
  email: bonnie@jones.com
billy:
  name: Billy Jones
  email: billy@jones.com
```

You would reference one of these preloaded records in your test methods by calling users(:billy). Typically, the fixture for Billy would be associated with a variety of other fixture records. Billy may belong to a team and may have taken a number of challenges, all of which would be useful for some subset of tests. Bonnie would also have a variety of traits that would allow other tests to use her record to stress those parts of the application.

Unfortunately, the fixture analogy breaks down in the translation between industrial engineering and software development. It can take weeks to produce a good set of physical fixtures for testing an aircraft wing, so it makes sense to reuse those fixtures as much as possible: The same fixtures would be used for testing a wide variety of wings.

With software, on the other hand, it takes relatively little time to adapt to the needs at hand. This is especially the case when using dynamic languages such as Ruby. Reusing a set of fixtures to test multiple classes in this environment leads to unnecessarily brittle and unreadable tests. We've all worked on applications where changing a detail of an existing fixture breaks tens or hundreds of seemingly unrelated tests. The common practice is then to treat existing fixtures as sacrosanct and to add new fixtures for every new set of tests. This leads to an explosion in the size of a fixture as well as duplication, as the purpose of each fixture becomes lost to posterity.

Say that developer writing new functionality involving user accounts wants to modify Billy's fixture slightly to suit his tests. In a test framework that relies on fixtures, doing this can easily break a large number of tests. The developer's only alternative is to add a new user fixture, with its own order and post associations. If you think about repeating this process with each new feature added to an application, you can see how the fixture explosion happens.

Another problem is that the definition for the network of records created by fixtures is spread out across a number of different fixture files in a test directory. Not only can you not see exactly what defines a fixture such as users(:sally) in your test method, but you have to examine each fixture file that may be associated with Sally to understand the entire object graph that your test is working with. This is a huge burden in terms of test readability and ultimately in terms of the developer's trust in the test suite.

Another issue with fixtures in Ruby on Rails is that fixture records are imported directly into the test database, without any validations. This is done for speed reasons but opens the door for having invalid seed data throughout your tests. This is most likely to happen when a new validation is added to a model in a fixture-based application.

Finally, fixtures do not go through the normal Active Record lifecycle. For example, columns that would be populated by after_save callbacks must be entered into a YAML file by hand. A common example of this is a `hashed_password` field in a `User` model. The cryptographic hash algorithm is generally repeated in the `User` model and in the `users.yml` fixture file. This is tedious and error prone, and it's a potential maintenance problem.

The following solutions discuss some very effective alternatives to fixtures that overcome these problems: using factories and modern BDD testing frameworks.

Solution: Make Use of Factories

Many patterns for creating related objects were formalized in the seminal work *Design Patterns: Elements of Reusable Object-Oriented Software* by Gamma, Helm, Johnson, and Vlissides. The factory is probably one of the most popular and well understood of those patterns.

A `Factory` class is responsible for creating objects of other classes. By encapsulating and centralizing the steps required to create associated objects, the `Factory` class allows you to keep the concerns of the rest of your classes pure and gives you a single place to make changes to that process when the class definitions change.

A Fixture Replacement

Factories can be a wonderful alternative to fixtures and all their related problems. Before we discuss how factories can help with the fixture blues, let's look at a simple factory implementation. A first attempt at introducing factories into a code base might look something like this:

```ruby
# file: test/test_helper.rb
class Test::Unit::TestCase
  require File.expand_path(File.dirname(__FILE__) + "/factory")
  # ...
end

# file: test/factory.rb
module Factory
  class << self
    def create_published_post
      post = Post.new(:body       => "lorem ipsum",
                      :title      => "Published post title",
                      :published  => true)
      post.save!
```

```
      return post
    end

    def create_unpublished_post
      post = Post.new(:body     => "lorem ipsum",
                      :title    => "Unpublished post title",
                      :published => false)
      post.save!
      return post
    end
  end
end
```

This defines a `Factory` module with class methods for creating different types of `Post` models. The `Factory` module would also have methods for every other type of model in the application. You would use `Factory` in your tests like this:

```
class PostTest < ActiveSupport::TestCase
  should "find all published posts on Post.published" do
    Factory.create_published_post
    Factory.create_unpublished_post
    Post.published.each do |post|
      assert post.published?
    end
  end
end
```

This is a great first step in using factories to DRY up your tests. Now when adding validations to your models, you only have to make changes to the methods in `Factory`. In addition, because the `Factory` methods use `ActiveRecord#save!`, you can be assured that the records are valid and that any computed attributes have been set correctly.

Unfortunately, you still have to create a new `Factory` method for every different type of `Post` you want to work with. This is much better than having to maintain the different fixture entries, but you can still improve on it. For one thing, it would be nice to be able to pass in the parameters to `Post.new` while maintaining the defaults specified in the `Factory` method. Also, this implementation doesn't have any implicit understanding of associations or unique constraints on columns.

Enter the FactoryGirl gem (http://github.com/thoughtbot/factory_girl). FactoryGirl makes factory definitions both easier and much more powerful. (You can find the full documentation for FactoryGirl on GitHub.) The following is an example of how you can use FactoryGirl in an application:

```
Factory.sequence :title { |n| "Title #{n}" }

Factory.define :post do |post|
  post.body        "lorem ipsum"
  post.title       { Factory.next(:title) }
  post.association :author, :factory => :user
  post.published   true
end
```

The accessors on `post` in the `Factory#define` block are interesting beasts. They define the default for each attribute on the model and can take values or blocks that are lazily evaluated. The `Factory#sequence` and `Factory#next` statements let you deal with attributes that must be unique, and the `association` method lets you define attributes on your model that should also be created via `Factory`.

The call signature for FactoryGirl is a little different from that of your home-brewed `Factory` module:

```
class PostTest < ActiveSupport::TestCase
  should "find all published posts on Post.published" do
    Factory(:post)
    Factory(:post, :published => false)
    Post.published.each do |post|
      assert post.published?
    end
  end
end
```

Because you can override the default values for the model's attributes, you no longer need to define a `Factory` method for both published and unpublished posts. It might still make sense to have multiple factory definitions for a single model, and FactoryGirl lets you do that.

The next section explores how to combine the `Factory` pattern with the concept of test contexts in order to clean up your tests even further.

Solution: Refactor into Contexts

We've seen how factories can help you break free of fixtures and improve your test base in terms of readability, flexibility, and integrity. Shoulda contexts reveal another way of removing fixtures without having to deal with the redundancy of repeatedly building your test records by hand in every test method.

The Malaise of Fixture-Oriented Tests

Convinced of the evils of fixtures, you may begin the task of removing them from your application's test suite. The first file you encounter resembles the much shorter version here:

```
def test_user_without_posts_should_return_false_on_has_posted
  user = users(:bob)
  assert !user.has_posted?
end

def test_user_without_posts_should_not_be_allowed_to_edit_post
  user = users(:bob)
  post = posts(:political_post)
  assert !post.editable_by?(user)
end

def test_user_with_posts_should_return_true_on_has_posted
  user = users(:sarah)
  assert user.has_posted?
end

def test_user_with_posts_should_be_allowed_to_edit_own_post
  post = posts(:political_post)
  user = users(:sarah)
  assert post.editable_by?(user)
end

def test_admin_user_should_be_allowed_to_edit_other_users_post
  post = posts(:political_post)
  user = users(:charlie)
  assert post.editable_by?(user)
end
```

This is a fairly straightforward test case, but it exemplifies one of the bad practices that fixtures encourage. These tests are making a number of assumptions about the fixture data—that :bob has no posts, that :sarah wrote a political post, and that :charlie is an administrator who did not write the political post. You would have to dig into both the users.yml and posts.yml files to figure out what's going on in any of these tests, and the situation gets progressively worse as the test suite grows larger.

Of course, you could find every fixture call and replace it with a call to ActiveRecord::Base#create!, passing in the parameters that define each record. Here's what this ends up looking like:

```
def test_user_without_posts_should_return_false_on_has_posted
  user = User.create!(:name => "Bob")
  assert !user.has_posted?
end

def test_user_without_posts_should_not_be_allowed_to_edit_post
  user = User.create!(:name => "Bob")
  assert !Post.create!(:title => "A Post").editable_by?(user)
end

def test_user_with_posts_should_return_true_on_has_posted
  post = Post.create!(:title => "A Post")
  user = User.create!(:name => "Bob", :post => post)
  assert user.has_posted?
end

def test_user_with_posts_should_be_allowed_to_edit_own_post
  post = Post.create!(:title => "A Post")
  user = User.create!(:name => "Bob", :post => post)
  assert post.editable_by?(user)
end

def test_admin_user_should_be_allowed_to_edit_other_users_post
  user = User.create!(:name => "Bob", :admin => true)
  assert !Post.create!(:title => "A Post").editable_by?(user)
end
```

These resulting tests are much more explicit than the originals. Each saved record clearly states everything you could want to know about it in the parameters. A developer working on these tests wouldn't have to go rummaging through a bunch of other files to figure out whether the user owns the post or what privileges the user has.

Unfortunately, this readability comes at the expense of test suite DRYness. Many of the test methods share the same bits of "setup" code. Imagine how another developer would have to deal with a new validation being added to the User model. That other developer would have to find and modify every call to User.create. That's time-consuming, error prone, and, in general, a huge maintenance headache.

This problem in general has led some developers to sprinkle their test cases with all kinds of ad hoc helper methods to create objects, set up mocks and expectations, or do other operations that happen in more than one test method. While these intentions are good, the results are scattered and inconsistent. A better approach would be to make use of a test framework that supports contexts.

Contexts

Using contexts is a way of grouping and gradually building setup code for a set of test methods. The following is an example of how contexts work:

```
context "A dog" do
  setup do
    @dog = Dog.new
  end

  should "bark when sent #talk" do
    assert_equal "bark", @dog.talk
  end

  context "with fleas" do
    setup do
      @dog.fleas << Flea.new
      @dog.fleas << Flea.new
    end

    should "scratch when idle" do
      @dog.idle!
      assert @dog.scratching?
    end

    should "not be allowed inside" do
      assert !@dog.allowed_inside?
```

```
      end
    end
  end
```

The context and should statements combine to create three test methods. Every should statement inside a context first runs the setup method for that context and for all the outer contexts. For example, the should "not be allowed inside" test runs both the setup that creates a dog and the setup that gives that dog a value for fleas before running its own assertions.

Essentially, these nested contexts are the same as the following explicit tests:

```
def test_a_dog_should_bark_when_sent_talk
  @dog = Dog.new

  assert_equal "bark", @dog.talk
end

def test_a_dog_with_fleas_should_scratch_when_idle
  @dog = Dog.new

  @dog.fleas << Flea.new
  @dog.fleas << Flea.new

  @dog.idle!
  assert @dog.scratching?
end

def test_a_dog_with_fleas_should_not_be_allowed_inside
  @dog = Dog.new

  @dog.fleas << Flea.new
  @dog.fleas << Flea.new

  assert !@dog.allowed_inside?
end
```

Using contexts can improve a test suite in many ways, the most dramatic of which is removing the redundant setup code that's copied and pasted between test methods. Armed with a test suite that supports nested contexts, you can rewrite the preceding tests and come up with this:

```
context "A user" do
  setup { @user = User.create!(:name => "Bob") }

  should "not be allowed to edit another user's post" do
    @post = Post.create!(:title => "A Post")
    assert !@post.editable_by?(@user)
  end

  should "return false on #has_posted?" do
    assert !@user.has_posted?
  end

  context "with a post" do
    setup { @post = Post.create!(:title => "A Post", :user => @user) }

    should "be allowed to edit the post" do
      assert @post.editable_by?(@user)
    end

    should "return true on #has_posted?" do
      assert @user.has_posted?
    end
  end

  context "with admin privileges" do
    setup { @user.update_attributes!(:admin => true) }

    should "be allowed to edit another user's post" do
      @post = Post.create!(:title => "A Post")
      assert @post.editable_by?(@user)
    end
  end
end
```

Although this example shows an increased number of test code lines, it also shows increased readability and maintainability. Most of the redundancy in the previous examples has been eliminated. If you had to change how a user was created, you'd have to do so in only one place. There is still some duplication in how posts are created, and we'll look at how to eliminate this duplication in just a bit. First, let's look at some of the other benefits of context-structured tests.

Hidden Jewels

By explicitly separating the setup code from the assertions, you can write a single focused test for each bit of functionality. This brings your test methods closer to the "one assertion per test" tenet that many respected testing experts practice. How often have you run across test methods like the following?

```
def test_get_to_show
  get :show, :id => @mother.to_param
  assert_response :success
  assert_template :show
  assert_nil flash[:warning]
  assert assigns(:mother)
  assert assigns(:children)
  assigns(:children).each do |child|
    assert child.good?
  end
end
```

This test was written by a developer who wanted to avoid repeating the get :show line across a series of tests. The result is a single test that is poorly named and that tests six different pieces of behavior. In addition, the rest of the assertions aren't run if one of them fails. This hides important debugging information from the developer.

A comparable example using contexts does not have these issues. It also promotes good BDD practices by forcing you to consider each bit of functionality as a separate part of the specification:

```
context "on GET to #show" do
  setup { get :show, :id => @mother.to_param }

  should "respond successfully" do
    assert_response :success
  end

  should "render the show template" do
    assert_template :show
  end

  should "not set the flash" do
    assert_nil flash[:warning]
  end
```

```
  should "assign to mother" do
    assert assigns(:mother)
  end

  should "only show good children" do
    assert assigns(:children)
    assigns(:children).each do |child|
      assert child.good?
    end
  end
end
```

This example also has the added bonus of producing very readable test names. A test failure would present the user with a test name like "on GET to #show should only show good children", which further encourages concise and focused test methods.

Join Forces for the Greater Good

As mentioned earlier, the code you're dealing with could still use some more DRYing up. While the details of creating a Post are repeated less using contexts, there is still some duplication. There will also almost assuredly be duplication of that bit of code across the different test files.

You might recognize that we addressed these concerns earlier in this chapter, in the section "Solution: Make Use of Factories." In fact, contexts and factories work together very well. Here's the same test file you've been working with, in this case refactored to make use of FactoryGirl:

```
context "A user" do
  setup { @user = Factory(:user) }

  should "not be allowed to edit another user's post" do
    assert !Factory(:post).editable_by?(@user)
  end

  should "return false on #has_posted?" do
    assert !@user.has_posted?
  end

  context "with a post" do
    setup { @post = Factory(:post, :user => @user) }
```

```
    should "be allowed to edit the post" do
      assert @post.editable_by?(@user)
    end

    should "return true on #has_posted?" do
      assert @user.has_posted?
    end
  end

  context "with admin privileges" do
    setup { @user.update_attributes(:admin => true) }

    should "be allowed to edit another user's post" do
      assert Factory(:post).editable_by?(@user)
    end
  end
end
```

The combination of contexts and factories may well be the pinnacle of current testing best practices. We've made use of this pattern in every application we've developed, and it hasn't let us down yet.

AntiPattern: Lost in Isolation

With all the benefits that using mocking can give you, it's important to be aware of the false sense of security mocking can instill. As you've seen, mocking allows you to isolate your tests, ensuring that you aren't testing more than one component at a time. While this can make your test suite more resilient to change, this resilience can be a liability.

Consider a simple domain where you have Posts and Watchers. A Post can have many watchers who need to be notified when the post is published. The post unit tests are as follows:

```ruby
# test/unit/post_test.rb
class PostTest < ActiveSupport::TestCase
  should_have_many :watchers

  context "a post" do
    setup { @post = Factory(:post) }

    should "send notify_all_of_published_post to its
            watchers when published" do
      @post.watchers.
            expects(:notify_all_of_published_post).
            with(@post)
      @post.publish!
    end
  end
end
```

The following model satisfies the test:

```ruby
# app/models/post.rb
class Post < ActiveRecord::Base
  has_many :watchers

  def publish!
    watchers.notify_all_of_published_post(self)
  end
end
```

The implementation here is fairly simple. Calling `@post.publish!` in turn calls `watchers.notify_all_of_published_post(@post)`. As discussed in the section "Solution: Learn and Love the `scope` Method" in Chapter 1, this is the same as calling `Watcher.notify_all_of_published_post` but against the subset of watchers that are attached to this post.

Notice that you've made use of mocking to test that the callback is being triggered. This means that the actual `notify_all_of_published_post` method is never called in the test. Instead, you ensure that the call is made by intercepting it with `#expects`.

The only part of the `watcher` model that concerns you for this example is that it has a `notify_all_of_published_post` class method:

```ruby
# app/models/watcher.rb
class Watcher < ActiveRecord::Base
  belongs_to :post

  def self.notify_all_of_published_post(post)
    # ...
  end
end
```

That method, of course, would be fully unit tested in itself.

Now let's look at what happens when one of your fellow developers comes in and decides that `notify_all_of_published_post` doesn't need the `post` passed in. After all, each individual `watcher` belongs to one and only one `post`; they shouldn't need any more information to do their job. The developer removes the `post` parameter and finds and fixes any failing unit tests for `notify_all_of_published_post`:

```ruby
# app/models/watcher.rb
class Watcher < ActiveRecord::Base
  belongs_to :post

  def self.notify_all_of_published_post
    # ...
  end
end
```

Seeing that all the tests pass, he then pushes his changes to the rest of the team.

Of course, the application is now broken. What went wrong?

The Post unit tests were still running under the assumption that notify_all_of_published_post required a parameter. The culprit is the line in the Post test that uses mocking:

```
@post.watchers.
       expects(:notify_all_of_published_post).
       with(@post)
```

This line now needs to be changed to reflect the new calling signature of the notify_all_of_published_post method:

```
@post.watchers.
       expects(:notify_all_of_published_post).
       with()
```

This is an example of the use of mocking causing gaps in the integration points of tests. An integration point is where module A (for example, the publish! method) interacts with module B (for example, the notify_all_of_published_post) method.

Mocking isolates tests from the implementations of other classes by acting as a buffer in these integration points. This means, however, that the integration points are now untested: You no longer know that module A knows how to talk to module B correctly.

Those new to mocking might argue that our developer is simply a lazy programmer: "Surely, he should have searched the code for the method name and inspected those tests by hand." Not only is this a lot to expect from a developer working in a large code base, but it's also infeasible in many situations. In many systems, and especially in Ruby and the Rails framework, method names are often commonly used words (such as find, all, and first). In addition, a highly dynamic language such as Ruby can also hide the method names through calls to send, define_method, and other tactics (as discussed further in the section "Solution: Make Magic Happen with Metaprogramming" in Chapter 1).

Solution: Watch Your Integration Points

Does the danger discussed in the preceding section hearken the end of the mocking "fad"? Not in the least. Experienced test developers know that a good test suite that makes use of heavy mocking absolutely must be driven by integration tests that don't use any mocking at all. As of late, the best way to produce these tests has been by using the Cucumber framework (http://cukes.info).

The cycle of developing a feature is as follows:

1. Write a user story in Cucumber that describes the feature.

2. Develop only enough of the controller to make this story pass. While developing this part of the controller, you're writing functional tests that mock out the lower layer (the models).

3. Develop only enough of the models to make the story pass. Again, this development is driven by unit tests, which may mock out interactions with other models.

You can think of this process as smaller TDD loops inside a larger BDD loop (the user story). By the end of this process, you are have a small, focused, and fast unit and functional tests that use mocking. You also have the reassurance of the user story to know that your integration points are tested.

Mock with Care

Story-driven development works well when it's used consistently throughout a project. We've found, unfortunately, that trying to add this methodology on top of existing code bases yields only marginal value. However, worse still is making heavy use of mocking in a project without supporting the features with any integration tests at all. Doing so only undermines the effectiveness of the tests—and the team's confidence in them.

AntiPattern: Mock Suffocation

Mocks and stubs are important and useful tools in the hands of a developer, but it's easy to get carried away. Besides lending a false sense of security, over-mocked tests can also be brittle and noisy.

Two of the greatest benefits of using mocks and stubs are the focus they lend to an exercise and the declarative nature of stubs in a setup. Consider the following example of a site with publicly viewable articles that users can rate:

```
context "given an article with an average score of 4" do
  setup do
    @article = Factory(:article)
    3.times { Factory(:vote, :article => @article, :score => 4) }
  end

  should "display the score on GET to show" do
    get :show, :id => @article.to_param
    assert_select '.score', '4'
  end
end
```

In this example, you don't want to display the average score for an article until it has at least three votes. In order to test that the score is displayed, you need to create the necessary votes.

This test has a number of problems. The practical speed issue of creating all these records in a context that might wrap multiple tests is undesirable, but there's a more philosophical issue at hand. While the main point of the setup is to have an article with a particular score, most of the setup is concerned with creating votes. The concept of a vote isn't actually relevant to this test and only serves as a distraction.

As you can see in the following code, using a stub produces a more declarative test case:

```
context "given an article with an average score of 4" do
  setup do
    @article = Factory(:article)
    @article.stubs(:score => 4)
    Article.stubs(:find).with(@article.id).returns(@article)
  end
```

```
    should "display the score on GET to show" do
      get :show, :id => @article.to_param
      assert_select '.score', '4'
    end
  end
```

Now the test is concerned only with the aspects of the business value it's proving—that the article has a score and that the score is displayed when you get the show page.

Unfortunately, it can be easy to fall into the habit of creating stubs without carefully considering the interface you want the tested system to obey. If you find that you need a great number of stubs just to get a test running, the fault may not be with the testing strategy; it may be with your production code.

In general, one of the main benefits of TDD is that the act of writing tests helps you think about the interfaces your classes should be exposing. If you have difficulty with a test, such as having to wade through the mock-and-stub stew, then it's likely that you have ailing interfaces, with your classes not exposing a consistent and self-contained API.

Solution: Tell, Don't Ask

If you find yourself stubbing out several methods on the same object, you might want to examine the interface you're using on that object. The following is an example of one of the most commonly used interfaces in Rails—saving an Active Record instance:

```
  if @article.save
    redirect_to @article
  else
    render :action => 'new'
  end
```

In order to test this interaction, you need to stub out only one method:

```
  @article.stubs(:save).returns(true)
```

The key here is the #save method, which validates the Article, saves it if it's valid, and then returns true or false to indicate success or failure. If you're familiar with other methods in the Active Record API, you know you could also write the example like this:

```
if @article.valid?
  @article.save!
  redirect_to @article
else
  render :action => 'new'
end
```

If you assume that all valid records should be savable, you might decide that the #save method is an unnecessary convenience method, given the existence of #valid? and #save!. However, the relationship between the controller and the model is now more complicated. This is revealed by the stubs that would be necessary to test the interaction:

```
@article.stubs(:valid?).returns(true)
@article.stubs(:save!)
```

The situation has become complicated because your controller is asking too many questions. The controller doesn't need to know if the article is valid; it just needs to know if it was saved successfully.

While Active Record is a truly useful framework, some of the features that create that utility also encourage long method chains and therefore promote a stew of mocks and stubs in tests.

Active Record associations allow you to access associated records and call class methods on those records easily and simply. Similarly, scopes (introduced as named_scope in Rails 2.x) allow you to break up bits of finder logic into chainable scopes, DRYing up finder methods and removing large swaths of SQL-building code.

However, using these chains outside a model introduces a lot of knowledge into your other classes. This makes refactoring more difficult. The telltale sign of this is often a large number of stubs in the tests.

Consider the following example, where you want to display "featured" articles on the front page of your site. In order to qualify, an article must be from the past week, must have at least one comment, and must have enough votes to merit a visible rating. Using a named scope allows you to write these three requirements nicely:

```
class Article < ActiveRecord::Base
  MIN_VOTES_TO_DISPLAY = 4
  FEATURED_CUTOFF_AGE = 7.days
```

```
scope :with_at_least_one_comment,
      where('articles.comments_count > 0')

def with_votes_at_least(minimum)
  where(['articles.votes_count >= ?', minimum])
end

def created_after(cutoff_date)
  where(['articles.created_at > ?', cutoff_date])
end
end
```

The controller can combine the chains like so:

```
class ArticlesController < ApplicationController
  def index
    @featured_articles = Article.
      with_at_least_one_comment.
      with_votes_at_least(Article::MIN_VOTES_TO_DISPLAY).
      created_after(Article::FEATURED_CUTOFF_AGE.ago)
  end
end
```

However, the `Article` model has now spilled into `ArticlesController`, tying the controller to three class methods and two constants. The tests for this scenario look even worse:

```
class ArticlesControllerTest < ActionController::TestCase
  context "given featured articles" do
    setup do
      chain = stub('chain')
      @featured_articles = [Factory(:article), Factory(:article)]
      Article.stubs(:with_at_least_comment).returns(chain)
      chain.
        stubs(:with_votes_at_least).
        with(Article::MIN_VOTES_TO_DISPLAY).
        returns(chain)
      chain.
        stubs(:created_after).
        with(Article::FEATURED_CUTOFF_AGE.ago).
```

```
        returns(@featured_articles)
    end

    context "on GET index" do
      setup { get :index }

      should assign_to(:featured_articles).with { @featured_articles }
    end
  end
end
```

The root of the problem is that the controller is digging into the `Article` model with gusto. You can clean this up by shoving that article logic back where it belongs:

```
class Article < ActiveRecord::Base
  def self.featured
    with_at_least_one_comment.
      with_votes_at_least(MIN_VOTES_TO_DISPLAY).
      created_after(FEATURED_CUTOFF_AGE.ago)
  end
end
```

Now the tests are much less noisy:

```
class ArticlesControllerTest < ActionController::TestCase
  context "given featured articles" do
    setup do
      @featured_articles = [Factory(:article), Factory(:article)]
      Article.stubs(:featured).returns(@featured_articles)
    end

    context "on GET index" do
      setup { get :index }

      should assign_to(:featured_articles).with { @featured_articles }
    end
  end
end
```

And the controller asks for only what it needs:

```
class ArticlesController < ApplicationController
  def index
    @featured_articles = Article.featured
  end
end
```

Stop Asking Questions

If you find yourself stubbing a number of methods for each object, look carefully at the methods you're stubbing. Are you asking too many questions? If so, stop asking your models questions and start telling them what needs to be done.

AntiPattern: Untested Rake

You've become a full-ranking test-first zealot, and you never commit code for which you haven't written tests first. But now you've hit your first stumbling block. You're asked to write a rake task, but you don't know how to drive the development of a rake task with tests.

There are two interrelated obstacles in testing rake tasks. One is that they are, by nature, scripts that live outside an application. This makes testing them much more complicated than testing a method on a class. The other obstacle is that rake tasks, more often than application code, perform operations across a network or against a filesystem. You must therefore take extra care in preventing side effects during test runs.

Consider the following rake task:

```
# lib/tasks/twitter.rake
namespace :twitter do
  task :search => :environment do
    puts "Searching twitter."
    Twitter.search("@tsaleh").each do |result|
      puts "Processing #{result.inspect}."
      alert = Alert.create(:body => result)
      alert.save_cache_file!
    end
    puts "All done!"
  end
end
```

One solution we've often seen is to simply point the rake task at a temporary directory or file and run it directly, using the system command:

```
# test/unit/twitter_task_test.rb
class TwitterTaskTest < ActiveSupport::TestCase
  # Required because the rake task is being
  # run outside of the transaction.
  self.use_transactional_fixtures = false

  context "rake twitter:search" do
    setup do
      # How slow is this going to be?  Very.
      @out = `cd #{Rails.root} && rake twitter:search 2>&1`
    end
```

```
        should "print a message at the beginning" do
          assert_match /Searching/i, @out
        end

        should "save some cache files" do
          # Search the filesystem for the cached files.
        end

        should "find all tweets containing @tsaleh" do
          # this one would be based entirely on luck.
        end

        should "print a message when done" do
          assert_match /all done/i, @out
        end
      end
    end
```

While this method works, it has drawbacks:

- The act of forking a process to test your rake tasks is both tricky and time-consuming. As test suites grow, the runtime of these tests begins to matter greatly.

- The crude nature of this technique means that extra care must be taken in preparing the files to be accessed and in removing any created or edited files after each test has finished.

- Because you are no longer in the same process as the code that you're testing, there is no way to make use of mocking and stubbing. This means some actions, such as network access, can neither be tested well nor stopped entirely (as they should be).

- Any database access performed by the rake task is done through a new connection that is different from the connection of the test process. This means that the transaction surrounding the test will have no effect on the rake task, and any modifications it made will remain in place after the test is finished.

- You must essentially trust that the rake task is already well behaved to believe that you won't be affecting other parts of the filesystem. In general, testing a rake task like this leaves you with no way of sandboxing its execution.

Solution: Extract to a Class Method

How do you test a rake task inside the same Ruby process? The trick is to understand that a rake task is nothing more than Ruby code disguised with domain-specific trappings. Therefore, you can move the entirety of the task into a class method. Usually, this method finds a home on one of the application models, but it can also be on a class of its own, as in the following example:

```ruby
# app/models/alert.rb
class Alert < ActiveRecord::Base
  def self.create_all_from_twitter_search(output = $stdout)
    output.puts "Searching twitter."
    Twitter.search("@tsaleh").each do |result|
      output.puts "Processing #{result.inspect}."
      alert = create(:body => result)
      alert.save_cache_file!
    end
    output.puts "All done!"
  end

  def save_cache_file!
    # Removes a file from the filesystem.
  end
end
```

You've now moved the bulk of the code into the model, which places it inside the class responsible for its behavior. This is generally good object-oriented programming practice, and it helps clean up and clarify the rake task:

```ruby
# lib/tasks/twitter.rake
namespace :twitter do
  task :search => :environment do
    Alert.create_all_from_twitter_search
  end
end
```

Testing the rake task is now as simple as testing any other class method:

```ruby
# test/unit/alert_test.rb
class AlertTest < ActiveSupport::TestCase
  context "create_all_from_twitter_search" do
```

```
setup do
  # Make sure none of the tests below hit the
  # network or touch the filesystem.
  Alert.any_instance.stubs(:save_cache_file!)
  Twitter.stubs(:search).returns([])
  @output = StringIO.new
end

should "print a message at the beginning" do
  Alert.create_all_from_twitter_search(@output)
  assert_match /Searching/i, @output.string
end

should "print a message for each result" do
  Twitter.stubs(:search).returns(["one", "two"])
  Alert.create_all_from_twitter_search(@output)
  assert_match /one/i, @output.string
  assert_match /two/i, @output.string
end

should "save some cache files" do
  Twitter.stubs(:search).returns(["one"])
  alert = mock("alert")
  alert.expects(:save_cache_file!)
  Alert.stubs(:create).returns(alert)
  Alert.create_all_from_twitter_search(@output)
end

should "find all tweets containing @tsaleh" do
  Twitter.expects(:search).
          with("@tsaleh").
          returns(["body"])
  Alert.create_all_from_twitter_search(@output)
end

should "print a message when done" do
  Alert.create_all_from_twitter_search(@output)
  assert_match /all done/i, @output.string
end
    end
  end
end
```

You no longer face all the issues involved with spawning a separate process.

You can now sandbox the tests for the rake task quite effectively, using your usual bag of tricks. You can stop unexpected network access and return mocked responses for expected ones. You can even make use of tools such as FakeWeb (http:// fakeweb.rubyforge.org) and `FileUtils::NoWrite`. Finally, because you're running inside the same process as the tests, any database access is completely encapsulated in the test's transaction.

As Simple As Possible, but Not Simpler

While it may seem that invoking the rake task directly via a system call is the simplest way of attacking the testing problem, the headaches quickly mount up. This is an example where a little thought, planning, and organization can go a long way toward easing your future testing burdens.

AntiPattern: Unprotected Jewels

We don't view TDD as just a safety net against bugs. It's a methodology for producing well-designed code, and it shows other developers that you view your work as a craft.

As discussed in Chapter 6, when deciding what plugins or gems to use in a project, one of the first and most important determiners of quality is whether the plugin comes with a full test suite. Good tests tell you that the plugin author took the code as seriously as you take the code in your application.

Writing a test suite for a gem or plugin is no easy task. Developers have a fairly straightforward template and scaffolding to use when testing a Ruby on Rails controller or model. There are even great integration testing libraries and patterns that are already well understood and adopted by the community.

Plugins and gems, on the other hand, are almost free form packages of code that can insert themselves into the Rails framework in a variety of ways. Because of this, there's really no silver bullet for creating a test scaffolding for your plugins.

The most common way of testing plugins and gems relies on the tests in the original application from which a plugin was extracted. This method is flawed in two ways. First, this keeps development of the plugin forever tied to the application, long after the application has lost its relevance. It removes the ability for developers from the community to make use of or add to the plugin's test base. Second, keeping the tests separate from the plugin makes it impossible for other developers to evaluate the quality of work.

The following solutions explore a variety of ways of testing plugins and gems that have worked well for us in the wild. First, we walk through writing tests for simple plugins that don't require the Rails framework at all. Then we look at pulling just the components we need, such as Active Record, into a test suite. Finally, we explore writing tests for plugins and gems that require the full Ruby on Rails stack.

Solution: Write Normal Unit Tests Without Rails

Often the simplest solution to a problem is the best one. While most Ruby on Rails plugins and gems are highly integrated with the framework, there are many times when that integration is trivial and is best ignored in the tests.

Take, for example, the following Lorem Ipsum plugin. It provides the Controller and View layers with a method, `lorem_ipsum`, that prints variable amounts of filler text. This plugin might be useful for producing quick prototype data while demonstrating an application to a client or investors. The majority of the logic of the plugin is contained in the `lib/lorem_ipsum.rb` file:

```
# lib/lorem_ipsum.rb
module LoremIpsum
  TEXT = "Lorem ipsum dolor sit amet, consectetur " +
         "adipisicing elit, sed do eiusmod tempor " +
         "incididunt ut labore et dolore magna aliqua. " +
         "Ut enim ad minim veniam, quis nostrud " +
         "exercitation ullamco laboris nisi ut aliquip " +
         "ex ea commodo consequat. Duis aute irure " +
         "dolor in reprehenderit in voluptate velit " +
         "esse cillum dolore eu fugiat nulla pariatur. " +
         "Excepteur sint occaecat cupidatat non proident, " +
         "sunt in culpa qui officia deserunt mollit anim " +
         "id est laborum."

  def lorem_ipsum(words = nil)
    if words
      TEXT.split[0..words - 1].join(' ') + "."
    else
      TEXT
    end
  end
end
```

An important thing to note is that none of this file requires or interacts with the Ruby on Rails framework. All of the plugin integration is contained in init.rb:

```
# init.rb
ActionController::Base.send(:include, LoremIpsum)
ActionView::Base.send(:include, LoremIpsum)
```

As you can see, the integration is kept to a minimum. This allows you to test the bulk of the plugin in isolation from the Ruby on Rails framework. To do this, you start off with a minimal test_helper.rb file:

```
# test/test_helper.rb
require 'rubygems'
require 'test/unit'
require 'shoulda'
require 'lorem_ipsum'
```

You can then unit test the LoremIpsum module as you would in any other non-Rails application:

```
# test/lorem_ipsum_test.rb
require 'test_helper'

class LoremIpsumTest < Test::Unit::TestCase
  include LoremIpsum

  context "lorem_ipsum" do
    setup { @output = lorem_ipsum }

    should "return some lorem ipsum text" do
      assert_match /lorem ipsum/i, @output
    end

    should "not include line breaks" do
      assert_no_match /\n/i, @output
    end
  end

  context "lorem_ipsum(3)" do
    setup { @output = lorem_ipsum(3) }

    should "return three words" do
      assert_equal 3, @output.scan(/\w+/).length
    end

    should "end in a period" do
      assert_equal ".", @output[-1, 1]
    end
  end
end
```

Note that because you're not relying on the code in init.rb, you must explicitly include the LoremIpsum module yourself. After that, it's just a matter of testing the behavior of a plain old Ruby module.

Having a simple test scaffolding in place makes it all the easier for you to maintain your code and for other developers to contribute to it. An overly complex and hard-to-grasp testing system creates a great barrier to entry for developers looking to contribute to your code.

Note that the tests shown in this section fail to cover the two lines in `init.rb`. While those lines aren't in any way insignificant, and you should always aim for full test coverage, the benefits of having a simple test setup like this far outweighs these faults. This simple and elegant style of testing a plugin is possible only because the majority of the plugin doesn't use any of the facilities provided by the Ruby on Rails framework. If at all possible, it's best to aim for this separation in your plugins. Not only does this separation allow you to test a plugin in isolation, it also increases your future flexibility. It gives you the option of releasing code as a gem or of using it in other non-Rails applications.

It is often the case, however, that you need to make use of some of the facilities that the Ruby on Rails framework provides. In such situations, you need to isolate the modules you require and include them piecemeal in your tests. The next section discusses just how to do this.

Solution: Load Only the Parts of Rails You Need

The preceding solution discusses writing tests for a plugin that bypass the Rails framework entirely. While this is a great strategy for simple plugins with little or no integration with the framework, extending this strategy to more complex plugins quickly leads to an unmanageable tangle of mocks and stubs.

While it might be tempting to pull out the big guns and embed a full Rails application into your test folder (which you will do in the next solution), there is a very maintainable and flexible middle ground. It's possible to include only the parts of the Rails framework that your plugin interacts with.

United We Stand

The Rails framework is a collection of gems that act in concert to help you build a database-backed web-based application:

- **ActionMailer:** Responsible for delivering templated emails.
- **ActionPack:** The controller and view components of a Rails application (the *M* and *V* of MVC).
- **Active Record:** The relational library we all know and love.
- **ActiveResource:** A REST-based port of Active Record for consuming third-party sites.

- **ActiveSupport:** A general-purpose collection of helpers and extensions.
- **Rails:** The library that binds the other gems into a coherent whole.

Most of these gems can be used in isolation quite easily. It's not uncommon to leverage Active Record when building a command-line script that manages database records.

Keep It Simple

Many plugins or gems actually interact with only one or two of the components listed in the preceding section. It would be heavy handed to include an entire Rails application in your plugin to test these components. Take, for example, a plugin named Slugalicious that adds pretty URL support to an Active Record model. At first glance, you might assume that this would touch the entire MVC stack. However, because of the Rails conventions surrounding #to_param, you can easily isolate such a plugin to just the Active Record library.

The trick to this involves reproducing just enough of the glue code from the Rails gem to get your models to talk to a database reliably. Here's what you have to do in the test helper file:

```ruby
# slugalicious/test/test_helper.rb
require 'rubygems'

# Only load ActiveRecord
require 'active_record'

# Grab some other gems to help with our tests
require 'shoulda'
require 'shoulda/active_record'
require 'factory_girl'

# Require the plugin file, itself
require 'slugalicious'

BASE = File.dirname(__FILE__)

# Configure Factory Girl
require BASE + "/factories.rb"

# Configure the logger
ActiveRecord::Base.logger = Logger.new(BASE + "/debug.log")
RAILS_DEFAULT_LOGGER = ActiveRecord::Base.logger
```

```
# Establish the database connection
config = YAML::load_file(BASE + '/database.yml')
ActiveRecord::Base.establish_connection(config['sqlite3'])

# Load the database schema
load(BASE + "/schema.rb")
```

The first few lines in the test_helper.rb file load the parts of the Rails framework
your plugin requires to run—in this case, just the Active Record gem. You also load
your testing tools of choice and then the plugin itself.

Next, you load the FactoryGirl definitions inside test/factories.rb, which for
your simple plugin is just the following:

```
#test/factories.rb

Factory.define :post do |f|
  f.title "New post"
end
```

The rest of the code in the test_helper.rb file is dedicated to setting up the
Active Record environment: loading the logger, configuring the database, and loading
the schema. Your database.yml file is configured to use the sqlite in-memory database feature. This frees you from having to configure a MySQL server for every
machine on which you want to run the tests, and it doesn't leave you with unnecessary
sqlite database files lying around. The following is a configuration for an sqlite in-
memory database:

```
#test/database.yml
sqlite3:
  adapter: sqlite3
  database: ":memory:"
```

The schema.rb file contains all the tables you need for your tests:

```
#test/schema.rb
ActiveRecord::Schema.define(:version => 1) do
  create_table :posts do |t|
    t.column :title, :string
```

```
      t.column :slug, :string
      t.column :body, :text
    end
  end
```

Now for the Easy Part

While at first glance, all the scaffolding necessary to test the Blawg plugin might seem quite complex, rest assured that the hard part of the road is behind you. The only task left is to write the tests themselves.

The complexity of this scaffolding setup should also serve as a warning to those attempting this technique for plugins that don't require it. We strongly encourage developers to use the simplest technique at their disposal. It's often the case that testing a plugin in the manner described earlier, in the section, "Solution: Write Normal Unit Tests Without Rails," is sufficient and preferable.

There is nothing special about the actual tests for the Slugalicious plugin, but we include them here for the sake of completeness:

```
#test/slugalicious_test.rb
class Post < ActiveRecord::Base
  # has title, slug, and body, as described in schema.rb
  include Slugalicious
end

class PostTest < ActiveRecord::TestCase
  setup { Post.destroy_all }

  should validate_presence_of(:slug)
  should     allow_value("one-two").for(:slug)
  should     allow_value("foo_bar").for(:slug)
  should     allow_value("foo"    ).for(:slug)
  should_not allow_value("f b").for(:slug)
  should_not allow_value("f.b").for(:slug)
  should_not allow_value("f|b").for(:slug)
  should_not allow_value("f'b").for(:slug)

  context "when there's an existing post" do
    setup { Factory(:post, :slug => "slug") }
    should validate_uniqueness_of(:slug)
  end
```

```ruby
should "set the slug from the title" do
  post = Factory(:post, :title => "This is a 'title'.")
  assert_equal "this-is-a-title", post.slug
end

should "set the slug to a uniq value" do
  post1 = Factory(:post, :title => "Title")
  assert_equal "title", post1.slug
  post2 = Factory(:post, :title => "Title")
  assert_equal "title-2", post2.slug
  post3 = Factory(:post, :title => "Title")
  assert_equal "title-3", post3.slug
end

should "be findable by the slug" do
  post = Factory(:post)
  assert_equal post.id, Post.find(post.slug).id
end

should "still be findable by the id" do
  post = Factory(:post)
  assert_equal post.id, Post.find(post.id).id
end

should "return the slug on to_param" do
  assert_equal "title",
              Factory(:post, :title => "Title").to_param
end
end
```

The Middle Road

The technique just described is clearly more complicated (and thus more of a maintenance hassle) than the previous solution, but when viewed against our next and final path, it seems almost elegant in its simplicity.

Extracting and isolating various parts of Rails to test a plugin is an effective technique when the plugin integrates with only a small portion of the framework. Many plugins, however, integrate and interact with the entire MVC stack—adding helpers to the views, modifying the controllers, and interacting with the models. In such a situation, the only good way of maintaining an effective test suite is to actually embed an entire Rails application inside the plugin's test suite. We discuss this technique next.

Solution: Break Out the Atom Bomb

Throughout the book, we strive to maintain a consistent theme of valuing simplicity in the solutions. Embedding an entire Rails application inside a plugin's test suite is a perfect example of a highly complex solution that you should avoid if at all possible. Unfortunately, at rare times this is the simplest—and maybe even the only—good way of testing a Rails plugin or gem.

Embed a Complete Rails Application in Your Tests

Some plugins interact with the entire Rails stack. For example, a blogging plugin could add an entire `posts` resource—model, controller, routes, and views. While it would be wonderful if you could use one of the previous techniques to test such a plugin, you would quickly find yourself mired in a tangle of mocks and overly complex testing harnesses. In such a situation, the heavy-handed solution of embedding a sample Rails application under the plugin's test directory turns out to be the simplest reasonable path.

The mechanics involved in embedding a Rails application in a test suit are actually less difficult than you might expect, and the level of indirection can be challenging to grasp. The strategy described in the following sections is to install a small fake Rails application under the plugin's test directory. Next, you will configure that application to point back to your plugin. Finally, you will develop your plugin by using normal TDD methodology—except that your tests will live inside the fake Rails application that's using your plugin, while your plugin code will be inside the `blawg/lib` and `blawg/app` directories, right where it belongs.

The Grunt Work

After generating a base plugin skeleton, you move into the `test` directory and run the `rails` command:

```
# cd blawg/test
# rails rails_root
      create
      create   app/controllers
      create   app/helpers
      create   app/models
      create   app/views/layouts
      ...
```

You should now configure the new application to run with a `sqlite` database. This allows you to run the tests without having to configure a local MySQL database and reduces the burden on would-be contributors. You can do this easily enough through the `database.yml` file:

```
# blawg/test/rails_root/config/database.yml
development:
  adapter: sqlite3
  database: db/development.sqlite3


test:
  adapter: sqlite3
  database: db/test.sqlite3
```

Note that while you don't have to configure a production environment, because of the way the Rails test system works, you do have to configure a development environment. Also, unless you're running this on OS X Leopard or later, you'll have to install the `sqlite3` gem:

```
gem install sqlite3-ruby
```

Next, you want your application to load the Blawg plugin as if it had been installed normally. A simple solution would be to use a symlink:

```
# cd blawg/test/rails_root/vendor/plugins/
# ln -s ../../../../ blawg
# ls blawg
lrwxr-xr-x  1 tsaleh  staff      12B Oct 20 17:18 blawg@ ->
../../../../
# ls blawg/
total 8
-rw-r--r--  1 tsaleh  staff     554B Oct 20 15:04 Rakefile
drwxr-xr-x  5 tsaleh  staff     170B Oct 20 16:39 app/
drwxr-xr-x  3 tsaleh  staff     102B Oct 20 16:50 config/
-rw-r--r--  1 tsaleh  staff      26B Oct 20 16:48 init.rb
drwxr-xr-x  3 tsaleh  staff     102B Oct 20 15:04 lib/
drwxr-xr-x  5 tsaleh  staff     170B Oct 20 15:36 test/
```

This works well enough on UNIX systems, but it doesn't work at all on Windows, which doesn't have the concept of a symlink. It also confuses some applications, such as TextMate, which will happily follow recursive symlinks until they run out of stack space.

A better way to deal with this is to use the Rails `config.plugin_paths` option to change the directory the application searches for plugins. You also explicitly configure the application to load only your plugin; you wouldn't want any other files or directories next to it confusing your tests. You set these configurations in the `environment.rb` file:

```
# blawg/test/rails_root/config/environment.rb
#...
Rails::Initializer.run do |config|
  # Point back to the plugin containing this rails_root
  config.plugin_paths = ["#{RAILS_ROOT}/../../../"]
  # Only load the plugin we're testing
  config.plugins = [ :blawg ]
  #...
end
```

Get Down to Business

Now that you're finished with the boilerplate code necessary to test your plugin, you can start with the real development. The intention with the Blawg plugin is that after installation, you'll be able to list and read blog posts by browsing to /posts. This requires a `Post` model, a `PostsController`, and some views and routes for the /posts resource.

Let's start with the `Post` model. You write the tests for the model inside the embedded Rails application as though it were a normal model in the application:

```
# blawg/test/rails_root/test/unit/post_test.rb
require 'test_helper'

class PostTest < ActiveSupport::TestCase
  should have_db_column(:title)
  should have_db_column(:body)

  should validate_presence_of(:title)
  should validate_presence_of(:body)
end
```

To run this test, you simply run the `rake` command from inside the application:

```
# cd blawg/test/rails_root
# rake test:units
(in .../blawg/test/rails_root)
...
  1) Error:
test: Post should have db column named body. (PostTest):
ActiveRecord::StatementInvalid: Could not find table 'posts'
...
```

The tests fail, as you expect it to, because there is no `posts` table in the database. At this point, you could write a migration generator for the Blawg plugin that would create this migration. You could even test-drive this fairly easily, as described in the rubyguides article on plugins (http://guides.rubyonrails.org/plugins.html#generators). That would be overkill for your purposes, though. Instead, you can simply document the contents of the small migration in the plugin's README file and add it to your application directly:

```
# blawg/test/rails_root/db/migrate/20091020224736_create_posts.rb
class CreatePosts < ActiveRecord::Migration
  def self.up
    create_table :posts do |t|
      t.string :title
      t.text :body
    end
  end

  def self.down
    drop_table :posts
  end
end
```

At this point, running the tests will show failures for not having a `Post` model defined. This is the first piece of code that you'll add to the plugin itself:

```
# blawg/app/models/post.rb
class Post < ActiveRecord::Base
  validates :title, :presence => true
  validates :body,  :presence => true
end
```

Note that in Rails 2.2.0, all you had to do to have the application automatically load your `Post` model was put it under `blawg/app/models`. This works with controllers, views, and helpers, as well as with the routes file (under `blawg/config`).

You now have passing unit tests, so you can move on to your controller. First you create the functional tests:

```
# blawg/test/rails_root/test/functional/posts_controller_test.rb
require 'test_helper'

class PostsControllerTest < ActionController::TestCase
  context "given a post" do
    setup { @post = Factory(:post) }

    context "on GET to /posts/:id" do
      setup { get :show, :id => @post.to_param }
      should render_template(:show)
      should respond_with(:success)

      should "find the post" do
        assert assigns(:post)
        assert_equal @post.id, assigns(:post).id
      end
    end

    ...
  end
end
```

To make these tests pass, you need a controller, a set of views, and a routes definition. Again, you can just put these under `blawg/app` and `blawg/config`. First, here is your controller:

```
# blawg/app/controllers/posts_controller.rb
class PostsController < ApplicationController
  def show
    @post = Post.find(params[:id])
  end
  ...
end
```

Here is the show view:

```
# blawg/app/views/posts/show.html.erb
<%= div_for @post do %>
  <h2 class="post_title"><%= h @post.title %></h2>
  <div class="post_body"><%= h @post.body %></div>
<% end %>
```

And here is the routes file, under the `config` directory:

```
# blawg/config/routes.rb
MyApp::Application.routes.draw do
  resources :posts
end
```

Take It Further

While the solution in the preceding section is clearly very heavy and complex, it does provide some nice features. It allows you to test the entire MVC stack, even using integration tests with webrat. It also allows you to test the interaction of your plugin when installed alongside other plugins, or with different application configurations.

You need to take care of one final detail. Having to run the rake task from inside the `blawg/test/rails_root` directory is unconventional and a likely point of confusion in the future. You can tie this up by replacing the default test task that comes configured in your Blawg `Rakefile` with the following:

```
# blawg/Rakefile
...
desc 'Default: run unit tests.'
task :default => :test

desc 'Test the blawg plugin.'
task :test do
  rails_root = File.join(File.dirname(__FILE__), 'test',
                         'rails_root')
  system("cd #{rails_root} && rake")
end
```

All you're doing here is delegating to the Rakefile in your embedded application.

Strive for Simplicity

Now you have three techniques at your disposal for testing Rails plugins: You can test them without using any of the Rails libraries; you can pull in only the individual Rails gems you need; and, finally, you can pull out the atom bomb and embed an entire Rails application in your test suite. You should turn to the next heaviest of these solutions only when it's clear that the preceding techniques aren't powerful enough for the needs of your plugin.

CHAPTER 8
Scaling and Deploying

Studies have shown that maintenance—that is, the processing of modifying existing operation software—typically consumes 60 to 80 percent of a software product's total lifecycle expenditures and over 50 percent of total programmer effort.

For many web applications, a lot of that expense and effort may be related to *scaling*, which is the capability of a system to handle an increasing amount of work gracefully or to be readily enlarged. The deployment strategies you use and must maintain also go hand in hand with scalability and the overall performance of your software system.

Typical Rails applications can employ a few simple strategies to ensure a solid deployment that can help to avoid common pitfalls and ensure a flexible system for the future without overly increasing up-front effort. In addition, some common Anti-Patterns throughout the application and database layer can contribute to scalability issues you can avoid and address in order to ensure a scalable system. This chapter provides insight into these issues to help you save time and money with software systems.

AntiPattern: Scaling Roadblocks

The concept of building for the actual environment on which you'll be deploying is prudent on its surface. If you'll be deploying to only one server for production, it doesn't make sense to prematurely spend extra engineering effort optimizing your code for multiple servers in a clustered configuration. This is absolutely the case for some scaling features you might try to add. However, there are some simple things you can do from the start with an application that don't add a significant amount of engineering overhead in the beginning but can save an enormous amount of time and effort in potential migration costs down the road.

Solution: Build to Scale from the Start

As with many other aspects of being a responsible developer, deciding when to build to scale from the get-go is a matter of striking a balance. With all development, you need to weigh the cost of implementing and maintaining a feature against the cost and likelihood of needing to add that feature to the application later in the development lifecycle. Some scaling features are clearly not worth worrying about early on, and some should be added to each application from the beginning.

Take dataset sharding, as an example. *Sharding* is the concept of breaking certain datasets into different sections and hosting each section on its own server to decrease the size of each server's dataset and load. The engineering effort needed to implement sharding from the start is far too high to justify in most cases. In addition, few real-world applications actually ever need to shard, no matter how much they must scale. It's simply not the right answer for every scaling problem, and therefore it's not something a responsible developer would add from the start.

Head in the Clouds

Unlike sharding, storage of assets is an area where several things can be put in place from the start to save a lot of time later on, when an application needs to grow from one server to many. These items, largely configuration options, add so little engineering overhead that implementing them from the start is a no-brainer.

The Rails community's preferred file attachment plugin is Paperclip (http://github.com/thoughtbot/paperclip). It offers several configuration options that, if done from the start, will make scaling to multiple servers much easier down the road.

Support for Amazon S3 is built into Paperclip. S3 is a distributed file store service that Amazon provides. If you don't store your images in S3 from the start and instead store them on the disk of your server, when your application changes to multiple servers, you must move your assets to S3 or to another shared filesystem, such as GFS or NFS. This process can be troublesome and time-consuming when you're dealing with thousands of files.

The following is the Paperclip configuration for storing files on disk on a single server:

```
has_attached_file :image,
                  :styles => { :medium   => "290x290>",
                               :thumb    => "64x64#" }
```

This is the same configuration with the files stored on S3:

```
has_attached_file :image,
                  :styles => { :medium   => "290x290>",
                               :thumb    => "64x64#" },
                  :storage => :s3,
                  :s3_credentials => "#{Rails.root}/config/s3.yml",
                  :path => ":class/:id/:style/:basename.:extension",
                  :bucket => "post-attachment-images-#{Rails.env}"
```

Maximum Occupancy

Most Linux-based filesystems have a limit of 32,000 files within each directory. With the Paperclip path definition in the preceding section (and the default, which is ":rails_root/public/:attachment/:id/:style/:basename.:extension"), you will run into this limit when you hit 32,000 attachments. This number may seem like far far away, but when you hit that limit, moving around and migrating 32,000 images won't be fun.

Fortunately, Paperclip has a built-in configuration option for dealing with this problem. Paperclip provides a path interpolation of :id_partition. This option changes where Paperclip stores the uploaded files; instead of storing all attachments in one directory, it splits up the id into a directory structure, ensuring that there are a limited number of files within each directory. For example, instead of storing the attachments for the post with id 1003 in /public/images/1003, it will store the attachments in /public/images/1/0/0/3. The new Paperclip configuration for this looks as follows:

```
has_attached_file :image,
                    :styles => { :medium    => "290x290>",
                                 :thumb     => "64x64#" },
                    :path =>
":rails_root/public/:class/:id_partition/:style/:basename.:extension",
                    :url =>
"/:class/:id_partition/:style/:basename.:extension"
```

And here's the same configuration with the files stored on S3:

```
has_attached_file :image,
                    :styles => { :medium    => "290x290>",
                                 :thumb     => "64x64#" },
                    :storage => :s3,
                    :s3_credentials => "#{Rails.root}/config/s3.yml",
                    :path =>
":class/:id_partition/:style/:basename.:extension",
                    :bucket => "post-attachment-images-#{Rails.env}"
```

Amazon S3 does not actually have the 32,000-files-per-directory limit (or "directories" at all, in fact). However, if you ever needed to move files or back them up to a storage system with this limit, you would run into many problems in doing so. Partitioning the data, even on S3, just makes sense because of the trouble it will save down the road.

Slice and Dice

Cloud deployment is easier today than ever before. With services such as Engine Yard (http://engineyard.com), Heroku (http://heroku.com), and Google App Engine (http://code.google.com/appengine/), you no longer need to maintain your own cluster configurations or keep track of and manage your own instances and provisioning and deployment involves one click (or command). In addition, the costs for an actual cluster in the cloud are comparable with what you might pay for a typical single server in a data center.

Yes, you can deploy to just one instance or server, but by deploying your applications to a clustered environment from the start, even if you only use one server there, you are sure to maintain ultimate flexibility in scalability and deployment. And the amount of effort and cost will be similar to what you'd spend on a more traditional server infrastructure.

AntiPattern: Disappearing Assets

In order to enable easy rollback of deployments, most deployment tools, such as the ever-popular Capistrano, will move old code to a timestamped directory and copy the latest code into its place. During this process, fixed assets on a server (such as user-uploaded content and configuration files) must not be moved along with the old release. While various manual or custom-built strategies may be employed to combat this problem, there is actually one provided by Capistrano.

Solution: Make Use of the System Directory

Capistrano provides the system directory, which is useful for preventing fixed assets on a server from being moved along with the old release. A top-level directory managed by Capistrano will look like this:

```
current -> releases/2010...
releases/
revisions.log
shared/
```

The shared directory contains a system directory, and Capistrano symlinks this system directory to RAILS_ROOT/public/system on each deployment of your application.

For example, if you're using Paperclip, the Rails community's preferred file upload attachment plugin, you'll configure the Paperclip attachment definition to store the uploads somewhere under the public/system directory, as shown here:

```
has_attached_file :image,
                  :styles => { :medium   => "290x290>",
                               :thumb    => "64x64#" },
                  :path =>
":rails_root/public/system/:class/:id_partition/:style/:filename",
                  :url =>
"/system/:class/:id_partition/:style/:basename.:extension"
```

Because the system directory is symlinked in public, everything in it is available for download, bypassing the Rails stack entirely. Therefore, you'll actually want to store any configuration files or other private information that should not be available for download in Capistrano's shared directory rather than shared/system. Storing items in these folders will ensure that they are preserved across application deployments.

AntiPattern: Sluggish SQL

The most common location of performance issues in the MVC framework is the database layer.

If you're anything like us, you got into Rails at least partially because of your love for the Ruby language. Ruby is a beautiful, expressive, and enticing medium for building code. SQL, that workhorse of relational algebra, is firmly and happily entrenched at the opposite side of this spectrum. SQL is a demanding boss, a field marshal, and is as unforgiving as it can be.

While most developers can recognize performance issues in their Ruby code at an early stage in their career, doing the same in SQL code requires a bit of experience and expertise. This section shows you some simple and common fixes you can implement to make quick gains against your SQL performance issues. We'll show you how to identify the need for indexes, as well as how to apply them. We'll show you when it's best to make use of SQL subselects, and finally, when you need to reconsider your domain model in general.

Solution: Add Indexes

Nearly all database servers you'll use in production support the concept of a database index, which is a data structure that speeds up database reads by serving as a lookup table for both ordering and querying.

Without indexes, querying a database becomes unreasonably slow once there are even only a few thousand records in the table. Database indexes are not tools to troubleshoot speed problems or data growing pains; they're fundamental tools that relational databases use to function correctly in the first place.

Unfortunately, it's all too easy to overlook adding indexes because they have to be added as a second step in your migrations. The following sections provide some guidelines for when to add indexes.

Primary Keys

Most SQL databases with the concept of a primary key will automatically create an index on the primary key column when it exists. In Rails, this is typically the id column in a table. Fortunately, because Rails tells the database that it's a primary key, you'll get the index for free—that is, created by the database. This is very important for a view for the show action, like /users/1, for example. The request comes in, and the query to "find user with id equal to 1" occurs very quickly because the users.id column is indexed.

Foreign Keys

Given the following User model, there will be a user_id column in the comments table, and the Comment model will use this column to determine the user that it belongs to:

```ruby
class User < ActiveRecord::Base
  has_many :comments
end
```

You should have an index on every foreign key column. When you make a page like /users/1/comments, two things need to happen. First, you look up the user with id equal to 1. If you've indexed primary keys, this index will be hit. Second, you want to find all comments that belong to this user. If you've indexed comments.user_id, this index will be used as well.

Because one of the biggest issues with indexes is remembering to add them, you might consider enforcing a code policy of only naming actual foreign key columns ending in _id. This will act as a hint that such a column needs to be indexed.

Columns Used in Polymorphic Conditional Joins

The following models set up a polymorphic relationship between comments and tags. Other models in this application can also have tags, and this is why they are polymorphic:

```ruby
class Tag < ActiveRecord::Base
  has_many :taggings
end

class Tagging < ActiveRecord::Base
  belongs_to :tag
  belongs_to :taggable, :polymorphic => true
end

class Comment < ActiveRecord::Base
  has_many :taggings, :as => :taggable
end
```

When you establish a polymorphic relationship like this one, you end up with a condition on a join in the resulting queries for doing lookups on these polymorphic records. For example, with the relationships shown above there will be queries like the following:

```
SELECT * FROM comments
  INNER JOIN taggings
   ON taggings.taggable_type = 'Comment' AND
      taggings.taggable_id = '3'
  INNER JOIN tags
   ON taggings.tag_id = tags.id
```

In this case, there should be a composite index on `taggings` on the columns `taggable_type` and `taggable_id` so that the initial lookup goes well. You should also index the `taggings.tag_id` column because this is a foreign key association:

```
class AddindexesToAllPolymorphicTables < ActiveRecord::Migration
  def self.up
    add_index :taggings, :tag_id
    add_index :taggings, [:taggable_id, :taggable_type]
  end
  def self.down
    remove_index :taggings, :column => [:taggable_id, :taggable_type]
    remove_index :taggings, :tag_id
  end
end
```

Columns Used in Uniqueness Validations

The `User` model shown here has a unique constraint on its `email` column:

```
class User < ActiveRecord::Base
  validates :email, :unique => true
end
```

In this model, every time you save a `User` record, Active Record runs a query to try to find other rows that have the same data in the email. It is much faster to do this comparison on indexed columns than on non-indexed columns; therefore, this column should have an index.

Columns Used for STI

With the single-table inheritance (STI) pattern in Active Record, there is a `type` column to store the parent class of a subclass. For example, if `AdminUser` inherits from `User` with STI, there will be a users table with a `type` column, which all `AdminUser` records will populate with the string `"AdminUser"` to indicate that those records are of that subclass. This means that every query that looks up `AdminUser` records is going to have at least a `WHERE users.type = 'AdminUser'` clause in it, and therefore the `type` column on that table should be indexed.

Columns Used by `to_param`

It's fairly common to introduce the concept of "pretty URLs" into an application. That is, instead of a location's URL being based on the `id` column of the location, it's based on the location's `city` column—for example, `/locations/springfield`. The `city` column is used as the lookup now, and it's important that it have an index. This column may be covered by other guidelines above that already gave it an index, but this is something to keep an eye out for to ensure that it's not missed.

Other Columns Used in **WHERE** Clauses

You don't want to index every column that can appear in the WHERE clauses of your SQL queries, but you do want to investigate each of them to understand how the queries will be run and whether indexes will be beneficial.

The following sections provide some common things to look for regarding potential indexes in your WHERE clauses.

State Columns

Say that in a system with an `Article` model, articles can be in Draft (not done yet), Submitted (done, awaiting approval), Published (approved), or Unpublished (approved then taken down) states. In this case, you're most likely going to have an interface for users that shows "all of your draft articles" so that the users can resume working on them and "all your submitted articles" so they can review their past wisdom. Or possibly you'll have an interface with a dropdown of all states to allow a listing on each state individually.

In this system with the `Article` model, you'll have an `articles.state` column, which will be a `varchar` column and hold one of the states as a string. You should consider indexing that column so that the queries to find comments in a certain state are indexed. If, as proposed, you have the interface list all the draft articles of a particular user, you'll want to do a composite index on `user_id` and `state`.

Boolean Columns

In the system with articles having a "submit for approval" concept, you need to add an "admin" concept for users, with the option to either be an admin or not be an admin. You also need an "all users who are admins" view so that you can see at a glance who is doing comment approval and click through to see what each has approved.

In this case, you need to add a Boolean column called `admin` to the `users` table. You should consider whether indexing Boolean columns is right for your application. For example, if you're using Boolean columns in a `WHERE` clause along with other conditions, it might be helpful to add the Boolean to the composite index. In addition, if the majority of users are not administrators, a page that is supposed to list only administrators will perform poorly without an index.

Consider indexing Boolean columns if they'll be queried and the values are heavily skewed in favor of either true or false and you are selecting the value that has the smaller number.

DateTime Columns

Assuming that published articles are listed with the most recent ones first, the query to find and list articles will likely have an `ORDER BY created_at DESC` clause. Or, if the home page shows any articles published this week, it may have a `WHERE created_at >= "2010-10-27 00:00:00"` clause. Given these clauses, it may be necessary to add an index on the `created_at` column.

You should determine how your date columns will be used in both `WHERE` and `ORDER` clauses and consider them for indexing.

What's the Downside?

If you haven't introduced indexes from day one, or if you are adding an index to a new column in a table that has many rows, the migration can take quite a bit of time. For example, adding a new index on a table with 12 million rows took us about 7 hours.

Also, you shouldn't just go about willy–nilly, adding database indexes to *every* column in every table in your database. There is a cost to the database to maintain those indexes, and every time an `INSERT` or `UPDATE` occurs, there is work to be done that would not need to be done without the index in place. It's important to do your homework before you go index crazy.

Seek and Destroy

How do you go about finding missing indexes and determining whether they should be added?

There are several Rails plugins you can use tools to identify missing indexes. The simplest of them is Limerick Rake (http://github.com/thoughtbot/limerick_rake), which provides a rake task db:indexes:missing. When run on your application, this task examines your database and identifies obvious missing indexes, primarily missing foreign key indexes.

You can also turn on MySQL slow query logging, which is described at http://dev.mysql.com/doc/refman/5.1/en/slow-query-log.html, and its sidekick log-queries-not-using-indexes. If you add the following to your MySQL configuration, your MySQL will take note of queries that take a long time or do not use any indexes:

```
log_slow_queries = /var/log/mysql/mysql-slow.log
log-queries-not-using-indexes
```

This log will serve as an important indicator of potential places for missing indexes.

There are also two Rails plugins that will print out EXPLAIN statements of every query used to render a page to the page itself. These can assist in identifying issues. The two plugins are Rails Footnotes (http://github.com/josevalim/rails-footnotes) and QueryReviewer (http://github.com/dsboulder/query_reviewer).

Finally, New Relic RPM (www.newrelic.com) is a Rails plugin that monitors an application's performance and sends the information to the New Relic RPM service for analysis and monitoring. You can then log into the service and drill down into the various layers of the MVC stack to see how much time is spent where. For diagnosing performance problems, including slow queries, New Relic RPM is an invaluable tool. We're not salespeople for them; we're just happy customers.

Solution: Reassess Your Domain Model

The number of rows you have in a table and the number of tables involved in an SQL query are two important factors that can undermine the speed of your queries. Furthermore, they can work in concert to *really* affect the performance of an application negatively. If you have many rows in many tables and you're joining across many tables in one query, you're going to have immediate performance issues.

Modeling your domain (and therefore your database tables) in a highly normalized fashion can contribute greatly to performance problems in many of your queries.
For example, examine the following models:

```
class State < ActiveRecord::Base
  validates :name, :unique => true
end

class User < ActiveRecord::Base
end

class Category < ActiveRecord::Base
  validates :category, :unique => true
end

class Article < ActiveRecord::Base
  belongs_to :state
  belongs_to :categories
  belongs_to :user
end
```

In order to query the articles of a particular state, category, and user, it would be
fairly typical to write the following query:

```
SELECT * from articles
  LEFT OUTER JOIN states ON articles.state_id=states.id
  LEFT OUTER JOIN categories ON articles.category_id=categories.id
  WHERE articles.category_id = categories.id
  AND states.name = 'published'
  AND categories.name = 'hiking'
  AND articles.user_id = 123
```

You would write this via `ActiveRecord#find` as follows:

```
Article.includes([:state, :category]).
        where("states.name"     => "published",
              "categories.name" => "hiking",
              "articles.user_id" => current_user)
```

Understandably, if there were very many articles, categories, and states, these joins would start to get very slow. With this in mind, the preceding query could be rewritten to avoid the joins as shown here:

```
SELECT * from articles
 WHERE state_id = 150
  AND category_id = 50
  AND user_id = 123
```

You could rewrite this using Active Record queries as follows:

```
published_state = State.find_by_name('published')
hiking_category = Category.find_by_name('hiking')
Article.where("state_id"    => published_state,
              "category_id" => hiking_category,
              "user_id"     => current_user)
```

The N+1 Problem

Take a look at the following view:

```
<table>
  <tr>
    <th>Title</th>
    <th>User</th>
    <th>State</th>
    <th>Category</th>
  </tr>
  <% @articles.each do |article| %>
    <% content_tag_for :tr, article do %>
      <td><%= article.title %></td>
      <td><%= article.user.name %></td>
      <td><%= article.state.name %></td>
      <td><%= article.category.name %></td>
    <% end %>
  <% end %>
</table>
```

This view loops through all the given articles and prints out the title, user name, state name, and category name of each one.

For each new state, category, and user on articles, a new query will be performed to look up and load the object. This could potentially be many queries and could cause this page to load too slowly.

You can solve this problem by using a strategy called *eager loading* that's built into Active Record. To do this, you change your query to retrieve the articles to use the `includes` scope:

```
Article.includes([:state, :category, :user])
```

This `includes` call eagerly loads the state, category, and user of each article by joining against the respective tables and loading all the data from it into the model instance. The preceding Active Record query would result in approximately the following SQL query:

```
SELECT * from articles
  LEFT OUTER JOIN states     ON articles.state_id    = states.id
  LEFT OUTER JOIN categories ON articles.category_id =
categories.id
  LEFT OUTER JOIN users      ON articles.user_id     = users.id
```

You're right back to the joins you started with in the first example!

Granted, for the sake of brevity and understandability here, the articles, states, categories, and users example is fairly trivial, and it might not result in slow queries. However, in most sufficiently complex applications, there won't be just these four models and the three joins they produce. There may be many more joins and many more rows in the database tables.

Also, while each of these problems can be addressed by manually massaging the queries produced by Active Record to avoid poorly performing joins, as a programmer, you ultimately want to be in a position to write the most straightforward and expressive code possible.

Learn to Love the Denormalized Dataset

The most straightforward solution to the problem presented in the preceding section is to recognize that the `Category` and `State` models aren't adding value. You can therefore eschew the above workarounds and complexity and simply denormalize the domain to eliminate those models altogether. Doing so results in an `Article` model with the following definition:

```
class Article < ActiveRecord::Base
  STATES = %w(draft review published archived)
  CATEGORIES = %w(tips faqs misc hiking)

  validates :state,    :inclusion => {:in => STATES    }
  validates :category, :inclusion => {:in => CATEGORIES}
end
```

The new query now pulls from only a single table, and it does not require subsequent queries to figure out the state and category names. It now looks like the following:

```
Article.where("state"    => "published",
              "category" => "hiking",
              "user_id"  => current_user)
```

Or, more idiomatically:

```
current_user.articles.find_all_by_state_and_category("published",
                                                     "hiking")
```

For full instructions and more information on this denormalization, see the sections "AntiPattern: The Million-Model March," in Chapter 2.

AntiPattern: Painful Performance

It's a frustrating experience for everyone, including the developer, management, and, most importantly, the customer when a website has performance problems. While it's true that a website can have performance problems introduced by the traffic load and the need to scale, you can make some straightforward changes in the way you write some code to greatly reduce simple performance problems.

Solution: Don't Do in Ruby What You Can Do in SQL

One of the most common performance pitfalls we see leading to slow application response times is doing operations on data in Ruby that can be done in SQL instead. The two most common causes for this are making a simple mistake, such as misunderstanding the Active Record API, and laziness.

Everybody Makes Mistakes

Simple mistakes are often caused by the unfamiliarity with or changes in the Active Record API. For example, there are three ways to get the number of items in an Active Record association:

```
@article.comments.count
@article.comments.length
@article.comments.size
```

All three of these methods will return the same correct number. However, each of them performs a dramatically different operation.

`@article.comments.count` executes an SQL count statement to find the number of items in the relationship. `@article.comments.length` is not defined on Active Record relationships, and therefore it falls through and causes all the records in the relationship to be loaded and causes length to be called on the resulting collection. `@article.comments.size` calls length on the collection of items in the relationship if it has already been loaded; otherwise, it calls count.

Each of the three different methods has a purpose, but unfamiliarity with the API or simple forgetfulness might cause a developer to call length. This could potentially load thousands of objects into memory and cause a very slow action.

Laziness

When it comes to using Ruby when SQL will do the job better, there are two types of laziness:

- The developer knows how to do it in SQL but does it in Ruby anyway.

- The developer doesn't know how to do it in SQL so instead does it in Ruby.

Both of these lead to slow application response times, but let's examine them individually.

The most common example of doing something in Ruby that can be done in SQL even though the developer knows how to do it in SQL seems to be sorting. For example, take the following case-insensitive sort of all users on an account by name:

```
@account = Account.find(3)
@users = @account.users.sort { |a,b| a.name.downcase <=>
b.name.downcase }.first(5)
```

This loads all users on the account into a collection from SQL and then sorts them all, using Ruby, by name. It lowercases each name so that the sort is case-insensitive, starting with the first five. In addition, as icing on the performance cake, sort also duplicates the original users array and returns a new sorted one, doubling the amount of memory used by this code.

You can write this by using SQL and the Active Record finders as follow:

```
SELECT * FROM users WHERE account_id = '3' ORDER BY LCASE(name)
LIMIT 5

@users = @account.users.order('LCASE(name)').limit(5)
```

> **Note**
>
> If you were actually going to perform the ordering and sorting shown here, you would do well to wrap it up in a named scope to enhance readability and separate concerns.

The second manifestation of laziness is doing something that is hard to do in Ruby because the developer didn't take the time to figure out how to do it in SQL.

Unfortunately, this results in poorly performing code in nearly every circumstance. The developer may think that it won't be an issue, but it often is.

No, it's probably not very much fun to spend all day composing a difficult SQL query. But it's not going to be very much fun dealing with the performance issue later either.

Take the following domain model, for example:

```ruby
class User < ActiveRecord::Base
  has_many :comments
  has_many :articles, :through => :comments
end

class Article < ActiveRecord::Base
  has_many :comments
  has_many :users, :through => :comments
end

class Comment < ActiveRecord::Base
  belongs_to :article
  belongs_to :user
end
```

In the application using the code above, the users want to see a list of their collaborators. A collaborator is another user who has commented on the same article that you have commented on and who is not the user himself. The developer isn't sure of the right way to program this functionality in SQL, so he decides to use Ruby instead and ends up with the following code:

```ruby
class User < ActiveRecord::Base
  has_many :comments
  has_many :articles, :through => :comments

  def collaborators
    articles.collect { |a| a.users }.flatten.uniq.reject { |u| u ==
self }
  end
end
```

This code works and returns the right list of collaborators, the entire collection of every article the user has commented on, and every user on all of those comments, including duplicates, and is loaded into memory. Then the array of arrays is flattened out, duplicates are removed, and the user himself is removed. The simple fact of the matter is that for any sufficiently large number of articles, users, and comments, this code is just not going to perform well.

Note that oftentimes a good indicator that Ruby is being used for something that SQL should be used for is that it contains calls to the `flatten` method. The preceding `collaborators` method can be rewritten using SQL (with Active Record finders):

```ruby
class User < ActiveRecord::Base
  has_many :comments
  has_many :articles, :through => :comments

  def collaborators
    User.select("DISTINCT users.*").
        joins(:comments => [:user, {:article => :comments}]).
        where(["articles.id in ? AND users.id != ?",
               self.article_ids, self.id])
  end
end
```

This results in the following SQL code:

```sql
SELECT DISTINCT users.* FROM users
  INNER JOIN comments
        ON comments.user_id = users.id
  INNER JOIN users users_comments
        ON users_comments.id = comments.user_id
  INNER JOIN articles
        ON articles.id = comments.article_id
  INNER JOIN comments comments_articles
        ON comments_articles.article_id = articles.id
  WHERE (articles.id in (1) AND users.id != 1)
```

As you can see, Active Record provides the capability to do more complex joins based on associations, and it prefixes the joined tables with unique prefixes if the same table is joined against more than once.

By using the tools described here, you should be able to perform complex queries while maintaining application response time.

Solution: Move Processing into Background Jobs

The majority of systems we've been involved with and written have eventually had something in them that does not fit well within the normal web request/response cycle. That is, the functionality takes too long to complete for the web page to be rendered to the user in a reasonable amount of time. These pain points can vary widely from application to application but tend to be a few common things:

- Generating reports

- Updating lots of related data in an associated object, based on a user action

- Updating various caches

- Communicating with slower external resources

- Sending email

When presented with any of the actions in this list, moving the processing into a background job is the common solution to the problem. You can take the action out of the response cycle altogether so that it is not executed at the same time as the original request.

There are two main strategies for executing tasks outside the response cycle: cron tasks and queuing.

cron Tasks

Moving extra processing into a cron task is a relatively straightforward process for those already familiar with the basic UNIX concepts of cron and scripting. Therefore, this can be a valid solution in some circumstances. The ideal circumstances for using cron tend to be when the work to be done can easily be identified, when the work can be done in batches, and when the amount of work to be done is fairly consistent between runs.

For example, retrieving the count on a large InnoDB table can take a very long time. In a system where it takes 3 minutes to get the count of rows in the table, but the total number of items is to be displayed on a web page, the total number of items should be cached.

Assuming that it's okay for the count to be slightly out of date, a cron script could be written to run every 30 minutes and regenerate the cache. In this scenario, the work to be done is easily identified. Simply calling count on the table will give you the new number.

However, if in order to use cron you must do a lot of complex operations, flagging, or queuing to identify which items need to be worked on in the background, using an actual queuing system, as explained in the following section, is a better option.

Queuing

Using a queue is the right solution when work to be performed is not easily identified, is not consistent, or isn't ideally suited for processing in batches.

A queuing system allows you to simply place a job to be performed on the queue whenever a job needs to be performed. For example, if a user requests that a very large CSV report be generated, you can place a job for doing this task in the queue and display a "Please wait" response to the user immediately.

There are a number of popular queuing systems for Rails. Two of the most popular and well supported are delayed_job (or DJ; http://github.com/tobi/delayed_job) and Resque (http://github.com/defunkt/resque). Both of these are libraries for creating background jobs, placing jobs in queues, and processing those queues. Resque is backed by a Redis datastore, and delayed_job is SQL backed.

Resque is heavily inspired by delayed_job and was built to power GitHub. We echo the sentiment of GitHub and Chris Wanstrath and highly recommend delayed_job to anyone whose site is not 50% background work. However, if you already have Redis deployed, you should consider using Resque. Because delayed_job is a straightforward, reliable system that is built on the technology stack most Rails websites already run (Rails and SQL), it should provide adequate queuing needs for most websites.

Once you've installed delayed_job into your application and followed the setup instructions in its README, you can add jobs to the queue by using two different mechanisms.

The first mechanism is to place any object that responds to perform onto the queue for later processing. Take, for example, the following SalesReport class:

```
class SalesReport < Struct.new(:user)
  def perform
    report = generate_report
    Mailer.sales_report(user, report).deliver
  end

  private
```

```
    def generate_report
      FasterCSV.generate do |csv|
        csv << CSV_HEADERS
        Sales.find_each do |sale|
          csv << sale.to_a
        end
      end
    end
end
```

If users should be able to request that a sales report be mailed to them, you can place this code in the `create` action of `ReportsController`, as shown here:

```
def create
  Delayed::Job.enqueue SalesReport.new(current_user)
end
```

The second mechanism provided by delayed_job is the `send_later` method on all objects. It has the same syntax as Ruby's `send` method, but instead of calling the method immediately, you place `Delayed::PerformableMethod` on the queue. This provides a slightly more ad hoc and flexible way of scheduling jobs in the queue. By using the `send_later` method, you can place the `generate_report` method shown earlier directly on the `Sale` model, without the need to create a separate class, as shown here:

```
class Sale < ActiveRecord::Base
  def self.generate_report(user)
    report = FasterCSV.generate do |csv|
      csv << CSV_HEADERS
      find_each do |sale|
        csv << sale.to_a
      end
    end
    Mailer.sales_report(user, report).deliver
  end
end
```

With this in place, your controller's `create` action would be as follows:

```
def create
  Sale.send_later(:generate_report, current_user)
end
```

Which syntax you choose is up to you. However, utilizing separate job classes is a good way to follow the Single Responsibility Principle and keep your classes clean, especially for more complex job logic.

Keep It Real

Backgrounding and queuing are reliable strategies for dealing with the inevitable slow actions that result from functionality that simply takes too long to perform. Once you have a queuing system in place, you can offload these tasks into the background and keep your application responsive for users. However, don't overdo it. If you push too many items into the background, often prematurely, your application will ultimately become overly complex and brittle. So be sure to exercise restraint when using queuing.

CHAPTER 9
Databases

With the Rails framework providing a simple ORM that abstracts many of the database details away from the developer, the database is an afterthought for many Rails developers. While the power of the framework has made this okay to a certain extent, there are important database and Rails-specific considerations that you shouldn't overlook.

AntiPattern: Messy Migrations

Ruby on Rails database migrations were an innovative solution to a real problem faced by developers: How to script changes to the database so that they could be reliably replicated by the rest of the team on their development machines as well as deployed to the production servers at the appropriate time. Before Rails and its baked-in solution, developers often wrote ad hoc database change scripts by hand, if they used them at all.

However, as with most other improvements, database migrations are not without pain points. Over time, a database migration can become a tangle of code that can be intimidating to work with rather than the joy it should be. By strictly keeping in mind the following solutions, you can overcome these obstacles and ensure that your migrations never become irreconcilably messy.

Solution: Never Modify the up Method on a Committed Migration

Database migrations enable you to reliably distribute database changes to other members of your team and to ensure that the proper changes are made on your server during deployment.

If you commit a new migration to your source code repository, unless there are irreversible bugs in the migration itself, you should follow the practice of never modifying that migration. A migration that has already been run on another team member's computer or the server will never automatically be run again. In order to run it again, a developer must go through an orchestrated dance of backing the migration down and then up again. It gets even worse if other migrations have since been committed, as that could potentially cause data loss.

Yes, if you're certain that a migration hasn't been run on the server, then it's possible to communicate to the rest of the team that you've changed a migration and have them re-migrate their database or make the required changes manually. However, that's not an effective use of their time, it creates headaches, and it's error prone. It's simply best to avoid the situation altogether and never modify the up method of a migration.

Of course, there will be times when you've accidentally committed a migration that has an irreversible bug in it that must be fixed. In such circumstances, you'll have no choice but to modify the migration to fix the bug. Ideally, the times when this happen are few and far between. In order to reduce the chances of this happening, you should always be sure to run the migration and inspect the results to ensure accuracy *before* committing the migration to your source code repository. However, you shouldn't limit yourself to simply running the migration. Instead, you should run the migration and then run the down of the migration and rerun the up. Rails provides rake tasks for doing this:

```
rake db:migrate
rake db:migrate:redo
```

The `rake db:migrate:redo` command runs the down method on the last migration and then reruns the up method on that migration. This ensures that the entire migration runs in both directions and is repeatable, without error. Once you've run this and double-checked the results, you can commit your new migration to the repository with confidence.

Solution: Never Use External Code in a Migration

Database migrations are used to manage database change. When the structure of a database changes, very often the data in the database needs to change as well. When this happens, it's fairly common to want to use models inside the migration itself, as in the following example:

```ruby
class AddJobsCountToUser < ActiveRecord::Migration
  def self.up
    add_column :users, :jobs_count, :integer, :default => 0
    Users.all.each do |user|
      user.jobs_count = user.jobs.size
      user.save
    end
  end

  def self.down
    remove_column :users, :jobs_count
  end
end
```

In this migration above, you're adding a counter cache column to the users table, and this column will store the number of jobs each user has posted. In this migration, you're actually using the User model to find all users and update the column of each one. There are two problems with this approach.

First, this approach performs horribly. The code above loads all the users into memory and then for each user, one at a time, it finds out how many jobs each has and updates its count column.

Second, and more importantly, this migration does not run if the model is ever removed from the application, becomes unavailable, or changes in some way that makes the code in this migration no longer valid. The code in migrations is supposed to be able to be run to manage change in the database, in sequence, at any time. When external code is used in a migration, it ties the migration code to code that is not bound by these same rules and can result in an unrunnable migration.

Therefore, it's always best to use straight SQL whenever possible in your migrations. If you do so, you can rewrite the preceding migration as follows:

```
class AddJobsCountToUser < ActiveRecord::Migration
  def self.up
    add_column :users, :jobs_count, :integer, :default => 0
    update(<<-SQL)
      UPDATE users SET jobs_count = (
        SELECT count(*) FROM jobs
          WHERE jobs.user_id = users.id
      )
    SQL
  end

  def self.down
    remove_column :users, :jobs_count
  end
end
```

When this migration is rewritten using SQL directly, it has no external dependencies beyond the exact state of the database at the time the migration should be executed.

There may be cases in which you actually do need to use a model or other Ruby code in a migration. In such cases, the goal is to rely on no external code in your migration. Therefore, all code that's needed, including the model, should be defined inside the migration itself. For example, if you really want to use the User model in the preceding migration, you rewrite it like the following:

```ruby
class AddJobsCountToUser < ActiveRecord::Migration
  class Job < ActiveRecord::Base
  end
  class User < ActiveRecord::Base
    has_many :jobs
  end

  def self.up
    add_column :users, :jobs_count, :integer, :default => 0
    User.reset_column_information
    Users.all.each do |user|
      user.jobs_count = user.jobs.size
      user.save
    end
  end

  def self.down
    remove_column :users, :jobs_count
  end
end
```

Since this migration defines both the Job and User models, it no longer depends on an external definition of those models being in place. It also defines the has_many relationship between them and therefore defines everything it needs to run successfully. In addition, note the call to User.reset_column_information in the self.up method. When models are defined, Active Record reads the current database schema. If your migration changes that schema, calling the reset_column_information method causes Active Record to re-inspect the columns in the database.

You can use this same technique if you must calculate the value of a column by using an algorithm defined in your application. You cannot rely on the definition of that algorithm to be the same or even be present when the migration is run. Therefore, the algorithm should be duplicated inside the migration itself.

Solution: Always Provide a down Method in Migrations

It's very important that a migration have a reliable self.down defined that actually reverses the migration. You never know when something is going to be rolled back. It's truly bad practice to not have this defined or to have it defined incorrectly.

Some migrations simply cannot be fully reversed. This is most often the case for migrations that change data in a destructive manner. If this is the case for a migration for which you're writing the down method, you should do the best reversal you can do. If you are in a situation where there is a migration that under no circumstances can ever be reversed safely, you should raise an `ActiveRecord::IrreversibleMigration` exception, as shown here:

```
def self.down
  raise ActiveRecord::IrreversibleMigration
end
```

Raising this exception causes migrations to be stopped when this down method is run. This ensures that the developer running the migrations understands that there is something irreversible that has been done and that cannot be undone without manual intervention.

Once you have the down method defined, you should run the migration in both directions to ensure proper functionality. As discussed earlier in this chapter, in the section "Solution: Never Modify the up Method on a Committed Migration," Rails provides rake tasks for doing this:

```
rake db:migrate
rake db:migrate:redo
```

The rake db:migrate:redo command runs the down method on the last migration and then reruns the up method on that migration.

AntiPattern: Wet Validations

Ruby on Rails generally treats a database as a dumb storage device, essentially working only with many of the common-denominator features found in all the databases it supports and eschewing additional database functionality such as foreign keys and constraints. But many Rails developers eventually realize that a database has this functionality built in, and they attempt to use it by trying to duplicate the validation and constraints from their models into the database. For example, the following User model has a number of validations:

```
class User < ActiveRecord::Base
  validates :account_id, :presence => true
  validates :first_name, :presence => true
  validates :last_name,  :presence => true

  validates :password, :presence     => true,
                       :confirmation => true,
                       :if           => :password_required?

  validates :email, :uniqueness => true,
                    :format     => { :with => %r{.+@.+\..+} },
                    :presence   => true

  belongs_to :account
end
```

You could attempt to create a database table to back this model that attempts to enforce the same validations at the database level, using database constraints. The (inadequate) migration to create that table might look something like this:

```
self.up
  create_table :users do |t|
    t.column :email,      :string, :null => false
    t.column :first_name, :string, :null => false
    t.column :last_name,  :string, :null => false
    t.column :password,   :string
    t.column :account_id, :integer
  end
  execute "ALTER TABLE users ADD UNIQUE (email)"
```

```
    execute "ALTER TABLE users ADD CONSTRAINT
user_constrained_by_account FOREIGN KEY (account_id) REFERENCES
accounts (id) ON DELETE CASCADE"
  end

  self.down
    execute "ALTER TABLE users DROP FOREIGN KEY
user_constrained_by_account"
    drop_table :users
  end
```

However, there are several reasons this doesn't work in practice. For one thing, not all databases support all the constraints that Active Record supports. For example, in MySQL, it's possible to enforce the uniqueness constraints on email, but none of the other constraints are fully possible without the use of stored procedures and triggers. For example, in the migration earlier in this chapter, there is only a constraint on NULL values in the first_name column. A blank string would still be allowed to be inserted.

If you are on a database that supports these constraints, you are then left to maintain them all by hand, in duplicate—a process that is tedious and error prone.

Active Record does not handle violations of database constraints well. It does not automatically read the constraints in the database. And if something is out of sync and a constraint in the database is hit, this will result in an exception that is not handled gracefully at the library level. The result is a failure the user sees or one that the programmer must handle, which is impractical.

Solution: Eschew Constraints in the Database

It's simply best to not fight the opinion of Active Record that database constraints are declared in the model and that the database should simply be used as a datastore.

Despite all of the above, you may find yourself working with a DBA who insists that foreign key constraints or other constraints be stored in the database, or you yourself may simply believe in this principle. In such a case, it is strongly recommended that you not attempt to do this by hand and instead use a plugin that provides support for this. One such plugin is Foreigner (http://github.com/matthuhiggins/foreigner/), which provides support for managing foreign key constraints in migrations. Several other well-supported plugins provide support for additional constraints, most of which will be specific to your database server.

There's Always an Exception

In the example we've been looking at in this section, the exception is NULL constraints coupled with default database values. Active Record handles these constraints perfectly, with the defaults even being picked up and populated in your model automatically. Therefore, the recommended way to provide default values to your model attributes is by storing the default values in the database. For example, if you want to default a Boolean column to true, you can do so in the database:

```
add_column :users, :active, :boolean, :null => false, :default =>
true
```

This will result in the active attribute on the user model being set to true whenever a new user is created:

```
>> user = User.new
>> user.active?
=> true
```

You can use this swell behavior to your benefit to simplify code and make your objects more consistent. In most applications, setting all Booleans to allow null and to default to false is preferred. That way, your Booleans will really have only two possible values, true and false, not true, false, and nil.

CHAPTER 10
Building for Failure

While most of us aren't building websites for banks, medical centers, or the NCSA, it's still important to focus on and be aware of the possible failure points of our applications. Doing so gives our products an attention to detail that will be appreciated by our user base and will evolve into real, tangible profits.

Building an application to handle various failure modes is simply another aspect of mindful, detail-oriented application design. Building for failure does not necessarily mean that the application must recover gracefully from all possible failures; rather, it means it should *degrade* gracefully in the face of uncertainty. A classic example of this is the "over capacity" error page sometimes presented to the (un)happy masses on Twitter. The error page displayed includes an endearing image of an exhausted cartoon whale being air lifted by a squadron of Twitter birds. Ironically, this failure image has become a positive icon of the modern web world. It's been seen on clothing and dishware, and it has even surfaced as a tattoo. The Twitter fail whale, concocted by a Twitter designer as a graceful way of conveying an internal technical failure to the end user, has its own fan club (http://failwhale.com).

There are very few concrete techniques for building an application that handles failure gracefully. There is no `fail_gracefully` gem to be installed. Rather, building for failure is a philosophy, a school of thought much like agile development. That being said, there are some good rules of thumb to keep in mind whenever working on your codebase, such as "fail fast" and "never fail silently." We'll be discussing each of these in the following solutions.

AntiPattern: Continual Catastrophe

A well-seasoned technical manager once said that the best developers started as systems administrators and that the best systems administrators started as developers. There are many reasons we believe this to be true, not the least of which is that systems administrators are trained with a healthy dose of paranoia.

While working as a systems administrator in a past, to-remain-unnamed position, one of the authors of this book came across the following snippet running nightly out of the root user's `crontab`:

```
cd /data/tmp/
rm -rf *
```

At first glance, you might not see an issue with this snippet. Clearly, it's there to remove temporary files from the system, a feature likely added to increase the system's reliability by keeping the storage array from overfilling.

As a systems administrator, this snippet kept me awake for nights. What would happen if I renamed the `data` directory `application`? The failure of the `cd` command would be ignored, and everything in the root user's home directory would be destroyed overnight. I fixed that script, but what other time bombs lay in wait for me the next morning?

`bash`, being designed for paranoid people such as myself, comes with `set -e` and the powerful `&&` operator to help address these kinds of ignored failures. You need to apply the same sort of techniques to your Rails code as well.

Solution: Fail Fast

The "fail fast" philosophy is applicable both in application code and in utility code such as rake tasks and other support scripts. It most clearly manifests itself as sanity checks placed toward the top of the execution stack.

Whoa, There, Cowboy!

For example, the following method from a `Portfolio` model has a collection of photo files:

```
class Portfolio < ActiveRecord::Base
  def self.close_all!
    all.each do |portfolio|
```

```
      unless portfolio.photos.empty?
        raise "Can't close a portfolio with photos."
      end
      portfolio.close!
    end
  end
end
```

The `Portfolio.close_all!` method closes all portfolios, which has the side effect of deleting all the photo files for each portfolio. Consider what happens when a user with 100 portfolios clicks the Close All button. If the 51st portfolio still has files in it, the user is left with 50 open portfolios and a general sense of confusion.

Even though the following version is less performant than the preceding, it produces a much more consistent end user experience:

```
class Portfolio < ActiveRecord::Base
  def self.close_all!
    all.each do |portfolio|
      unless portfolio.photos.empty?
        raise "Some of the portfolios have photos."
      end
    end

    all.each do |portfolio|
      portfolio.close!
    end
  end
end
```

In this version above, you ensure that all the portfolios are empty before closing any of them. This helps avoid the half-closed scenario above. It still leaves room for race conditions if the user uploads more photos while the method is running, but you can alleviate this via database-level locking.

Improve the User Experience

While raising an exception prevents the inconsistency outlined in the above scenario, it doesn't present a very good user experience, as it allows the user to close all portfolios and simply presents a 500 error screen when that action fails. You can address this with some judicious extraction and double-checking at the Controller and View layers.

The first thing to do is to extract the sanity check into another class method on Portfolio:

```
class Portfolio < ActiveRecord::Base
  def self.can_close_all?
    ! all.any? { |portfolio| portfolio.photos.empty? }
  end

  def self.close_all
    raise "Can't close a portfolio with photos." unless
can_close_all?

    all.each do |portfolio|
      portfolio.close!
    end
  end
end
```

Like most other method extraction refactorings, this has the added benefits of making the class easier to test and increasing the readability of the code in general. Now you can make use of this predicate class method in your views like this:

```
<% if Portfolio.can_close_all? %>
  <%= link_to "Close All",
              close_all_portfolios_url,
              :method => :post %>
<% end %>
```

And, as a third check, you can add a before_filter to your controller action:

```
class PortfoliosController < ApplicationController
  before_filter :ensure_can_close_all_portfolios,
                :only => :close_all

  def close_all
    portfolio.close_all!
    redirect_to portfolios_url,
                :notice => "All of your portfolios have been
closed."
  end
```

```
      private

    def ensure_can_close_all_portfolios
      if Portfolio.can_close_all?
        redirect_to portfolios_url,
                      :error => "Some of your portfolios have photos!"
      end
    end
  end
```

While the business logic is properly extracted into a single method (`can_close_all?`), the repeated checks in this above might seem a bit redundant. Situations in which you need to guard against irreversible actions call for this layered approach.

Readability

A further benefit of pushing sanity checks toward the top of your execution stack is readability. It's easy to see, in the following example, what sanity checks are being run:

```
  def fire_all_weapons
    ensure_authorized!
    ensure_non_friendly_target!
    ensure_loaded!

    weapons.each {|weapon| weapon.fire! }
  end
```

If the sanity checks are scattered throughout the execution stack, the purpose is obscured, hindering the readability and maintainability of the codebase.

Consistency Breeds Trust

As is the case with all the other solutions in this chapter, using the "fail fast" philosophy helps ensure that your application will behave consistently in the face of adversity. This, in turn, is one of the pillars of producing a user base that trusts you and your application.

AntiPattern: Inaudible Failures

An important part of the motivation behind building for failure is the user experience of the end user. Functionality that is error prone or inconsistent leaves the user not trusting your software. Oftentimes, we've seen code samples that look something like the following:

```ruby
class Ticket < ActiveRecord::Base
  def self.bulk_change_owner(user)
    all.each do |ticket|
      ticket.owner = user
      ticket.save
    end
  end
end
```

The purpose of this code is fairly clear: `Ticket.bulk_change_owner(user)` loops through each ticket, assigning the user to it and saving the modified record.

You can modify the `Ticket` model by adding a validation to ensure that each ticket's owner is also a member of that ticket's project:

```ruby
class Ticket < ActiveRecord::Base
  validate :owner_must_belong_to_project

  def owner_must_belong_to_project
    unless project.users.include?(owner)
      errors.add(:owner, "must belong to this ticket's project.")
    end
  end

  ...
end
```

It's important to always keep the end user in mind when working on absolutely any part of an application.

Consider, for example, what happens when a user attempts to assign another user to a bunch of tickets across multiple projects. `Ticket.bulk_change_owner` works fine for any ticket whose project has the user being assigned as a member and silently swallows validation errors for all other tickets. The end results are an inconsistent and buggy experience for the users and an unhappy customer for you.

Solution: Never Fail Quietly

The precise culprit in the `bulk_change_owner` method in the preceding section is in the inappropriate use of `save` instead of `save!`. However, the underlying issue is the silent swallowing of errors in general. This can be caused by ignoring negative return values, as you've done above, or by accidentally swallowing unexpected exceptions through overzealous use of the `rescue` statement.

Embrace the Bang!

In the code above, `Ticket.bulk_change_owner` should have been originally written to use the `save!` method—which raises an exception when a validation error occurs—instead of `save`. Here's the same code as before, this time using `save!`:

```ruby
class Ticket < ActiveRecord::Base
  def self.bulk_change_owner(user)
    all.each do |ticket|
      ticket.owner = user
      ticket.save!
    end
  end
end
```

Now, when the exception happens, the user will be made aware of the issue (you'll see how later in this solution). There is still the issue of having updated half of the tickets before encountering the exception. To alleviate that, you can wrap the method in a transaction, as in the following example:

```ruby
class Ticket < ActiveRecord::Base
  def self.bulk_change_owner(user)
    transaction do
      all.each do |ticket|
        ticket.owner = user
        ticket.save!
      end
    end
  end
end
```

Make It Pretty

In the preceding section, the user is made aware of the fact that a problem occurred, and you no longer have the problem of inconsistent data. However, showing a 500 page isn't the best way to communicate with your public.

One quick way of producing a better user experience is to make use of the Rails `rescue_from` method, which you can leverage to display custom error pages to users when certain exceptions occur. While you could add your own exception for the `Ticket.bulk_change_owner` method, you'll keep it simple for now and just rescue any `ActiveRecord::RecordInvalid` exception that finds its way to the end user:

```
class ApplicationController < ActionController::Base
  rescue_from ActiveRecord::RecordInvalid, :with => :show_errors
```

Never Rescue `nil`

A mistake we commonly see in the wild involves developers accidentally hiding unexpected exceptions through incorrect use of the `rescue` statement. This always involves using a bare `rescue` statement without listing the exact exceptions the developer is interested in catching.

Consider this snippet of code, which calls the `Order#place!` method:

```
order_number = order.place! rescue nil
if order_number.nil?
  flash[:error] = "Unable to reach Fulfillment House." +
                  " Please try again."
end
```

The `Order#place!` method contacts the fulfillment house in order to have it ship the product. It also returns the fulfillment house's internal order number. The code makes use of an inline `rescue` statement to force the returned order number to `nil` if an exception was raised while placing the order. It then checks for `nil` in order to show the user a friendly message to ask them to try again.

Let's take a look at the implementation for the `Order#place!` method:

```
class Order < ActiveRecord::Base
  def place!
    fh_order = send_to_fulfillment_house!
    self.fulfillment_house_order_number = fh_order.number
    save!
```

```
      return fh_order.number
    end
  end
```

Here, the `Order#place!` method is calling the `send_to_fulfillment_house!` method, which is where the earlier example expected the exception to originate. Unfortunately, the `place!` method also calls `save!`, and there lies the rub.

The `order_number = order.place! rescue nil` line not only swallows any network errors that occurred during the `send_to_fulfillment_house!` call, it also cancels any validation errors that happened during the `save!` call. To make matters worse, the flash message instructs the user to attempt to place the order again, which means the fulfillment house will end up sending multiple products to the user because of a simple validation error on your end.

The root issue is using a blanket `rescue` statement without qualifying which exceptions to catch. The correct solution, as shown in the section "AntiPattern: Fire and Forget" in Chapter 5, is to collect the exceptions you want to catch in a constant and rescue those explicitly.

Big Brother Is Watching

Producing a consistent and trustworthy user experience is just one benefit of writing code that fails loudly. The other critical benefit has to do with instrumentation. Consider the `before_save` callback on the `Tweet` model shown here:

```
class Tweet < ActiveRecord::Base
  before_create :send_tweet

  def send_tweet
    twitter_client.update(body)
  rescue *TWITTER_EXCEPTIONS => e
    HoptoadNotifier.notify e
    errors.add_to_base("Could not contact Twitter.")
  end
end
```

Here, you let the user know that you had issues contacting Twitter (a very rare situation, indeed) by setting a validation error. In addition, you record that fact via the Hoptoad (http://hoptoadapp.com) service to ensure that the development team is aware of any connectivity issues or of general downtime with the external service.

> **Note**
>
> In the examples in this chapter, we've used Hoptoad, the
> most popular error logging service for Rails applications.
> However, there are other services and plugins, such as excep-
> tion_notification (http://github.com/rails/exception_notifi-
> cation), Exceptional (http://getexceptional.com), and New
> Relic RPM (http://newrelic.com).

The Takeaway

You should never ignore exceptions and negative return values. Instead, you should
bubble them up to both the end user and to a monitoring system. Doing so ensures
that your user's experience remains consistent, which, as we've said before, is key to
building a relationship of trust between users and your application. In addition, it
removes your team's blindfold and keeps you aware of the errors your users experience.

Index

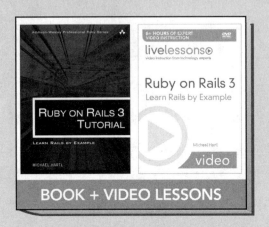

BOOK + VIDEO LESSONS

ISBN: 9780132492546

Master Rails 3.x programming fast, with hours of world-class video training and today's best Rails tutorial book in one value-priced bundle!

 Bundle is available at informit.com and retail.

Both the video and tutorial are available in Safari Books Online.

Addison Wesley

REGISTER

THIS PRODUCT

informit.com/register

Register the Addison-Wesley, Exam Cram, Prentice Hall, Que, and Sams products you own to unlock great benefits.

To begin the registration process, simply go to **informit.com/register** to sign in or create an account. You will then be prompted to enter the 10- or 13-digit ISBN that appears on the back cover of your product.

Registering your products can unlock the following benefits:

- Access to supplemental content, including bonus chapters, source code, or project files.
- A coupon to be used on your next purchase.

Registration benefits vary by product. Benefits will be listed on your Account page under Registered Products.

About InformIT — THE TRUSTED TECHNOLOGY LEARNING SOURCE

INFORMIT IS HOME TO THE LEADING TECHNOLOGY PUBLISHING IMPRINTS Addison-Wesley Professional, Cisco Press, Exam Cram, IBM Press, Prentice Hall Professional, Que, and Sams. Here you will gain access to quality and trusted content and resources from the authors, creators, innovators, and leaders of technology. Whether you're looking for a book on a new technology, a helpful article, timely newsletters, or access to the Safari Books Online digital library, InformIT has a solution for you.

informIT.com

THE TRUSTED TECHNOLOGY LEARNING SOURCE

Addison-Wesley | Cisco Press | Exam Cram
IBM Press | Que | Prentice Hall | Sams

SAFARI BOOKS ONLINE

informIT.com
THE TRUSTED TECHNOLOGY LEARNING SOURCE

InformIT is a brand of Pearson and the online presence
for the world's leading technology publishers. It's your source
for reliable and qualified content and knowledge, providing
access to the top brands, authors, and contributors from
the tech community.

✦Addison-Wesley   **Cisco Press**   EXAM/**CRAM**   **IBM** Press.   **QUe**   **PRENTICE HALL**   **SAMS** | Safari Books Online

LearnIT at InformIT

Looking for a book, eBook, or training video on a new technology? Seek-
ing timely and relevant information and tutorials? Looking for expert opin-
ions, advice, and tips? **InformIT has the solution.**

- Learn about new releases and special promotions by
  subscribing to a wide variety of newsletters.
  Visit **informit.com/newsletters**.

- Access FREE podcasts from experts at **informit.com/podcasts**.

- Read the latest author articles and sample chapters at
  informit.com/articles.

- Access thousands of books and videos in the Safari Books
  Online digital library at **safari.informit.com**.

- Get tips from expert blogs at **informit.com/blogs**.

Visit **informit.com/learn** to discover all the ways you can access the
hottest technology content.

Are You Part of the IT Crowd?

Connect with Pearson authors and editors via RSS feeds, Facebook,
Twitter, YouTube, and more! Visit **informit.com/socialconnect**.

informIT.com
THE TRUSTED TECHNOLOGY LEARNING SOURCE   PEARSON

✦Addison-Wesley   **Cisco Press**   EXAM/**CRAM**   **IBM** Press.   **QUe**   **PRENTICE HALL**   **SAMS** | Safari Books Online

Try Safari Books Online FREE

Get online access to 5,000+ Books and Videos

Safari Books Online

FREE TRIAL—GET STARTED TODAY!
www.informit.com/safaritrial

Find trusted answers, fast
Only Safari lets you search across thousands of best-selling books from the top technology publishers, including Addison-Wesley Professional, Cisco Press, O'Reilly, Prentice Hall, Que, and Sams.

Master the latest tools and techniques
In addition to gaining access to an incredible inventory of technical books, Safari's extensive collection of video tutorials lets you learn from the leading video training experts.

WAIT, THERE'S MORE!

Keep your competitive edge
With Rough Cuts, get access to the developing manuscript and be among the first to learn the newest technologies.

Stay current with emerging technologies
Short Cuts and Quick Reference Sheets are short, concise, focused content created to get you up-to-speed quickly on new and cutting-edge technologies.

 Addison Wesley
 AdobePress
 ALPHA
Cisco Press
 FT Press
 IBM Press
lynda.com
Microsoft Press
New Riders

O'REILLY
 Peachpit Press
 PRENTICE HALL
 Que
 Redbooks
 SAMS
 SAS Publishing
 Sun

 WILEY

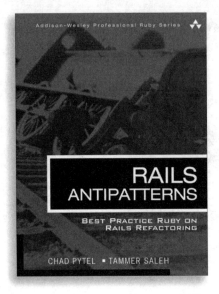

FREE Online Edition

Your purchase of *Rails™ AntiPatterns* includes access to a free online edition for 45 days through the Safari Books Online subscription service. Nearly every Addison-Wesley Professional book is available online through Safari Books Online, along with more than 5,000 other technical books and videos from publishers such as Cisco Press, Exam Cram, IBM Press, O'Reilly, Prentice Hall, Que, and Sams.

SAFARI BOOKS ONLINE allows you to search for a specific answer, cut and paste code, download chapters, and stay current with emerging technologies.

Activate your FREE Online Edition at www.informit.com/safarifree

> **STEP 1:** Enter the coupon code: XVJDKFH.

> **STEP 2:** New Safari users, complete the brief registration form.
> Safari subscribers, just log in.

If you have difficulty registering on Safari or accessing the online edition, please e-mail customer-service@safaribooksonline.com

AdobePress ALPHA Cisco Press FT Press IBM Press lynda.com Microsoft Press New Riders

O'REILLY Peachpit Press PRENTICE HALL Que Redbooks SAMS SAS Publishing Sun WILEY